D0296034

Look Back in Pleasure: Noël Coward Reconsidered

for Graham Payn
friend of Noël Coward

Look Back in Pleasure: Noël Coward Reconsidered

edited by Joel Kaplan and Sheila Stowell

Methuen

Published by Methuen 2000

1 3 5 7 9 10 8 6 4 2

First published in Great Britain in 2000
by Methuen Publishing Limited,
215 Vauxhall Bridge Road, London SW1V 1EJ

Copyright © Joel Kaplan and Sheila Stowell 2000

Joel Kaplan and Sheila Stowell have asserted their rights under the Copyright,
Designs and Patents Act, 1988, to be identified as the authors of this work

Methuen Publishing Limited Reg. No. 3543167

A CIP catalogue record for this book
is available from the British Library

ISBN 0 413 75500 2

Typeset in Goudy by MATS, Southend-on-Sea, Essex

Printed and bound in Great Britain by
Creative Print and Design (Wales), Ebbw Vale

Contents

Acknowledgements

We would like to thank the trustees of the Noël Coward Estate and members of the Noël Coward Centenary Committee, especially Philip Hoare, Michael Imison, Sheridan Morley and Graham Payn, for their encouragement and support. We are grateful, as well, to the University of Birmingham, the British Academy and Chiltern Railways for significant financial help, and to Methuen Ltd and Warner/Chappell Music Ltd for permission to quote from Coward's plays and songs. Our greatest debt, of course, is to our contributors and to those individuals whose involvement made possible the Noël Coward Conference from which this volume arose: Professor Maxwell Irvine, Vice-Chancellor, University of Birmingham; Professor N. J. H. Dent, Head, School of Humanities; Dr Clive Field, Head, Library Services and Information Technology; C. L. Penny, Special Collections; seminar chairs Steve Nallon, Russell Jackson and Dan Rebellato; Peter Greenwell; Julie Batham; Joyce Heathcote; and, above all, Amanda Cadman, conference administrator. A note of personal thanks to Fran and Flora – they know who they are.

All profits from the sale of this volume will be contributed to a bursary fund for postgraduate students studying Drama and Playwriting at the University of Birmingham.

Foreword

The 1999 Noël Coward Centenary, of which the Birmingham University Conference which this book celebrates was a major part, was, I believe, the greatest ever such event organised on stage and screen worldwide for any British writer or artist of any kind.

Those of us who are the Trustees of the Coward Estate and therefore centrally involved in the Centenary's organisation cannot, however, take too much credit here; although by then almost thirty years beyond the grave, it was as usual Noël himself who had organised its triumph.

Consider this: if you were celebrating a centenary of Cole Porter, all you really have are the songs; if of Terence Rattigan, just the plays. But with Noël, it was always different. The playboy of the West End world, jack of all entertainment trades and Master of most, left behind him plays, films, songs, short stories, paintings, poems, a novel, a ballet, memoirs, diaries and travelogues (not to mention some recently unearthed home movies of his travels in the Far East early in the 1930s), all of which were there to be celebrated, and all of which were. I alone was lucky enough to host celebrations of his plays, songs and films in Singapore, Hong Kong, Bangkok, London, Antibes, Los Angeles and New York, and there were many others that even I missed – an account of some of the Centenary productions will be found in the following pages.

But of everything we did in his name, I believe the setting up of a Coward study centre at the University of Birmingham, of which this conference effectively proved the unofficial opening ceremony, was perhaps the most significant and certainly far-reaching.

All of us who loved, knew and worked with Noël (I was his first biographer back in 1967; my grandmother Gladys Cooper created his *Relative Values* on stage and had been a wary friend since the early 1920s) were aware that with this Centenary, and the 20th century of which Coward was the most articulate and ambitious showbiz voice, something was coming to an end. Noel had been the angry young man of the 20s, the cynical satirist of the 30s, the fervent patriot of the 40s, the American exile of the 50s and the grand old man of the 60s; what would happen to him with the ending of the century he so defined and delineated?

Graham Payn, Noël's lifelong friend and executor of his Estate, was rightly concerned that Noël's remarkable career and reputation should be safeguarded for a new century; as I turn sixty, I am also aware that Coward's guardians aren't getting any younger. It was, we felt, crucial that there should be some kind of study centre where directors, actors, critics, historians, academics and audiences could go to see his papers, look at the original costume drawings and reviews and writings about him. A study centre akin, in fact, to the one that Christopher Bigsby set up so admirably a decade or so ago for Arthur Miller at the University of East Anglia.

Thanks to Joel Kaplan and David Edgar at Birmingham, we now have just that; no longer will those in search of the Coward archive have to trawl through several private collections in London and Switzerland and New York. The centrality is all; the centre will of course take some time to develop, and it will be some time before it can be considered a complete resource.

But, as these essays indicate, we are well on the way. As I listened to these papers, delivered over a two-day seminar in November 1999, I couldn't help recalling that when I had started to write Noël's life, back in the middle 1960s, I was seriously advised by several agents, colleagues and even publishers that there was no future in Coward and that I should find myself an alternative obsession. It wasn't until I began talking to John Osborne and Harold Pinter, supposedly then the dramatists who had replaced him, and discovered their ardent admiration for Noël, that I began to think that maybe his future was safe after all. Now, nearly forty years on, we know that it is.

Sheridan Morley

Introduction

The present volume had its origin in the first ever Noël Coward Conference, hosted by the University of Birmingham's Department of Drama and Theatre Arts in November 1999. The Conference, which was in part held to celebrate the designation of the University as the ultimate repository of the Noël Coward Papers, was in turn one of a series of events, official and unofficial, that constituted the Noël Coward Centenary. The commemoration of the hundredth year of Coward's birth had actually begun a year earlier, in 1998, with the broadcast on BBC2 of Adam Low's *Arena* trilogy on Coward's life and work, the release of Neil Tennant's *Twentieth Century Blues* (an album of Coward songs by, among others, Elton John, Paul McCartney, Marianne Faithfull and Robbie Williams) and the unveiling by Queen Elizabeth, the Queen Mother, of Angela Conner's statue of Coward in the foyer of the Theatre Royal, Drury Lane.

The Centenary proper saw the unveiling of two further Coward statues, in New York and Jamaica, the reissuing by Methuen of most of Coward's published work and, above all, an ad hoc festival of Coward's plays, familiar and unfamiliar, across the length and breadth of the United Kingdom: *Cavalcade* at The Glasgow Citizens Theatre, *Present Laughter* at the West Yorkshire Playhouse (Leeds), *Nude with Violin* at Manchester's Royal Exchange, *The Young Idea* at the Chester Gateway, *Blithe Spirit* at the Salisbury Playhouse, *Easy Virtue* at the Chichester Festival, *Ace of Clubs* at the Wimbledon Studio and, in central London, a concert performance of *After the Ball* at the Peacock Theatre as part of the Covent Garden Festival of Music, *Song at Twilight*, first at the King's Head and then at the Gielgud, *Private Lives* at the Royal National Theatre and *Hay Fever* at the Savoy. These proceedings were supplemented by BBC Radio 4's production of six plays from *Tonight at 8.30*.

North America's contribution to the festivities included a concert performance of *Sail Away* at New York's Carnegie Hall, featuring its original lead, Elaine Stritch, a Broadway revival of *Waiting in the Wings* with Lauren Bacall and Rosemary Harris, and Christopher Newton's sumptuous restaging of *Easy Virtue* at Canada's Shaw Festival. In the United Kingdom the year culminated in a Celebrity Gala at the Savoy and the announcement by Graham Payn and the Coward Estate that Noël Coward's legacy would be made accessible to future generations of students, scholars and theatre practitioners by depositing on permanent loan at the University of Birmingham Coward's manuscripts, papers and related memorabilia.

The University's Noël Coward Conference was an attempt to provide a focal point for these events. Over a period of two days the Department of Drama and Theatre Arts was able to bring together a distinguished group of scholars, critics, directors and actors – many involved in the productions cited above – to reassess from a range of complementary viewpoints Coward's contribution to English culture and the stage.

Most of the twelve essays that make up Part One of this volume were presented in an earlier form as conference papers. Some attempt a revaluation of Coward's place in theatre history and his role in the development of a modern stage language. Arguing that what sets Coward apart from his predecessors is a richly self-referential use of stage technique, playwright David Edgar sees Coward as a bridge between traditional and modernist comedy, a figure who borrows from Wilde but prefigures Beckett and looks forward to writers such as Mark Ravenhill, Martin Crimp and Patrick Marber. Each operates, Edgar claims, not by creating new genres, but by placing existing ones in inverted commas. The Wilde connection is also pursued by Jean Chothia and Peter Raby. The former sees Coward as a 'metatheatrical subversive' whose challenges to comic closure have their counterparts in both the cinema of the 1930s and the darker worlds of Harold Pinter, while the latter presents Coward's country house comedies as the culmination of a stage tradition that began in the 1890s and had at its mid-point the leisured heathenism of H. H. Munro. A different path is traced by Frances Gray who draws upon Roland Barthes and the dance language of Fred Astaire to create a new vocabulary for exploring Coward's use of stasis and movement. Considering the relationship between the performer and the performed self, Gray sees in Coward's best work a radical use of the actor's body to create moments that are at the same time intensely private and self-consciously public. Each finds in Coward a major and provocative stage writer whose experiments with dramatic form and language demand our attention. Indeed, the starting point for all is a firm rejection of 'received' theatre history which, until the past decade, had cast Coward, together with Terence Rattigan, as a welcome casualty of the Osborne revolution.

Other contributors have chosen to focus upon Coward's self-marketing and his uncanny ability to define the decades in which he worked. Here the recurring motif is the trinity of class, gender and nation, as Coward is considered in terms of his status as cultural icon as well as his impact upon a large and popular public. The ways in which Coward helped shape a national sense of culture defined by reticence, taste and duty is examined by Philip Hoare. Finding in Coward a rebel who became an institution – a telling comparison with Elvis is drawn – Hoare sees the persistent power of a piece like *Still Life* residing in Coward's ability to exploit his own sublimated sexuality, evoking for later eras a time when emotions were kept firmly under control. Alan Sinfield historicises the process. Exploring the manner in which Coward successfully cultivated two audiences, one broadly boulevard the other specialised and sexually dissident, Sinfield places Coward's repudiation of effeminacy within the context of both an emerging queer consciousness and an inter-war debate about the kind of place England should be.

Coward's construction of Englishness is in turn taken up by Dan Rebellato, Peter Holland and Russell Jackson. Rebellato's starting point is the marginalisation of land and old money in late-Victorian Britain and the consequent emergence of etiquette as a device for keeping parvenus at bay. The reduction of 'culture' to a series of performance acts, Rebellato argues, allowed Coward to use rudeness as an ideological tool exposing the failure of 'good society' to deal with the new worlds of the 1920s and 1930s. For Holland class itself is another set of theatrical turns. Beginning with Coward's review sketches and history plays, and paying particular attention to *Still Life* and its cinematic embodiment in *Brief Encounter*, he takes issue with the notion that the playwright's satire and snobbery are directed exclusively at working-class targets. Jackson concludes the story at the lag end of Coward's career, setting forth the manner in which the playwright, disillusioned and spurned by the reviewers, sought out ideal 'English' communities. Turning his back upon the post-war Welfare State, and savaging both the critics and the new playwrights of the 1950s, Jackson's 'Shaftesbury Avenue Coriolanus' found his 'world elsewhere' in the colonies, in the armed forces, and in a sentimentalised and depoliticised vision of Cockney London. These, together with the theatre itself, became for Coward the last repositories of decency, fellowship and 'English' common sense.

The challenges of performance as well as Coward's place in the twenty-first century are taken up in a third group of essays. By focusing upon Coward's France rather than his England, John Stokes is able to underscore the dangers of repackaging Coward as a modernist. Surveying the mawkish yoking of sex and sentimentality that characterises works like *Bitter Sweet* and *Conversation Piece*, as well as the contribution of boulevard star Yvonne Printemps to Coward's craft and sensibility, Stokes identifies a side of the playwright easy to overlook in our headlong rush to make him our contemporary. Yet if these works represent today the least palatable side of Coward – the Centenary, to be sure, kept clear of both – a recognition of their overlap with, say, the Deauville setting of *Private Lives* allows us to gauge better the complex and often contradictory nature of Coward's art.

The tension between interpretation and authenticity provides
a link between the very different essays of Dominic Vlasto and
Michael Coveney. Looking at Coward's songs, Vlasto, a
musicologist, stresses the manner in which Coward's accompanists helped shape his performance legacy. He is also
concerned with the conventions of light music, making, in the
end, a plea for both the theatrical nature of Coward's songs and
the interpretative freedom of contemporary artists. Michael
Coveney, theatre critic for the *Daily Mail*, and former critic for
the *Observer* and the *Financial Times*, concludes the section by
making a similar plea for Coward on stage. Tracing the current
reassessment of Coward back to the ground-breaking work of
Philip Prowse and Sean Mathias in the 1970s and 80s, Coveney
offers an overview of some of the centenary year's most
innovative productions. Calling attention to both the revival of
neglected work – Sheridan Morley's *Song at Twilight*, Marianne
Elliott's *Nude with Violin* and Deborah Shaw's *The Young Idea* – as
well as the controversial revisiting of more familiar pieces –
Prowse's *Cavalcade*, Philip Franks's *Private Lives* and, above all,
Declan Donnellan's *Hay Fever* – Coveney speaks, in a phrase that
provoked much controversy at the Conference, of the need to
'rescue Coward from Coward'. If Coward is to be taken seriously
as a playwright with something to say about the way in which we
live our lives, Coveney argues, then directors and performers
must be allowed to treat him as 'outrageously' as they do
Shakespeare or Brecht.

Many of the points raised in the above papers were debated at
the Conference in two round-table sessions for theatre
practitioners. Participants, drawn from a number of the year's
most significant revivals, included Philip Franks (*Private Lives*),
Corin Redgrave (*Song at Twilight*), Christopher Newton (*Easy
Virtue*, Shaw Festival), Malcom Sinclair (*Hay Fever*) and Sue
Wilson (*Tonight at 8.30*). Excerpts from their comments open
Part Two.

They are followed by four interviews with practitioners unable
to attend the Conference itself. The first, with Judy Campbell,
looks at the challenges of being directed by Coward and playing

opposite him in *Present Laughter*, *This Happy Breed* and *Blithe Spirit* in the 1940s. The remaining three, with Philip Prowse (*Cavalcade*), Maria Aitken (*Easy Virtue*, Chichester Festival) and Juliet Stevenson (*Private Lives*), consider from a practitioner's point of view some of the key productions of the centenary year. Yet while each engages in a highly individual way with the problems of staging Coward in our time, it is important to note some essential common ground. Each draws, at the outset, a central distinction between the need to get Coward's rhythms right and the pointlessness of adopting what Aitken condemns as 'imitation poshness'. And all talk, in one form or another, of discovering 'alternative texts', 'darker worlds' or 'real characters' beneath Coward's polish. It is a paradox nicely caught in Prowse's observation that Coward's 'subtextual other plays' can only be found by doing things exactly as Coward wished. It may be, as some critics have argued, that Strindberg, Pinter and Beckett provide a more resonant context for staging Coward today than the expected trio of Congreve, Sheridan and Wilde. But the directors and performers who bring us new readings still talk of timing, precision and clarity – and offer radical rethinkings that follow to the letter the most minute of Coward's directions. 'Listen to him,' Philip Franks cautions both critics and fellow directors. 'He knew what he was doing.' At the Conference such cross-talk underscored the manner in which Noël Coward, some quarter-century after his death, had become a subject for serious debate. This volume, it is hoped, will extend the discussion.

JK, SS

PART ONE
Noël Coward Reconsidered

Noël Coward and the Transformation of British Comedy

David Edgar

In Adam Low's 1998 *Arena* documentary on Noël Coward, there is a scene in which Arnold Wesker watches a recording of a Royal Court fund-raising gala in which Coward is marvellous but clearly miserable as the restaurant owner in an extract from Wesker's *The Kitchen*. Less emblematic but even more delicious is the story, told in Philip Hoare's biography, of Coward's visit to the Court to see David Storey's grittily realistic Rugby League play *The Changing Room*. His attention drawn to the male genitalia on display in the bath scene, Coward remarked that 'fifteen acorns are hardly worth the price of admission'.[1]

This was pretty much Coward's verdict on the playwrights who emerged in the wake of John Osborne's *Look Back in Anger* (Wesker included) and largely their verdict on him. And despite a revival of interest in his early work in the 1960s (which he dubbed 'Dad's Renaissance'), Coward has been regarded since 1956 as being on the losing side of a final struggle between the frothy commercialism of mid-century British theatre and a renewal of stern theatrical didacticism, which saw its lineage not in Noël Coward but Bertolt Brecht.

Well, what a change is here. The 1998 centenary of Brecht's birth was marked by a virtually invisible minifest in Manchester and a single touring production of *Squire Puntila and his Man Matti*. The following year, Coward's centenary saw new

productions of *Private Lives* at the National, *Present Laughter* at
the West Yorkshire Playhouse, *Nude with Violin* at the
Manchester Royal Exchange, *Easy Virtue* at Chichester, *The
Young Idea* at the Chester Gateway, *Cavalcade* at the Glasgow
Citizens, and both *Hay Fever* and *Song at Twilight* in the West
End. Had a playwright, academic or critic been spirited forward
from the Sixties or Seventies, in the manner of John Craven in
Post-Mortem (1930), he might well have speculated how things
had come to this pass. Or whether, indeed, anent '*Peace in Our
Time*', the other side had really won the war.

A number of reasons have been advanced for Dad's second
renaissance feeling more like a restoration. The first is that the
condemnation of Coward and others was based on an under-
estimation of his seriousness: for *Guardian* critic Michael
Billington, Coward's exploration of 'the thin dividing line
between sex and savagery' in *Private Lives* (1929) puts him on a
par with Strindberg.[2] A rather different argument is presented by
Dan Rebellato in *1956 And All That*, a deconstruction of the
Osborne revolution which boasts a photograph of Coward's *Blithe
Spirit* (1941) on the cover. In the spirit of Coward's 1961 appeal
to the self-expressive young playwrights of the Royal Court
school to 'consider the public',[3] Rebellato charts the way in
which the post-1956 Royal Court disempowered the audience,
from the abolition of the writer's curtain call (at which the
audience could boo) to the emergence of the authorial pro-
gramme note and press interview (read in respectful silence).
And as the greatest change in the Eighties and Nineties in the
theatre – as in British culture as a whole – has been a shift of
power from the producer to the consumer, it's no surprise that
audiences have flocked back to a playwright whose stated purpose
is to give them a good time.

But Rebellato's most provocative thesis is that the Royal
Court's mission was to challenge a theatre culture unhealthily
dominated by gay men. At their first meeting, Royal Court
director George Devine told John Osborne that 'the blight of
buggery . . . could be kept down decently by a direct appeal to

seriousness and good intentions from his own crack corps of heterosexual writers, directors and actors'.[4] In this analysis, 1956 was not so much a revolution against the Establishment as an Arts Council-promoted counter-revolution against 'the linguistic perversity of a homosexuality which seemed on the point of constituting itself as an oppositional subculture, destabilising the vital unities which seemed the foundation of a strong national identity' (as in *Look Back in Anger*, Jimmy Porter calls for 'something strong, something simple, something English').[5] But by attacking the ambiguity, private language, encoding and subtext inherent in a culture that could not speak its real name, Rebellato argues, the Royal Court roundheads were attacking precisely what gave mid-century drama its theatricality.

Coward's plays clearly fall into this category. True, the 1926 *Semi-Monde* presents gay and lesbian relationships as part of its dance of shifting sexual liaisons in the public rooms of a Paris hotel; his 1965 *Song at Twilight* is about a writer confronted by his homosexual past. But *Semi-Monde* was not performed in Coward's lifetime and *Song at Twilight* premièred in the dying days of British theatre censorship. In between, it is argued, gay relationships and gayness itself appear in heavy disguise: analogised with drugs in *The Vortex* (1923), concealed under Gilda's, Leo's and Otto's mutating geometry in *Design for Living* (1932), they can only now come out into their own.

But while the reassertion of audience power, a reassessment of Coward's seriousness as a playwright and a restoration of theatricality endorsed by an impeccably progressive political cause all clearly contribute to the extraordinary revival in his fortunes as a playwright, the plays themselves tell a separate, if parallel, story. By their elevation of form over content, his best work provides a bridge between a great dramatic genre in its dotage and the modernist experiments in the post-war years.

This is most clearly seen by comparing Coward's major and minor work. Most of his contemporary plays are either comedies of manners or episodic plays about the history of his time. The first lot are generally regarded as good (all the revivals bar one are drawn from the group) and the second as problematic.

Coward didn't like propaganda in the theatre, unless disguised so brilliantly that the audience mistakes it for entertainment. Nonetheless, both *Cavalcade* (1931) and *This Happy Breed* (1939) are overtly Conservative political plays written in the Brechtian epic manner: the scenes are set at a number of key moments in which the lives of fictional families are touched by major political events over thirty and twenty years of history respectively. The 1947 '*Peace in Our Time*' is written on the same principle, but is set in a fictional (and, when Coward wrote it, immediate) past in which Britain had lost the war and been occupied by the Nazis. Here the base group is not a family but the regulars of a London pub and, as the play covers only five years, the gaps are smaller. But the fundamental dramaturgical challenges of this strategy remain the same. These are (a) to avoid each scene consisting largely of exposition of what's happened since the last scene, (b) to find ways for people to be touched by public events in a way that allows them to discuss them plausibly and (c) to provide genuinely causal links between the events of the play.

Surprisingly, for someone of such structural virtuosity and adeptness, Coward never really gets on top of any of these challenges. In *This Happy Breed*, a number of the scenes consist entirely of catching up on what's happened to the Gibbons family in the scene change, often by way of characters telling each other what they already know. If the play has a plotting spine it is the Gibbons' daughter Queenie's rejection of solid and dependable Billy in favour of dreams of a more exciting life, her leaving home for a married man, her disowning by her mother, and her own subsequent disillusion and abandonment. When she returns to the hearth at the end of Act Three, Scene One, we have a right to expect that she will say something to her mother, her father and to us about her shattered ideals. She says precisely three words – 'hallo', 'mum' and 'yes' – and we never see her again.

While in *Cavalcade*, the ooh-er revelation of the *Titanic* lifebelt on the deck of the hitherto unspecific ocean liner is anticipated none too subtly by the line: 'It's too big, the Atlantic, isn't it?' In '*Peace in Our Time*', too, Coward fails to find ways for his people to be genuinely touched by public events: the action stops for a series of six set-piece discussions about why Britain lost the war, the nature of patriotism, the efficacy of democracy and the requirement for resistance, only one of which – the last – actually speaks to the current choices faced by the characters.

But the most telling problem with Coward's political plays is the talk. Coward's best dialogue consists either of insiders speaking in inverted commas to outsiders who don't understand them, or of two insiders playing off each other, picking up each other's phrases, coding and recoding them, and batting them back. In the political plays the conversation is largely between outsiders and none of this happens. True, characters take up words and phrases used by other characters; but they do it without any transformation beyond the clichéd, nothing is coded and the phrases don't travel. In *This Happy Breed*, the temporarily anti-capitalist Sam accuses Queenie of 'complacency, arrogance and a full stomach'; to which Queenie responds: 'You leave my stomach out of it!' While in *Calvacade* there is a trope that teeters tantalisingly on the edge of a wonderful Cowardian joke, only to deflate like a bursting balloon:

> JOE: Mum, could I ever be a policeman?
> JANE: Perhaps, darling – if you're good.
> JOE: Are all policemen good?

It's worth thinking for a second what Sholto or Sorel or Amanda or Elvira would have done with *that*. What Jane actually says is 'Yes, dear, as good as gold'.

This deadening literalness is perhaps best exemplified in a dramatic situation which recurs again and again in Coward: a sexual encounter which happens while characters are talking about something else. Famously, in *Private Lives*, Amanda and Elyot edge closer to their sexual reunion through a discussion of the delights of foreign travel; in *Present Laughter* (1934), Garry Essendine and Joanna Lyppiatt come to congress via a debate on the comparative merits of various London concert halls; while in *Still Life* (1935), Laura and Alec discover their mutual chemistry through a lecture on the virtues of preventive medicine. In *This*

Happy Breed, when Frank wants to claim his conjugal rights with
Ethel, he says, 'give us a kiss'.

For what appears to desert Coward in the dialogue of these
plays is precisely his capacity for subtext and thus his
theatricality. In overall structural terms their theatrical weakness
is demonstrated by comparison with another political play, also
deemed a failure (in this case by Coward himself).

Never performed in Coward's lifetime, *Post-Mortem* is to the
First World War what '*Peace in Our Time*' is to the Second,
although from the opposite political point of view. The play
begins in the trenches of World War One. An intelligent, charming and liberal young officer (John Craven), who while realistic
about the bloodiness and waste of the war is convinced that some
good must come out of it, is pitted against Perry Lomas, a dull,
humourless and prolix advocate of the 'ultimate futility' school.
Having suggested that one may well discover the truth about
one's life in the split second before dying (and that this may have
something to do with the circularity of time), the nice guy is shot
and, as the life ebbs away from him, looks up at the cynic and says
that he's still sure he's right, and now he'll know. The next seven
scenes are set in 1930 and consist of Craven's ghost visiting his
engagingly unfazed mother, former girlfriend, father, old com-
rades and indeed old sparring partner, who has written a book
attacking the retrospective romanticisation of the war that he
predicted all those years ago and, facing calumny in the press, is
preparing to commit suicide in his miserably shabby flat. There is
a truly awful scene involving the ghost's newspaper proprietor
father and a rather wonderful one in which the response of the
hero's girlfriend, her vapid chums and her husband Bertie to the
presence of a First World War officer in their midst demonstrates
both their character and the response of their archetype to the
continued moral questions raised by the war. So, at the end of the
play, the hero returns to the moment of his death and
demonstrates by echoing one of his lines that against all the odds
he has come round to the 'war is futile', 'life's a joke', 'it was all
worthless' position, the one advocated by the least attractive
outsider in the play.

This is of itself a clever twist and it happens in a scene which also reveals that Scenes Two to Seven of this eight-scene play have taken place not in the future but in the split second between the end of Scene One and the beginning of the single-line Scene Eight. In this, Coward anticipated Terry Johnson's *Hysteria*, in which the whole action takes place in the last seconds of Freud's life. He also draws on ideas about the circularity of time used by J. B. Priestley in his time plays. But unlike Priestley who, having established his game plan in *Dangerous Corner*, *Time and the Conways* and *An Inspector Calls*, rolls out a predictable course of events remorselessly, Coward wrong-foots the audience and thus makes more surprising and in some ways more effective use of the form.

Coward was right that *Post-Mortem* contains some of the worst scenes he ever wrote. But its structural ingenuity is a vital clue to his place in the story of twentieth-century drama and his current appeal. In 1977 Kenneth Tynan claimed that *The Young Idea* (1921) 'contains the first line that distinguished Coward from all his predecessors in English comedy: "I lent that woman the top of my thermos flask and she never returned it. She's shallow, that's what she is, shallow."'[6] Tynan was certainly referring to a kind of self-conscious, knowing wit in which insider speaks unto insider (on the stage and in the audience). But this self-consciousness goes far beyond the individual line: it represents Coward's answer to the challenge that the twentieth century posed to traditional theatrical genre.

From fifth-century Athens until the end of the nineteenth century the vast majority of comedies consisted of a young man and a young woman overcoming parental objections to their liaison and getting married. Due to the immense social changes of the Victorian era, that model ceased to be of dominant contemporary relevance well before the First World War. As often happens at the point where something petrifies, classic comedy took on its most perfect form in *The Importance of Being Earnest* (which has two pairs of lovers, a move from the town into an idyllic countryside, a pretend death and the brilliantly original twist that the male half of one obstructed relationship is the

obstacle to the other one). But from then on, and in the absence
of any genuinely innovatory comic form until after the Second
World War, comedy had either to rejuvenate other forms (as
Jarry and Brecht in different ways went back to the folk tale), to
find contemporary variations on elements of the old model (as
arcadian comedies are transposed from magic forests to ocean
liners or package holidays), or to do something new with what
was already there.

Bernard Shaw's answer to this problem was to take the old
format and reverse it – he has his young people face parental
obstacles and simply defy them or, more often, abandon the
game, usually for ideological feminist reasons. Although not a
feminist, Coward too starts out by taking the old structure and
upending it – in *The Young Idea, The Vortex* (1923) and *Hay Fever*
(1924) it's the parents who behave irresponsibly and the children
who complain. But then, suddenly, in the comedies but not the
political plays, Mum and Dad disappear.

From *Private Lives* (1929) onwards, Coward comes up with a different obstacle for his orphaned couples to overcome: instead of
being external and parental, it's inside, within the couples themselves. Neither financial nor parental problems figure in Elyot's
and Amanda's marriages nor, indeed, their lives; their problem is
each other. There is a trace of economics in *Design for Living*, and
a kind of parent in Gilda's outsider husband Ernest, but essentially
the contest is between a *ménage* and its *trois*. While in the later
comedies the question becomes not what women are worth but
whether they are worth it, in *Present Laughter* the hero wants them
to be absent and in *Blithe Spirit* he wishes they were dead.

The way Coward dramatises these conflicts is not actually by
great psychological insights – the issues that pull Amanda and
Elyot apart in the second act of *Private Lives* are the pretty typical
ones of past lovers: sex, drink and the loudness of the gramophone. The real originality lies in the use of the dramaturgy.
Whatever Tynan meant, the thing that Coward does for the first
time is to convey meaning entirely by the manipulation of our
expectations of what happens in the theatre.

To put this case, it is necessary to make a distinction. In the last scene of *Still Life* (later reworked as the film *Brief Encounter*) we are led to expect a great parting scene between the adulterous lovers, but are denied it by the unexpected appearance of a third party. This is a great theatrical idea, but it is also, and primarily, an observation of something that happens in real life (and, indeed, Chekhov uses the climactic romantic moment that goes phut in both *The Three Sisters* and *The Cherry Orchard*). On the other hand the fact that neither of the central characters says a word for the last three pages of *Private Lives* relies absolutely for its effect on it being in a play. Obviously, in the 1924 sketch *Class*, the fact that a couple of nobs are confronting the crisis of their daughters living in sin in 'a squalid room in the east end', immediately followed by the same situation being played out by an 'ow's-yer-father Cockney family in 'a beautifully furnished dining-room in Mayfair', makes its argument about the essential equivalence of family attitudes across classes that would not exist at all without the theatrical device of placing them one after the other. And while the vividly theatrical 'Manner of the Word' game at the beginning of Act Two of *Hay Fever* could be observed in real life, the conversion of the fake melodrama of the family's behaviour into the words of an actual melodrama is essentially and exclusively a device in a show.

In the second act of *Design for Living*, Coward draws our attention to the only scene in the play between the two male sides of the play's triangle by the simple device of creating and then denying a theatrical expectation that the woman is going to appear, with Otto's line: 'If Gilda came in now she'd be surprised all right, wouldn't she?' This is satisfying not as an observation of real life (in which no doubt they've been alone together many times before) but as a shared acknowledgement between playwright and audience that the meaning of *Design for Living* is contained in its geometry: all the possible couple combinations must be played out before us to demonstrate their incompleteness before the essentially triangular fullness of their relationship is presented to us whole. As Peter Holland points out,[7] such relationships have historically proved notoriously hard to bring into dramatic equilibrium and *Design for Living* is perhaps the first ever play to hold the balance between three sides by leaning them inwards. In the same way, *Hay Fever* is not just about a game, it *is* a game: the mathematics of Act Two, in which every member of the Bliss family enters into a liaison with someone else's weekend guest, are a dramatisation of the essentially performative nature of their behaviour. By the time of *Present Laughter* the meta-theatricality has become archly self-conscious: by repeating the shoving of embarrassing female guests through doors into spare rooms in each act, Coward transforms a mechanism into a metaphor; unfortunately, he feels the need to draw further attention to the device by having one character inform another that 'she feels as if she were in a French Farce and is sick to death of it'.

But the play that does all this most perfectly is *Private Lives*. The artificiality of Coward's project is demonstrated clearly by the binary construction of the first act, in which each con-versation within and between the two honeymooning couples on the implausibly coincidental adjacent balconies echoes the other (and is meaningless without it) from foreign travel to sunbathing to gambling. We learn from the different ways in which the same topics are addressed by newly wed Elyot with Sybil and newly wed Amanda with Victor that the once-wed Elyot and Amanda are people who are happy speaking in code and Sybil and Victor are not. But not only are Amanda and Elyot encoding away, so is the dramaturgy: after Elyot maniacally attempts to persuade his new wife to leave their honeymoon hotel at once, we don't need to be told what Victor and Amanda are talking about when they arrive in mid-argument, because we know from the rest of the scene that the same thing is going on in both pairings.

Of course, playwrights before Coward encoded themes or phrases which they would set up, reiterate, pay off and echo for comic or ironic effect. But no one before Coward built a play out of them. One example – one of dozens – is the concept of flippancy, which Amanda sets up in Act Two as a call to arms against the puritans ('Laugh at them. Be flippant . . . Flippancy brings out the acid in their damned sweetness and light'), a prediction which is fulfilled when Victor accuses Elyot of flippancy in Act Three and is delightfully paid off at the climax of the play when Sybil tells Victor he couldn't be flippant if he tried. The repeat of the word not only enhances the story, it tells it. So, when the escaped Amanda and Elyot have obligingly reiterated the code of 'Solomon Isaacs' as an emergency stop mechanism at moments of potential catastrophe, we know that when one of them and then the other has used it successfully, the first one will try it a third time and it will fail, not because of the observable psychology of the situation but because that's how things happen in plays. In this sense Coward's plumbing is on the outside, like the Pompidou Centre: his plays consist of what they are about.

This self-referential use of theatrical technique is what sets Coward apart from what precedes him, and sets great Coward apart from the plays in which his touch is less sure. It makes him part of a progression that leads on to Priestley's time plays, in which the mechanics are even more obviously the message. But in this sense Coward also anticipates those playwrights who stretched the form to snapping point and created a genuinely new dramatic genre thereby. Coward thought *Waiting for Godot* ridiculous, but a man who wanted his audiences to take his meaning from his juggling of theatrical devices cannot wholly spurn a writer who expresses what he wants to say by defying the most basic theatrical convention of all. By doing the same thing twice in different ways in his sketch *Class*, Coward prefigures *Godot* and *Happy Days*, and enables the development of *Play*, in which Beckett does the same thing twice in the same way. Thus it's no surprise that Coward admired Beckett's leading British disciple: the content of Aston's huge speech at the end of Act Two of Pinter's *The Caretaker* is not Cowardian in content or tone, but its unexpectedness and theatricality are. *The Home-coming* is about family games, outsiders becoming insiders, and shared and unshared codes. And although he didn't live to see it, the reversed time structure of *Betrayal* addresses a Coward theme through a self-consciously theatrical device, akin to the flash-forward at the core of *Post-Mortem*.

If Coward was a bridge between traditional and modernist

comedy, then why has he come back with such a vengeance now? Perhaps it is because, at this moment, the genres that have sustained the century show signs of petrification and, predictably, are more concerned with the cunning manipulation of old forms than finding new ones. The bewildering cross-pollination of television forms, the increasingly convoluted attempts by romantic comedy writers to find ever more ingenious ways of postponing the inevitable, the multiplication of each successful movie formula into seemingly uncontrollable chains of sequel and prequel all point to a time when old forms are failing to speak effectively to the age. Like Coward before them, many of the best of new British playwrights are not creating new genres but taking the existing ones and either putting them in inverted commas or turning them inside out. So plays like Mark Ravenhill's *Shopping and Fucking*, Patrick Marber's *Closer* and Martin Crimp's *Attempts on Her Life* explore disjuncture through what happens between scenes rather than within them, express unconnectedness with the theatre's tools of connection and challenge the centred individual in an art form which has the individual at its centre.

In this, they are following Brecht's project, but they are using Coward's technique. And if they do represent a synthesis between the two traditions that came into contest in 1956, this could not have happened without the institutional changes brought about by one of the contesting parties. Covertly homophobic and misogynistic the Royal Court of the late Fifties may have been, but it was the Court and not the West End which provided a site for the women writers who emerged in the Eighties and many of the young gay male writers who emerged a decade later. From Tony Kushner's *Angels in America* at the beginning of the decade to Mark Ravenhill's *Some Explicit Polaroids* at the end of it, contemporary gay writing has been defined not by meta-theatrical conjuring, but by a new attempt to synthesise the personal and the political. But the ingenious double couplings at the core of both plays demonstrate that these writers have built on discoveries about how to write modern comedy which Coward pioneered.

(Most of this contribution appeared as 'Be Flippant' in the *London Review of Books*, 9 December 1999.)

NOTES

1. Philip Hoare, *Noël Coward* (London: Sinclair-Stevenson, 1995), p.512.
2. Michael Billington, 'Love and violence', *Guardian*, 14 May 1999.
3. Quoted in Hoare, p.466.
4. Dan Rebellato, *1956 And All That* (London: Routledge, 1999), p.215.
5. Ibid., p.191.
6. Quoted in Hoare, p.114.
7. 'Noël Coward and comic geometry' in Michael Cordner, Peter Holland and John Kerrigan (eds), *English Comedy* (Cambridge: CUP, 1994), pp.267–87.

'It's All a Question of Masks'

Philip Hoare

In one of the seemingly endless compendia created to celebrate and summarise the passing of a century, *Brief Encounter* was voted number two in a list of the hundred best British films in September 1999. That week, a leader in the *Independent* newspaper, attempting to come to terms with this apparently retrogressive barometer of British popular culture, asked 'Should we conclude that the country is hopelessly nostalgic? That it is still obsessed with the last war?'[1]

The very fact of the film's survival is remarkable enough, let alone its extraordinary and continuing popularity. Ostensibly, *Brief Encounter*'s tale of a would-be extramarital affair in a mythic mid-century English suburbia, memorably portrayed by a love-torn Celia Johnson and Trevor Howard as Laura and Alec, would seem to be supremely irrelevant now, little more than an excuse for camp parody. But the fact that the rolling chords of Rachmaninov's Second Piano Concerto and the luminous close-ups of Johnson and Howard have the ability to affect contemporary audiences almost as much as they did half a century ago is a tribute not only to the art of David Lean, but to the story's original creator. As much as any of his other works (and perhaps more so, because it survives where theatre is evanescent), the film is a shining testament to the talent of Noël Coward.

Yet the question remains: how far does our chronological distance from *Brief Encounter* – and the play that inspired it, *Still Life* from *Tonight at 8.30* – conspire with the mores of an ironic age to render any real connection with its creator's spirit and intention virtually impossible? As we move into a new century, are we just too far away from Noël Coward, and what he meant, either to appreciate or preserve for a new generation his sterling genius? Indeed, should we attempt to preserve it at all?

Noël Coward, the twentieth century's quintessential Englishman, was able to conjure deep emotion in a superficially facile manner which epitomises what is seen as a national characteristic: that of almost disdainful reticence. The cloud of steam which wreathes the characters as they part on the railway platform seems to be the veil of English reticence falling over the love they must end, for their own good and that of their respective families and, indeed, of Britain itself. As the *Independent*'s leader noted, 'The repressed sexual longing in *Brief Encounter* still gives cold railway stations a hint of romance.'[2]

To some it also reeks of complacence, of a blind acceptance of social stasis and the status quo, and perhaps of the arrogant (and now redundant) superiority of the nation state. As Frances Gray notes in her critique of Coward, he 'took Laura's return to suburban normality for granted'.[3] In both play and film, the cosy suburbia of the Kardomah tearooms, Boots lending library and Laura's stalwart husband sitting by the fireside with *The Times* crossword calls her back from the edge of emotional anarchy; back to the old, reassuring middle England of restraint and duty. Unlike Coward's more sophisticated heroines from the inter-war Society fantasies of *Private Lives* and *Easy Virtue*, divorce is not an option for Laura Jesson.

As a child of the Victorian century, Noël Coward believed implicitly in duty; it was the bedrock of his birthright. The country might have proscribed his sexuality and censored his work, yet he still felt – almost perversely – the age-old ties that bound him. As early as 1925 Coward had declared that 'England's played out' and that he intended to make his creative life in America (and was shortly after arrested for throwing flower baskets in the street), yet he would remain irrevocably and emotionally associated with England – even when it rewarded his wartime work for the Secret Service by fining him for contravening currency regulations on his propaganda trips to the USA, and when a long-deserved knighthood was 'sabotaged' by political elements working against him – the stirrings of a new national ethos which would seek to render him, and his values, obsolete.[4]

It was only with his mother's death in 1954 that Coward claimed to feel released from his atavistic contract with his homeland. He told Joyce Carey, his confidante, 'I think on the whole that I have not done badly by England and I also think that England has not done very well by me.'[5] Yet ten years later, in 1965, he was declaiming imperially to a reporter from the *Sunday Express*, 'I *am* England and England is me.'[6] Such hubristic statements were an expression either of a deluded ego, or of one who realised how far he had helped shape a national sense of culture – a sensibility which was defined by reticence. With his upper lip perennially stiff, his face a solemn mask of apparent responsibility betrayed only by the creases around his eyes, duty, taste and behaving well were the gods to whom Coward prayed (he didn't believe in the other sort).

These, then, were the ruling values that created *Still Life* (its very title seemed to reference stasis) and which made *Brief Encounter*. As social documents, the latter had a historical context which was perhaps more urgent, cogent and pressing than the former. Lean's and Coward's film dealt with adultery at a time when it was a serious issue: the steady pre-war world was threatened by moral anarchy; as husbands and lovers were engaged in the arena of war, women were vulnerable to affairs. Marital infidelity was a theme Coward had explored for much of the two previous decades, albeit in the fantasies of Mayfair and the Côte d'Azur; now, social changes brought the adulterous dilemmas, the 'what ifs' of *Private Lives* and *Easy Virtue* to the Home Counties. Indeed, in Coward's original play, the would-be lovers consummate that which in Lean's film is kept at bay.

Then (and perhaps more so now) both film and play seemed to access a sense of break point with the world of Coward's early work – challenged as they were by post-First World War neurosis – and an ever more uncertain future after the Second World War. For both *Still Life* and *Brief Encounter*, England's reassuring Metroland was already under threat from a second world war, which changed society as irrevocably as the first had done. Coward's plays, songs and short stories stood as both a symptom and valediction of an in-between period bookended by global conflagration; the 1940s saw the last of that burst of creativity, with *Blithe Spirit* (another comment on wartime mortality, as well as a supremely sophisticated working out of Coward's themes of fidelity) and the collaborations with Lean.

It was as though the reality of war had brought Coward's career to a premature close, and his values could not survive. (As the dust died down, the critic Beverley Baxter would ask, not altogether rhetorically, 'Did Noël Coward survive the war?').[7] In this scenario *Brief Encounter* becomes a fascinating – and perhaps unsung – creative bridge between the fantasies and inter-war delusory optimism of British theatre and popular culture, and the starker tone of the post-war culture that followed it. The close-ups of Johnson and Howard may be made misty by steam, but there is a sharp focus to their composition, a polarising black and whiteness that seems to put an end to the fantasy of the era they have left behind.

The fact that Coward's writing career peaked creatively in the Forties (and in many ways his part in the Second World War sealed his reputation as the representative of all that was English) makes it pertinent, at the end of a troubled century, to examine why *Brief Encounter* still works. Evidently a sense of nostalgia underlies its popularity – perhaps the film was nostalgic even as it was premièred – a reassuring backward glance. It represented a country united not only in the shared experience of cinema (at a time when thirty million went to the movies each week, and when the National Anthem was still played at the end of the evening), but in a shared experience of life – and death – that the Dunkirk spirit (so acutely caught by Coward in his Blitz soundtrack of 'London Pride') had underlined. Famously, the *Luftwaffe*'s bombs had levelled class barriers; inevitably Coward's work sought to reflect that new spirit of equality, albeit with varying degrees of success.

In his works of the late Thirties to mid Forties, Coward – his finger ever on the *Zeitgeist* – sought to meld a patriotic, mythic sense of a greater self with social 'realities' which were often abstracted from his own lowly, transpontine background. Just as his first film with David Lean, an extended tribute to his beloved Navy and his great contribution to war propaganda, *In Which We Serve* (1942) had been probably the first British film to employ bad language to give it a sense of reality (and a gritty sexuality in which Coward, a frequent 'grey funnel' traveller, had revelled); and *This Happy Breed* (filmed 1944) had addressed – perhaps a little less convincingly – socio-political issues with uncomfortable incursions into the General Strike from the lower-middle-class, Clapham-residing Gibbons family (distant cousins of *Still Life's* buffet staff and dialogue precursors of the banter of Albert and Myrtle, whose 'refained' accent is so beautifully and damningly undermined by the line, 'There go me Banburys'), so in 1945 *Brief Encounter's* sexual expression was considered so passionate that its producers feared it would not pass the censor.

It was 'the first film which dealt with middle-aged love outside marriage', wrote the film historian James Robertson. 'Duties and responsibilities to others ultimately triumph over sexual desire and emotion, but had the ending been otherwise, the BBFC [British Board of Film Censors] might not have been so tolerant . . .'[8] Ironically, in the light of its contemporary standing, it was also regarded as a somewhat unBritish piece: its producers thought it would do better in Europe – as it did, winning the *Prix Internationale de Critique* at Cannes in 1946.

Yet now these stilted words and emotions seem vaguely camp, Cowardian versions of reality. In *In Which We Serve* Coward, playing Captain Kinross, the Mountbatten character, returns home to Alix, his wife (Celia Johnson, the perfect interpreter of Forties Coward). She asks: 'Is there going to be a war?'

'Yes, I think there is,' he replies.

'Does the chintz look all right?' asks Johnson.

'Absolutely first class,' says Coward.

Or a sunset bridge scene with Captain Kinross and his second-in-command which might well be an out-take from *Private Lives*:

'Someone sent me a calendar like that last Christmas, sir.'

'Did it have a squadron of Dorniers in upper right-hand corner?' says Coward.

'No, sir.'

'That's where Art parts company with Reality,' replies Coward.

'I believe you're right, sir. Cigarette?'

The irony of Coward's comments on art and reality underpins such scenes with the exquisite omnipotence of his fantastic creations. Perhaps you had to have been there truly to suspend disbelief: in the twenty-first century it is hard for anyone not of that era, or versed in its ways, to take such writing seriously; the very enunciation of the words seems hopelessly lost in a black-and-white world which we had left behind long before John Major's 'classless' society of the early Nineties or the apparent homogeneity of Blairite Britain.

Certainly for some critics the original playing of Coward and Gertrude Lawrence in *Still Life* required more than a suspension of disbelief: '[W]hen [Coward] wrote himself into the role of ardent heterosexual lover (*Still Life*, which he himself called the 'most mature' of the one-act plays in *Tonight at 8.30*),' writes John Lahr, 'the characterisation is wooden . . . Only when Coward is frivolous does he become in any sense profound.'[9] Yet now it is that very stiff-upper-lip sensibility that still appeals, partly to a camp sensibility, admittedly; but also because it evokes a time when emotions were as yet under control in an unglobally warmed world; love in a cold climate. At one point in *Brief Encounter* Laura declares, 'Do you know, I believe we should all behave quite differently if we lived in a warm, sunny climate all the time. We shouldn't be so withdrawn and shy and difficult.'

In an age when all-pervasive irony distances us from emotion, it seems almost impossible to reclaim the meaning of Coward's work. We live in a time when the presenter of a peak-time TV quiz show can be a drag queen, and when fine art has become so self-referential in concept that it can only be viewed through an ironic lens and a tankful of formaldehyde. Coward himself had addressed – with a characteristic and deceptive lack of seriousness – such aesthetic issues in his post-war *Nude with Violin* with its

satirical 'isms' inspired by Pollock and the Abstract
Expressionists. In a Fifties caught up in the splash-pattern
newness of petroleum culture and what Coward called 'Nescafé
Society', he was already reactionary and old-fashioned. Fifty years
later, in our sophisticated, anthropophagite culture, surely the
very essence of his era seems to have evaporated. The modern
notion of irony seems too hard-edged to apply to the role model
of the Bright Young Things, and camp was not something the
sexually reticent Coward dealt in – publicly, at least (privately, he
wasn't above sashaying around his Gerald Road apartment in
Gladys Calthrop's turban and high heels).

But at the end of his life, perhaps finally persuaded by a newly
liberated and questioning era, Coward seemed to revise his
opinion on the value of reticence. In my turn-of-the-century
Chambers Twentieth-Century Dictionary, published in the year of
Coward's birth, one of the definitions of the word is 'concealment
by silence'.[10] In an extraordinary and rather wonderful feat of
creative self-reference and deflection, Coward's last complete
play, *Song at Twilight* (1965) became an intricately woven tribute
to his own reticence – yet at the same time a public notification
of his lack of hypocrisy – while being a critique of that of
Somerset Maugham, on whom the play's irascible main character
is based. Hugo Latymer, a married, aged writer, is suddenly faced
with evidence of his true sexuality produced by a former (female)
lover. 'Homosexual tendencies in the past?' she retorts. 'You're
queer as a coot and you have been all your life.' As Lahr writes,
'[Coward's] straight-talking about homosexuality – the issue
disguised as drug-taking in *The Vortex* and the code behind the
frivolity in his great comedies – was as far as he could go toward
dropping his legendary reticence.'[11]

A generation previously Virginia Woolf had reported – in one
of her gossipy letters to her sister – on an encounter with Coward
at Sibyl Colefax's salon in 1928: 'He says the English theatre is so
degraded that he will not produce any serious work here in
future,' she wrote to Roger Fry. 'He says the middle classes make
his life a burden. Old women in Gloucester write and abuse him
for immorality. Lord Cromer [the Lord Chamberlain] can force

him to leave out any sentence, or ban the whole play. He says they are infinitely more civilised in America and Berlin. So he is off to produce his plays in New York. There he makes £1000 a week, and he can say what he likes.'[12]

Such Bloomsbury-laden comments seemed to set a fascinating prognosis of 'serious work' for the playwright; but it was one which would, for the denizens of Gordon Square and Gower Street, remain unfulfilled. Coward never really came to terms with the more radical issues with which he had flirted in the Twenties and Thirties, from *The Vortex* through to *Semi-Monde* and *Post-Mortem*. Perhaps that guise bored him (and he was a man notoriously easy to bore) and, finding it unentertaining, he moved on.

It is no coincidence that the latter two plays, as radical – indeed, as ironic as they are, were never performed in Coward's lifetime. Rather than stage *Post-Mortem*, he brought his blockbusting spectacular *Cavalcade* to Drury Lane, a production which seemed to underline all the reactionary politics apparently required to deal with the seriousness of the oncoming decade, with its forelock-tugging and degenerate lower classes and tributes to how exciting it was to be British, even in those unstable times.

Little wonder that Bloomsbury, in the shape of Woolf (who had lately professed herself 'in love' with Coward and pressed him to write more adventurously – although, as her letters about him and his 'Surbiton'[sic] background indicates, she was quite as class-obsessed as he appeared to be) dropped him like a hot brick.[13] Or that Ethel Mannin, Sean O'Casey and even Beverley Nichols denounced Coward in print for his pandering to the middle classes. 'We are meant to deplore the passing of servility in servants,' wrote Mannin after seeing the play. 'All around me were fat, white, bejewelled and befurred women who one felt sure were thanking Mr Coward for showing . . . that servants are no longer what they were . . . If only one could have felt that Coward was making this point as a challenge to class distinctions, if only he had . . . used the opportunity to put *the upper classes* in their place for once . . . but Noël Coward is now a very successful young man, and sometimes success makes people forget, so that they instinctively ally themselves on the side of money and power.'[14]

There was truth in Mannin's critique, but it was the state of her subject's persona that was, and is, perhaps more interesting. To some, Coward's attitude was that of a man afraid to affect his popular image; a man in denial, not only of his humble origins, but of his sexuality, his very emotional interior. For them the creative compromises and personal masquerade were – are – a mark of cowardice. For others they were a matter of discretion and an interior life not predicated on the exposition of one's sexual desires as a badge of identity. As a character in *The Vortex* tells the neurotic anti-hero whose cocaine addiction was even then seen as a mask for his homosexuality, 'The great thing in this world is not to be obvious, Nicky – over *anything*!'

Like Wilde – the last writer to be as well known for the way he looked as for what he wrote – Coward's innate 'good taste' was part of the masquerade. But unlike Wilde – whom he denounced, a little ungraciously given what he had inherited from the Irishman, as a 'silly, conceited, inadequate creature . . . a dreadful self-deceiver' – Coward did not transgress that boundary.[15] He had so refined his art that subtlety and exquisite artifice disguised its emotion. As Leo says 'grandiloquently' in *Design for Living*, 'It's all a question of masks, really: brittle, painted masks. We all wear them as a form of protection; modern life forces us to.'

Thus construed, *Still Life/Brief Encounter* becomes a cover for Coward's own personal vulnerability, for the brief encounters which made up his emotional life. Perhaps it is this underlying analogy that has lent the film – and much of the rest of Coward's work – its stringent relevance. The way Coward's image informed his work, and vice versa, seems a very modern manner of artistic mediation. And thus reassessed, he begins to acquire a sense of the ironic, which may in fact underlie the true reason for his survival, even into a new century.

There was a telling incident when Coward and Cecil Beaton were both travelling on the same transatlantic liner. Beaton, the arch social climber, had felt in Coward's shadow ever since he saw *The Vortex* while at Cambridge. Now he was mocked by Coward for his effeminate voice, the way he walked, the clothes he wore. 'It is important not to let the public have a loophole to lampoon you,' Coward explained, evidently with the ghost of Wilde in his mind. 'He studied his own "façade" carefully,' wrote Beaton:

> his voice was definite, harsh, rugged. He moved firmly and solidly, dressed quietly . . . 'You should appraise yourself,' he advised. 'Your sleeves are too tight, your voice is too high, and too precise. You mustn't do it. It closes so many doors . . . It's hard, I know. One would like to indulge one's own taste. I myself dearly love a good match, yet I know it is overdoing it to wear tie, socks and handkerchief of the same colour. I take ruthless stock of myself in the mirror before going out. A polo jumper or unfortunate tie exposes one to danger.

Beaton added, 'He cocked an eye at me in mockery.'[16]

It is a mark of Coward's social success in sublimating his sexuality – or, more rightly, using it to his own ends – that Beaton was to acknowledge in his style summary of the era, *The Glass of Fashion*, the extent to which Coward influenced the way a generation dressed, acted and spoke. 'All sorts of men suddenly wanted to look like Noël Coward,' he wrote,

> – sleek and satiny, clipped and well groomed, with a cigarette, a telephone, or a cocktail at hand . . . Men enjoyed imitating the exaggerated, clipped manner of certain leading actors and adopted the confident manner of those who are aware of their charms . . . Coward's influence spread even to the outposts of Rickmansworth and Poona. Hearty naval commanders to jolly colonels acquired the 'camp' manners of calling everything from Joan of Arc to Merlin 'lots of fun', and the adjective 'terribly' peppered every sentence.[17]

Coward's persona had become an integral expression of Englishness, adopted even by royalty in an act of camp mimesis, like the Prince Regent copying Beau Brummel, the ultimate

confirmation of the playwright's social ascendancy. Writing in
the *Guardian* on the hundredth birthday of the Queen Mother,
historian Hywel Williams noted, 'She brought into the royal
family a very 1920s style of brittle suppression, which was part of
a wider culture. Embarrassed by Victorian ardour and emotion,
its ancestors in literature are Oscar Wilde and Ronald Firbank.
Suddenly, it was smart to be hard. The Queen Mother's coeval
and friend Noël Coward developed the style as a clipped
heartlessness that has sunk deep into Windsor consciousness'.
Thus did Coward's influence spread across the sexes; Williams
went on to describe the then Duchess of York as 'an
emasculating femme fatale', as though she were a Coward
heroine herself.[18]

Using all available media Coward adeptly propagated his
image to sell his work in a manner which – in his famous post-
Vortex recumbent photo session for *The Sketch* in 1925 – almost
consciously updated Wilde's sofa-lounging pose for Sarony's lens
in 1882 (and was subsequently revisited by Truman Capote on
the dust jacket of *Other Voices, Other Rooms*). Like Wilde and
Capote, Coward sold his 'decadence' across America, and back in
Britain was responsible for cocktail shakers in a million suburban
homes. The remarkable transition from decadent to patriot – of
which Coward's work of the 1940s represents the high point –
was already achieved by the mid Thirties, when the author of
Cavalcade was firmly established as a national role model. My
father, born in Bradford in 1915 and brought up in the
Depression, nonetheless slicked back his hair like Coward and
continued to do so all his life, just as Teddy Boys who quiffed their
hair in the Fifties retain the same hairdo. As a rebel become
national institution, Noël Coward was the Elvis Presley of his day
– even to the extent that he revived a flagging career by appearing
in cabaret at the Desert Inn, Las Vegas: 'Las Vegas, Flipping,
Shouts "More!" as Noël Coward Wows 'Em in Café Turn', as
Variety succinctly put it.[19]

As a performer, emotion for Coward was usually kept hidden
under a silk dressing gown, behind the trails of smoke from a
cigarette holder; it was all the more effective, then, when he

allowed it to appear. In 1929 Coward wrote the defining lyric of 'If Love Were All'. Sung by the heroine of *Bitter Sweet*, it is in Coward's voice (and in the Pet Shop Boys' telling modern version of the song) a *cri de coeur*:

> Life is a very rough and tumble
> For a humble
> Diseuse,
> One can betray one's troubles
> never,
> Whatever
> Occurs,
> Night after night.
> Have to look bright,
> Whether you're well or ill.

In the blinding glare of the limelight he faced for almost all his life, it was hard to discern the shadows in between.

Thirty years later, in the late Fifties, the ageing Bright Young Thing made a rearguard lunge against the Angry Young Men:

> I don't care for the present trends either in literature or the theatre. Pornography bores me. Squalor disgusts me. Garishness, vulgarity and commonness of mind offend me, and problems of social significance on the stage, unless superbly well presented, to me are the negation of entertainment. Subtlety, discretion, restraint, finesse, charm, intelligence, good manners, talent and glamour still enchant me.[20]

Coward was an exemplar of an era in which emotion was masked because so much emotion had been suffered – in the First World War. The enormity of the war itself seemed to have had an effect on the British psyche. Just as returning soldiers had to retreat behind taciturnity in the face of the horror of their experience, so language, for Coward and his generation, became a defensive weapon, protecting a damaged interior. It is no coincidence that his speech was so clipped and quickfire that it sounded like a

Gatling gun, or that what was said was so often the opposite of
what was meant.

Private Lives is more emotional because of the suppression of
the characters' emotions. Lahr writes that 'Coward the lover
knows that too much talk about feeling kills romance'.[21] In
matters of love, reticence, after all, is a come-on. 'Words. Words.
Masses and masses of words!' says an exasperated Myra in Hay
Fever. 'We none of us ever mean anything,' confesses an equally
exasperated Sorel in the same play. Both works in this respect
anticipate Leo's comment about masks in Design for Living. Our
ironic age may be a barrier between us and Coward; but we begin
to realise that his own age dealt so deeply in irony that this is a
credible reason for the currency of his work. He erected his own
barrier of English cynicism – the product of his own culture, both
personal and popular – which made the eruption of romance in
Still Life and the film it became so much more affecting.

It is characteristic that the most emotional scene in the film, as
in the original play, is where the doctor describes various lung
diseases to the housewife as a mask for the attraction between
them. 'The thing I like best about Brief Encounter', Coward would
later comment, 'is that the love scene is played against the
words . . .'[22] Writing in the New York Times in January 1999,
journalist Ariel Swartley noted:

> In our current culture of revelation, it strikes us as a shame
> that for all his logorrhea, Coward never quite came out and
> said what he meant, or who he was. That privacy cost him
> love, and the energy he invested in maintaining his front
> made him more callous than he might have been to those
> less amusing than him, including people of other races and
> financial strata. And yet he broke through language barriers
> we've forgotten ever existed.[23]

In 1969, at the end of a life spent almost entirely in the public
eye, Coward declared: 'One's real inside self is a private place,
and should always stay like that. It is no one else's business.'[24]
As the centuries stand back to back and the world is as

uncertain as ever, the values of Coward's world are being reappraised, to some, a lost world in which one is not defined by one's sexual exploits or ability to externalise emotion; in which one could be oneself, without recourse to self-exposure; the sense of an interior life, and Woolf's room of one's own. The now unknown and unknowable past – a past which art can nonetheless help us to understand – held certain prejudices of which we are well rid; and some of Coward's gestures – artistic and personal – against both established authority and new ways of seeing can certainly appear infantile, the product of an implacably contrary mind. His public acceptance of the status quo sits ill with his private rejection of it: his work often projects a complacency born of conformity, which does not concord with his own subversion and rebelliousness: *The Vortex* versus *Cavalcade*. Others must kowtow; he could, and did, escape (itself a leitmotif of his life).

Underlying this necessary creative paradox there was always a danger of appropriation by forces with vested interests. Looking back thirty years to 1931, when *Cavalcade* was taken up by the *Daily Mail* and trumpeted as a call to arms of right-thinking patriots, Coward wrote: 'I had been assured on all sides that I had done a great service for England by writing it and producing it at such a timely moment [i.e. when a depressed Britain had come off the Gold Standard]. I suppose I believed all this? It is difficult to believe that I did. But perhaps the laurels rested comfortably enough on my head and I accepted the tributes without irony . . .'[25] His viewpoint may have lacked irony, but that year he inscribed a copy of the play's text (which had been serialised by the *Mail*) to Esme Wynne-Tyson: 'From a National Hero'[26] and his neglected, if not hapless younger brother, Erik, noted acerbically to their mother, 'Noël is getting a Cadillac, is he? For all his supposed patriotism, he seems to prefer most American things. I can't think why . . .'[27]

Coward may have spent more than half his life out of the country, in virtual exile, but at the end of the twentieth century he remained under threat from the bland colonisation of the English heritage industry, of his books and recordings sold in

Past Times' shops, condemned to eternal 'am-dram' productions
and Saturday matinées playing to blue-rinsed matrons – the
same ladies, perhaps, about whom he had confided to Roddy
McDowell when proscribing references to his homosexuality in
Sheridan Morley's biography: 'There are still a few old ladies in
Worthing who don't know . . .'[28] Posthumously Coward was in
danger, as D. W. Harding wrote of Jane Austen, one of Coward's
favourite writers, of becoming 'an ironist sentimentalised by
[his] admirers'.[29]

It was this preconception of Coward that my own biography,
published in 1995, tried to redress, while not disdaining the value
of his appeal to the generation to which he had tailored his art –
an art that was always cut to the cloth of popular culture.
Through the Eighties and Nineties there was a discernible
movement to reassess and reconfigure Coward, most actively in
the work of new directors – Philip Prowse, Sean Mathias, Declan
Donnellan, Philip Franks – and new interpretations: an overtly
camp *Semi-Monde*, a sexed-up *Design for Living*, a post-modern
Hay Fever, and – perhaps most shocking of all – a seriously
minded *Private Lives*. In 1998 the three-and-a-half-hour BBC2
Arena documentary film sensitively directed by Adam Low and
the *Twentieth-Century Blues* album, intelligently assembled by
Neil Tennant, appeared. The ensuing media coverage claimed
Coward as a godfather to the queasy phenomenon known as
'Cool Britannia', a politically and culturally convenient way to
find a place for him in Blairite Britain.

With the end of the Nineties, it seemed, Coward had been cut
loose from Old England, from the 'hopeless nostalgia' that
concerned the *Independent*, set free (perhaps even from himself)
in a classless, devolved country (he was, after all, one-quarter
Irish and one-half Scottish). A year later, at the very end of the
decade, in the centenary of his birth – the occasion for these
papers – both confirmed and questioned these posthumous
developments in Coward's remarkable ability to provoke debate
three decades after his death in 1973 – not in some English
country pile, but in a decolonialised Jamaica where Bob Marley
was already making records in downtown Kingston.

In the Nineties culture of self-reference and self-revelation, of obsession with fame and infamy, our age appeared no more mature than the inter-war period when the very notion of modern celebrity was invented (not least by Coward himself). As we begin to gain a new perspective on a decade we have left behind, we see similar patterns; the same mores and delusions which Coward so exquisitely captured, censured and appeared to condone. Having reached the end of a century, it seemed we had yet to grow up.

A cartoon, published around the time of *Cavalcade*'s enormous success, depicted the infant Noël in his perambulator, making notes for his future epic. 'Coward was Slighty in *Peter Pan*, and you might say that he has been wholly in *Peter Pan* ever since,' as Tynan wrote in 1961,[30] adding later, 'Whether by genetic luck or environmental good judgement, Noël Coward never suffered the imprisonment of maturity.'[31] Standing in the wings of the century, he remains a shadowy, ageless paradox. And that, the ghost of Noël Coward – a sprightly male Elvira in a brown evening suit – is an entirely fitting image for a shadowy, paradoxical age still wreathed in the steam from Milford Junction.

NOTES

1. The *Independent*, 23 October 1999.
2. Ibid.
3. Frances Gray, *Noël Coward* (London: Macmillan, 1987), p.66.
4. G. B. Stern, letter to Esme Wynne-Tyson, 28 May 1925, quoted Philip Hoare, *Noël Coward* (London: Sinclair-Stevenson, 1995), p.149.
5. Noël Coward, letter to Joyce Carey, undated but 1955, quoted Hoare, p.418.
6. Clive Hirschhorn, interview, *Sunday Express*, 23 May 1965.
7. Hoare, p.486.
8. Hoare, p.359.
9. John Lahr, *Coward the Playwright* (London: Methuen, 1982), p.3.
10. *Chambers Twentieth-Century Dictionary* (London: Chambers, 1899), p.798.
11. Lahr, p.154.
12. *Leave the Letters Till We're Dead: The Letters of Virginia Woolf*, Vol. IV, ed. Nigel Nicolson (London: The Hogarth Press, 1984), p.523, quoted Hoare, p.200.

13. *A Change of Perspective: The Letters of Virginia Woolf*, Vol.III, ed. Nigel Nicolson (London: The Hogarth Press, 1977), p.471, quoted Hoare, p.199.
14. *New Leader*, 29 January 1932, quoted Hoare, pp.235–6.
15. *The Noël Coward Diaries*, ed. Graham Payn and Sheridan Morley (London: Weidenfeld & Nicolson, 1982), p.135.
16. *Self-Portrait With Friends: Selected Diaries of Cecil Beaton*, ed. Richard Buckle (London: Weidenfeld & Nicolson, 1979), pp.11–12, quoted Hoare, p.201.
17. Cecil Beaton, *The Glass of Fashion* (London: Cassell, 1954), pp.153–4, quoted Hoare, p.141.
18. *Guardian*, 22 June 2000.
19. *Variety*, 15 June 1955.
20. *Sunday Times*, 22 January 1961.
21. Lahr, p.64.
22. *File on Coward*, ed. Jacqui Russell (London: Methuen, 1987), p.87.
23. Ariel Swartley, *The New York Times*, 10 January 1999.
24. Noël Coward, interview with Hunter Davies, *Sunday Times*, 28 December 1969.
25. Noël Coward, *Past Conditional* (London: Methuen, 1986), p.251, quoted Hoare, pp.234–5.
26. Erik Coward, letter to Violet Coward, 14 June 1932, quoted Hoare, p.235.
27. Hoare, p.235.
28. Hoare, p.509.
29. Jonathan Bate, introduction to Charles Lamb, *Elia and the Last Essays of Elia* (Oxford & New York: OUP, 1987), p.xiii (note).
30. Kenneth Tynan, *Curtains* (London: Longmans, 1961), quoted Lahr, p.161.
31. Kenneth Tynan, *New Yorker*, 24 January 1977, quoted Hoare, p.202.

Noël Coward and Effeminacy

Alan Sinfield

This is Quentin Crisp in *The Naked Civil Servant* on the 1920s:

> The men of the twenties searched themselves for vestiges of effeminacy as though for lice. They did not worry about their characters but about their hair and their clothes. Their predicament was that they must never be caught worrying about either. I once heard a slightly dandified friend of my brother say, 'People are always accusing me of taking care over my appearance.' The sexual meaning of behavior was only sketchily understood, but the symbolism of clothes was recognized by everyone. To wear suede shoes was to be under suspicion. Anyone who had hair rather than bristle at the back of his neck was thought to be an artist, a foreigner, or worse.[1]

This is very reminiscent of Coward's advice to Cecil Beaton in 1929, quoted in Philip Hoare's splendid biography:

> Your sleeves are too tight, your voice is too high and too precise. You mustn't do it. It closes so many doors ... It's hard, I know. One would like to indulge one's own taste. I myself dearly love a good match, yet I know it is overdoing it to wear tie, socks and handkerchief of the same colour. I

take ruthless stock of myself in the mirror before going out.
A polo jumper or unfortunate tie exposes one to danger.[2]

Again, rehearsing with Marlene Dietrich in 1935, Coward
exhorted her: 'Marlenah! I must not appear effeminate in any
way. Do be a dear – watch out for anything that could be
considered less than "butch", if you see me being at all "queer",
tell me immediately.'[3]
So Coward was anxious about this. He well might be. What is
striking to me, and I suspect to other people of my generation and
background, is that Coward, Beaton, Dietrich and the entire set
have always seemed as camp as Christmas. To my lower-middle-
class, scholarship-boy, CND, Sixties, Gay-Lib sensibility,
Coward's persona *in its entirety*, and all his characters and
everything to do with his kind of theatre, appeared bathed in
effeminacy. It hardly occurred to me that Coward might regard
himself as 'straight-acting' (as contact ads today sometimes
promise and demand).
In the period of Gay Liberation, taking off from the change in
the law in 1967 and the Stonewall Riot in 1969, Coward offered
a troubling model. After all, in *Song at Twilight* (1966) Carlotta
remarks that sanctions against homosexuality are out of date, but
Hugo propounds the view of Coward and most of his ilk: 'Maybe
so, but even when the actual law ceases to exist there will still be
a stigma attached to "the love that dare not speak its name" in the
minds of millions of people for generations to come. It takes more
than a few outspoken books and plays and speeches in Parliament
to uproot moral prejudices from the Anglo-Saxon mind.'[4]
Most upper-class queers, we thought, had done nothing to
promote law reform; they had contributed more to gay shame
than to gay pride. The theatre we valued most in the 1970s was
campaigning – avant-garde, Brechtian, agit-prop – the mode of
Gay Sweatshop. We couldn't make up our minds – and still can't
– as to whether effeminacy was old-fashioned and self-oppressed,
gender-bending and subversive, or nothing much to worry about
either way.
Further study of Coward's work complicates the position but

only partly changes it. I had been inclined to celebrate the song 'We All Wore a Green Carnation' from *Bitter Sweet* (1929), as an exuberant triumph of sanctions busting, in which Coward's genius overwhelms the Lord Chamberlain to achieve a moment of queerness rampant:

> Haughty boys, naughty boys, dear, dear dear!
>> Swooning with affectation.
>> Our figures sleek and willowy,
>> Our lips incarnadine,
>> May worry the majority a bit.
>> But matrons rich and billowy,
>> Invite us out to dine,
>> And revel in our phosphorescent wit.[5]

However, the song makes better sense in the way Hoare proposes: as 'Noël's comment on the Uranian decadents, purveyors of a camp sensibility he eschewed', signalling 'disdain for the more obvious members of the homosexual fraternity'.[6] *Bitter Sweet* contains another song in similar mode, 'Tarara boom-de-ay', in which the four 'exquisites' again admit to being ineffectual:

> We merely spend our time preventing
>> Some earnest stripling
>> From liking Kipling
>> Instead of Wilde.
> Now that we find the dreary nineteenth century is closing,
> We mean to start the twentieth in ecstasies of posing.[7]

Two things seem plain: that Coward's repudiation of effeminacy was insecure and that his notion of the impression he was making involved some wishful thinking. In practice, it was very difficult for men of his generation to dissociate effeminacy and homosexuality. There was a discourse, drawing upon Walt Whitman, Edward Carpenter and 'uranian' writers, which asserted male same-sex practice as quintessentially manly.[8] Edward Carpenter, E. M. Forster, Goldsworthy Lowes Dickinson and J. R. Ackerley sought to proclaim this idea. However, gender inversion was intrinsic to 'homosexuality' as it was being constructed in the wake of Wilde and the dawning light of Freud, and these men never quite managed to expel a residuum of effeminacy from the concept of queerness. Mostly they ended up manifesting effeminate manners while insisting that they were not really like that. Robin Maugham, according to Bryan Connon,

> could never relax in the company of effeminate men in public unless he was too drunk to care. Like Willie [Somerset Maugham] he did not understand why some homosexual men felt compelled to behave flamboyantly to challenge total strangers with their brand of sexuality. Camping about with friends in private was a different matter, though he never felt entirely at ease with this, but to be anything other than masculine in public was a betrayal of the male ethos.[9]

Actually, it is the chosen partner who was usually expected to bear the burden of explicit masculinity. Because he was often from the lower classes and therefore supposed to be manly by definition, he might easily be co-opted into this fantasy role. Coward's fondness for soldiers and sailors fits this pattern.

Yet personal sexuality is not enough to account for what is happening in Coward, his image and his work. After all, we think of the 1920s as a time when women cut their hair in a boyish manner and many upper-class young men, partly influenced by Coward himself, purposively cultivated a camp style. Martin Green argues that such frivolity manifested a disillusionment with the 'Victorian' seriousness and responsibility that were seen as having produced the war and, even more, the phoney attitudes that accompanied it: 'They refused to grow up into men of responsibility, fathers of families and of the state, soldiers.'[10] Samuel Hynes discusses right-wing operations such as the prosecution of Rose Allatini's pacifist–gay novel *Despised and Rejected* (1918) and the trial incited by the performance of Maud

Allan in *Salome* (1918). Hynes argues that such manoeuvres

> intensified and solidified what was worst and most repressive
> in wartime English society, and by so doing helped to create
> a post-war sub-culture of outsiders, composed of an odd
> mixture of persons – opponents of the war, artists,
> homosexuals – whom the war spirit had identified as
> subversive. . . . Oscar Wilde had seemed dead in 1914, and
> pacifism had scarcely been born. But in 1918 both were alive
> and vocal.[11]

These stances of conformity and dissidence were processed as
masculine and feminine, and were consolidated through the
division at public schools and upper-class universities into
hearties (or athletes) and aesthetes. By 1930, in his book
Degenerate Oxford?, Terence Greenidge was presenting such a
split as generally acknowledged. An element of the feminine was
civilising, he thought, but not too much. There were dangers, in
particular 'the mass-production of effeminate men' whose 'feet
will be shod with gay suede shoes. They will speak with artificial
voices of a somewhat high timbre, also they will walk with a
mincing gait.'[12] The Oxbridge pattern fed back into public
schools. At Harrow, where Terence Rattigan was a pupil, it
became fashionable for boys in rebellion against school values to
proclaim their genuine or affected homosexuality.[13] The sissy –
that despised other of the Victorian boys' story – returned to
challenge the system.

While Crisp is right, therefore, to say that it was important for
men generally not to appear feminine, this doesn't mean that no
one did. Rather, some did and some didn't, and it was very
important which you were. There was a contest about the kind of
place England should be, and it was focused partly through ideas
of gender and sexuality. While Coward did not want to suffer the
consequences of outright queer manner, he did want to cultivate
the dissident potential of the aesthete. In the plays, this produces
a complex pattern of gesture and denial.

In *The Vortex* (1923) Nicky is the aesthete – just back from composing music in Paris; 'extremely well dressed'; 'tall and pale, with thin, nervous hands'.[14] Tom, conversely, is 'athletic and good looking', the stage direction says; 'one feels he is good at games and extremely bad at everything else.' Florence prefers Tom's cigarettes to Pawnie's because they are 'a special rather hearty kind'. Helen finds his dancing 'too athletic'. 'Anyhow,' Pawnie replies, 'I'm sure he's a success at the Bath Club (pp.201–2).' Tom finds Nicky pretty baffling (he is not terribly bright). 'It seems so funny you being in love with that sort of chap,' he tells Bunty. 'You know – up in the air – effeminate (pp.196–8).' Indeed, Bunty herself is obliged to inform Nicky that he is unpromising as a marital partner: 'You're not in love with me, really – you couldn't be! (p.217).' Nicky is certainly more amusing, though. Tom has been at Sandhurst, the upper-class training college for officers: 'Such a pretty place,' Nicky remarks.

However – and this is Coward looking for the best of both worlds – Nicky is not as effeminate as Pawnie. The latter is described as 'an elderly maiden gentleman' who makes 'a "Fetish" of house decoration' (p.167). His conversation is decadent and effete: for instance, when he remarks that Florence is 'a couple of hundred years too late – she ought to have been a flaunting, intriguing King's mistress, with black page boys and jade baths and things too divine – (p.170)'. He even contrives to flirt with Tom:

> TOM (*shaking hands*):   How are you?
> PAWNIE: Very well, thank you – how sweet of you to ask me? (p.174)

Harry Benshoff, in his study of homosexuality and the horror film, calls the deployment of figures such as Pawnie 'inoculation': the extreme queer tends to protect the moderate queerness of others.[15]

In *Design for Living* (1933) the assertion of difference is more confident. 'We have our own decencies. We have our own ethics. Our lives are a different shape,' Leo declares (p.462). Yet, if this

involves an element of effeminacy attaching to Leo and Otto, at
least they are not as queer as Ernest. He is said to be rather precise
in manner, distrustful of women, a permanent spectator,
'sterile'.[16] He loves the three principals a lot – though Gilda 'a
little less than Otto and Leo', she notes, 'because I'm a woman
and, therefore, unreliable'. But then, his way of loving is limited
anyhow: 'Your affection is a scared thing, though. Too frightened;
too apprehensive of consequences (pp.352–3).' Ernest's queerness makes the heterosexual interests of Leo and Otto more
plausible. His marriage to Gilda is mocked: 'You're a dear old pet,
Ernest, and we're very, very fond of you and we know perfectly
well that Gilda could be married to you fifty times and still not be
your wife (p.453).'

In *Present Laughter* (1942) Garry Essendine is reported to have
close liaisons with men as well as women. A young man went to
the Slade School because Garry allowed him to think he
'minded so passionately about his career'; an Indian whom he
met in a bar in Marseilles 'was wonderful'.[17] There is an admiral's
son: Garry 'swore to him that if he left the Navy [he]'d give him
a job on the stage' – 'Absolutely marvellous, if it's the one I think
it is [which other ones were there?], vast strapping shoulders and
tiny, tiny hips like a wasp – .' Old gentlemen in the city will back
Garry in plays, especially if they are not married (pp.224, 244).
However, Roland Maule, who pursues Garry obsessionally,
seems peculiarly queer. He has been studying psychology, he tells
Garry, 'because I felt somehow that I wasn't at peace with myself
and gradually, bit by bit, I began to realise that you signified
something to me. . . . I feel much better now because I think I
shall be able to sublimate you all right (pp.206, 174–5).' He feels
better still on his next visit: 'Couldn't I stay a little longer, you
see every moment I'm near him I get smoother and smoother and
smoother, and my whole rhythm improves tremendously
(p.213).' But Garry tries to avoid Roland, so Garry can't be all
that queer.

Coward's trick, then, is to distance himself from effeminate
queerness even while deploying it. In fact, as I try to show in *Out
on Stage*, he manages to attract two audiences at once: a general

boulevard audience that finds naughtiness titillating, and a more specialised audience of sexual dissidents for whom he and his work were actively constitutive of a newly emergent gay sub-culture.[18] Coward's plays, I believe, did not merely reflect ideas of gayness; they afforded a reference point through which many men cultivated their own ideas of who they were.

Coward's main cover in this manoeuvre was that effeminacy didn't necessarily mean 'homosexual'. This is the argument of my book, *The Wilde Century*. The exposure and conviction of Wilde contributed crucially to the establishment of the dominant twentieth-century metropolitan idea of the queer man. Even so, effeminacy, aestheticism and a dandified manner did not correlate *inevitably* with queerness. Effeminacy was, first of all, a class manner – one which had been accepted by the upper classes as the middle class constituted itself around usefulness, morality and seriousness (hence the importance of being earnest). The proprietress of a local diner was suspicious of Quentin Crisp's friend although 'his airs and graces were far less pronounced than mine'. This is because the friend was local, whereas Crisp was 'a real gentleman'.[19]

The fussy, fastidious bachelor remained a broadly plausible upper-class figure, therefore. In many plays he spends time with women, involved in gossip; he is useful as a commentator and facilitator because he isn't party to the heterosexual pairing off which is usually the central theme. He may be traced back to Sheridan's *School for Scandal*, and has only faintly queer characteristics in Somerset Maugham's *Mrs Dot* (1908) and *Jack Straw* (1908). An element of stigma did attach to him, as to sissy-boys, mannish spinsters and tomboys – violators of gender hierarchy. But people did not think, necessarily, that anyone who wasn't manifesting some kind of heterosexual enthusiasm must be queer. Consider, for instance, Charles Marsden in Eugene O'Neill's *Strange Interlude* (1927).[20]

But this was changing. Even for the innocent or the resistant, effeminacy tended to signal homosexuality. The plausibility of this linkage was increased by the spread of psychological theories. Freud dismissed notions of a female soul in a feminine body, but he cultivated the idea that lesbians and gay men manifest 'a certain arrest of sexual development'.[21] And the 'arrest' occurs at the point of Oedipal development where the individual is caught in the 'wrong' gender identity. In a note added to the *Three Essays on the Theory of Sexuality* in 1910, Freud declares:

> In all the cases we have examined we have established the fact that the future inverts, in the earliest years of their childhood, pass through a phase of very intense but short-lived fixation to a woman (usually their mother), and that, after leaving this behind, they identify themselves with a woman and take *themselves* as their sexual object. That is to say, proceeding from a basis of narcissism, they look for a young man who resembles themselves and whom *they* may love as their mother loved *them*.[22]

The homosexual behaves as his mother did (or as he wanted her to). Carole-Anne Tyler glosses: 'If a man desires another man, he must do so as a woman.'[23]

Theatre was one of the places where these new ideas circulated. In *The Prisoners of War* (1925) by J. R. Ackerley, young Conrad doesn't have a framework for understanding Adelby's suggestion that his problem might be related to 'what clever people call your ego'. Conrad thinks this means he's selfish; nor does he see the relevance of Adelby's suggestion that pacing the pattern in the carpet might be significant.[24] However, the audience is expected to get the point.

In *The Vortex* Nicky's 'weak' father and attachment to his mother would prompt the thought of homosexuality. 'I've grown up all wrong,' he says. 'Of course it's your fault, Mother – who else's fault *could* it be? (p.237).' Nicky's confrontation with his mother over her adultery is very like Hamlet's – George Street, the Lord Chamberlain's reader, thought Coward might plead Shakespeare as a precedent – and the buzz idea was that Hamlet had an unresolved 'Oedipus complex'.[25] Freud's remarks in *The Interpretation of Dreams* (translated in 1913) had been developed by Ernest Jones in a notorious essay of 1910 (reprinted in 1923).

T.S. Eliot, in his *Hamlet* essay of 1919, adduced also Shakespeare's sonnets: '*Hamlet*, like the sonnets, is full of some stuff that the writer could not drag to light, contemplate, or manipulate into art. And when we search for this feeling, we find it, as in the sonnets, very difficult to localize.'[26] I think we all know what that is.

'I do not know whether the author of the play knew our psychological concept of homosexuality,' Abraham Brill, leading proponent of psychoanalysis in the USA, remarked of Otto and Leo in *Design for Living*, 'but all the essential factors of it were cleverly depicted. The narcism [*sic*] was expressed by making the two men look and dress almost exactly like; they even kiss each other.'[27]

Increasingly an audience, and specially a gay audience, learnt to read these codes, even as they were doing in their own sub-cultural interactions. The indeterminacy over effeminacy and sexuality was both the anxiety and the opportunity for Coward. He tried to maintain a distance between himself and manifest queerness. Nonetheless, a strategic cultivation of effeminacy enabled him first to stake out an oppositional stance, then to invoke and partly to constitute an emergent gay sub-culture. He found homosexuality embedded in, perhaps trying to emerge from, a more general concept of bohemian-leisured exuberance, and elaborated that formation and its language in a way that strengthened the potential for a discreet queer identification.

Nor is the gendering of gayness a resolved issue. At the end of the twentieth century Andrew Sullivan, in *Love Undetectable*, is still keen to distance himself from 'insecure gay adults' who will 'always cling, to a greater or lesser extent, to the protections of gender mannerisms, of excessive masculinity or caricatured femininity'.[28]

NOTES

1. Quentin Crisp, *The Naked Civil Servant* (New York: Plume, 1977), pp.21–2.
2. Cecil Beaton, *Self Portrait with Friends* (London: Weidenfeld & Nicolson, 1979), pp.11–12, quoted in Philip Hoare, *Noël Coward* (London: Sinclair-Stevenson, 1995), p.201.
3. Hoare, *Noël Coward*, p.268.

4. Noël Coward, Song at Twilight, in Coward, Plays: Five (London: Methuen, 1983), pp.417–18.
5. Noël Coward, Bitter Sweet, in Coward, Play Parade (London: Heinemann, 1934), pp.156–7.
6. Hoare, Noël Coward, p.206.
7. Coward, Bitter Sweet, pp.149–50.
8. See Alan Sinfield, The Wilde Century (London: Cassell, 1994), pp.109–17.
9. Bryan Connon, Somerset Maugham and the Maugham Dynasty (London: Sinclair-Stevenson, 1997), p.167.
10. Martin Green, Children of the Sun (London: Constable, 1977), p.152.
11. Samuel Hynes, A War Imagined (London: Bodley Head, 1990), p.234; see Philip Hoare, Wilde's Last Stand (London: Duckworth, 1997), pp.188–9, 202–7, 227–31.
12. Terence Greenidge, Degenerate Oxford? (London: Chapman and Hall, 1930), p.107.
13. Michael Darlow and Gillian Hodson, Terence Rattigan (London: Quartet, 1979), p.40.
14. Noël Coward, The Vortex, in Coward, Play Parade, p.183.
15. Harry M. Benshoff, Monsters in the Closet (Manchester: MUP, 1997), p.188.
16. Noël Coward, Design for Living, in Coward, Play Parade, pp.400–1.
17. Noël Coward, Present Laughter, in Coward, Plays: Four (London: Methuen, 1983), pp.151, 222.
18. Alan Sinfield, Out on Stage (New Haven: Yale University Press, 1999), chapter 5. I argue also that Coward contributed significantly to the use of 'gay' in England.
19. Crisp, Naked Civil Servant, p.53.
20. See Sinfield, Out on Stage, pp.114–19.
21. Quoted in Kenneth Lewes, The Psychoanalytic Theory of Male Homosexuality (London: Quartet, 1989), p.32.
22. Sigmund Freud, Three Essays on the Theory of Sexuality, in The Penguin Freud Library, Vol. 7, On Sexuality (Harmondsworth: Penguin, 1977), p.56.
23. Carole-Anne Tyler, 'Boys Will Be Girls: the Politics of Gay Drag' in Diana Fuss, ed., Inside/Out (New York: Routledge, 1991), p.34.
24. J. R. Ackerley, The Prisoners of War, in Michael Wilcox, ed., Gay Plays, Vol. 3 (London: Methuen, 1988), pp.105–6.
25. W. David Sievers, Freud on Broadway (1955; New York: Cooper Square, 1970), p.133.
26. T. S. Eliot, Selected Prose (Harmondsworth: Penguin, 1963), pp.101–2. Arthur Hopkins 'produced the memorable Freudian Hamlet with John Barrymore in 1922': Sievers, Freud on Broadway, p.47.
27. A. A. Brill, Freud's Contribution to Psychiatry (New York: Norton, 1944), p.133; quoted by Sievers, Freud on Broadway, p.217.
28. Andrew Sullivan, Love Undetectable (London: Chatto, 1998), p.153.

Noël Coward's Bad Manners

Dan Rebellato

So many of Noël Coward's plays were set in country houses that it is unsurprising that his reputation should have become tainted with the values of an upper-class milieu. John Pick, in *The West End: Mismanagement and Snobbery*, accuses Coward of shameless social climbing and his chapter cataloguing instances of upper-class prejudice is brutally entitled 'The Rank and Snobbery of Sir Noël Coward'.[1] Certainly, some of Coward's own pronouncements, especially in the waspish later years of his diary, do little to discourage such an association: 'I have a Ritz mind,' he once unblushingly declared, 'and always have had.'[2]

Upper-class manners find their way into some of the plays and at times the observance of etiquette stifles a more profound understanding of the social dynamics Coward is portraying. *'Peace in Our Time'* (1947) imagines a counter-factual Britain under Nazi occupation. In a pub near Knightsbridge the locals are joined by Albrecht, a Nazi officer, who attempts to curry favour by buying a round. He proposes a toast:

> ALBRECHT (*lifting his glass*):   Heil Hitler.
> *Albrecht drinks. There is a silence. Chorley begins to lift his glass and then stops.*
> GEORGE (*gently*):   That was a mistake, Mr Richter – a psychological error.
> ALBRECHT (*icily*):   In what way?
> GEORGE: It places us in an embarrassing position.[3]

The moment ludicrously reduces a fascist invasion of Britain to a species of vast social gaffe. Other plays like *Relative Values* read like thin imitations of Somerset Maugham, and suggest that Coward had become imaginatively impoverished by his limited social circle and intellectually compromised by its etiquette.

The origin of his alleged infatuation with the aristocracy was his invitation in 1915 to Hambleton, the Rutlandshire country seat of Mrs Astley Cooper, an eccentric member of the landed gentry. 'This was', as Cole Lesley has written, 'Noël's first taste of "county".'[4] Philip Hoare states, 'Hambleton was pivotal to Coward's progress. It identified a social goal, a standard to which he could aspire now that he knew what life among his "betters" was like.'[5] What these accounts do not acknowledge is that there was no uncomplicated 'country life' for Coward to imbibe. During the First World War, life among the nobility and gentry was in the midst of a wholesale transformation, affecting every level of aristocratic life. By attending to the dynamics of this shift I hope to show a different side of Coward: the playwright as mischievous social critic, with a complex and satirical relation to the class he is supposed always to have wished to join.

The author of *Etiquette for Gentlemen* (1923) described the 1914–18 war as 'shattering to all conventional ideas'.[6] Ursula Mary Lyon went further, describing it as 'a cataclysm' which precipitated 'an apparent upheaval of all accepted standards'.[7] The war had hit the British nobility very hard; of the peers and their sons who went to war, one in five did not return.[8] The emotional devastation of this loss was mixed with the disruption it caused to the institution of primogeniture; the carefully maintained system of handing land, wealth and property from eldest son to eldest son was ravaged by the war.

Yet this does not explain the widely articulated feeling that *all* social values were in crisis, as suggested by Colonel Whittaker in *Easy Virtue* (1925) who remarks that 'everything's changing nowadays'.[9] Indeed, the human casualties of war were perhaps a scapegoat for the wider decline experienced by the British upper classes over the thirty years preceding it.

At the end of the 1870s the British aristocracy had the greatest accumulation of power, wealth and status of any comparable social group in Europe and the source of this was land. Some seven thousand families owned four-fifths of the British Isles. Land conferred celebrity, generated regular income, and gave its owners control over parliamentary representation, access to ministers and a quasi-feudal stranglehold on local adminis-tration.[10] They dominated not only the Lords but the Commons too. The London Season was organised partly to marry off their children, but also to entertain the leading party grandees and thereby steer the course of national politics.

All this changed in the 1880s. The growth in world trade meant an increasing supply of cheap goods from America, Canada, South America and the Antipodes. Coupled with a series of bad harvests, this led to a sharp downturn in the income to tenant farmers and a consequent squeeze on the rents which had financially underpinned the leisured life of the country gentleman. In England, between the mid-1870s and mid-1890s, average rents fell by twenty-six per cent. At the same time, the exponential growth in industry and commerce was creating both new forms of wealth, independent of land, and a new class clamouring for greater access to government. So as British agricultural production suffered in competition with foreign land, land itself was politically marginalised. The 1884–5 Third Reform Act, by enfranchising many county voters, further marginalised the landowning class. The Lords did themselves few favours when they attempted to block passage of the bill, giving rise to unprecedented levels of public hostility. Within a decade land had become an economic and political liability. As Lady Bracknell remarks in Wilde's The Importance of Being Earnest (1895), 'Land has ceased to be either a profit or a pleasure. It gives one position and prevents one from keeping it up. That's all that can be said about land.'[11]

The landowners responded by trying to reorganise their hold-ings, selling off assets, renting out their town houses and putting portions of their country estates on the market. But if it was the aristocracy who had to sell, it was the rising industrial class who could afford to buy, and quickly the prized exclusiveness of country life and high society was challenged. High society's most stuffily self-regarding periodical, *The Queen*, sighed, 'nowadays it is sufficient merely to acquire these symbols (yacht, house, grouse moor, racehorses, cars) to be admitted to Society'.[12]

Dismayed by this challenge to its own prestige and power, Old Money had to respond to New Money and their weapon of choice was etiquette. If the 'merely wealthy' could now buy land and property, the ascendency of the nobles had to be vested in something you couldn't buy. One of the most bohemian of the pre-war aristocratic sets, 'The Souls', 'prided themselves above all on their intellect, their aesthetic sensibility, their unique interpretation of the taste and manners of their time'.[13] This turn inwards from an authority guaranteed by riches to one based on personal values is characteristic of a wider shift in the aristocracy's understanding of itself.

Etiquette promised the nobility a means of determining the social ground on which all people, newly or anciently wealthy, would have to move. The newly prosperous had 'stormed the citadels of social exclusiveness, and flaunted their parvenu wealth with opulent and irresistible vulgarity'.[14] The handbooks of polite manners promised to check this excess, declaring: 'One rule should be theirs from the very start. No ostentatious display.'[15] With every faux pas, every subtle correction, every adoption of new behavioural codes, the parvenus would be put back in their place, one which yielded to the aristocrat as arbiter of civilised values.

What made etiquette such a promising ideological tool is that the codes were self-protecting. The admonition not to make a scene made it impossible to challenge, or even to acknowledge, the rules of etiquette, which had always to be *tacitly* observed. As one authority put it, 'The perfection of manners is "no manner".'[16] Another comments, 'The manners of the best-bred people are those which are thrust the least upon the notice of others.'[17] The parvenu, persuaded to adopt aristocratic manners, would thereby prevent himself from questioning their value, because the rules of etiquette, like a good butler, were held to function best when virtually invisible. Using polite manners to forestall social change was nothing new; manners books and primers on etiquette had always insisted that politics was an unfit subject for the polite drawing room, a stricture which had shielded high society from direct criticism since the first Reform Act. As Andrew St George writes, 'Manners are social control self-imposed; and etiquette is class control exercised.'[18]

The specific class origins of this codified behaviour were further disguised by a rhetoric which treated them as generally accepted rules, adopted for the good of society as a whole; one handbook considers etiquette to be 'an accumulation of universally accepted rules of conduct whereby the whole world is made kin'.[19] All etiquette books of the early twentieth century came bristling with prolegomena characterising the current rules of good behaviour as the pinnacle of civilisation. In 1922, Mary Woodman's *Correct Conduct* (tellingly subtitled 'Etiquette for Everybody') explained that:

> When savages and cavemen held sway in the land, each individual lived for himself and he pleased himself how he lived. With the march of civilization, the thought for others became more and more a part of people's natures, until, today, nobody can pretend to be a reasonable subject unless he models his actions upon the accepted notions of those with whom he comes into contact.
>
> The laws which guide men's actions in these matters form our code of etiquette, and it will be seen that life could not proceed in an orderly manner were this code to be ignored.[20]

The passage is typical in its mixture of dubious history and implicit warnings of chaos. In 1900 the anonymous author of *Complete Etiquette for Ladies and Gentlemen* informs us that while etiquette may at first have been merely functional, 'with advancing civilization would come, of necessity, increased refinement, opulence, and leisure'.[21]

Most late-nineteenth century men and women would surely have paused before characterising their life as one of refinement, opulence and leisure, yet nonetheless etiquette was promoted as class-neutral, the product of general cultural advancement. When G. R. M. Devereux writes that to acquire perfect etiquette 'one must have a knowledge of the observances of well-bred society',[22] the unabashed equation of good manners with the conduct of 'well-bred society' lays bare the class basis of these apparently universal rules of social demeanour.

Yet this awesome promotion of etiquette to the role of conduit for all that is best in the human spirit was part of a wider political strategy. As protests against the Lords and calls for their abolition mounted in the 1880s, Tory defenders of aristocratic privilege worked out a new defence: that the aristocracy embodied the civilised values of the country as a whole and had therefore a duty to protect those values against any government which might tyrannically try to pursue narrower interests. Lord Curzon put it more nonchalantly: 'All civilisation has been the work of aristocracies.'[23]

Crucially, this civilisation was located in aristocratic breeding, in their inherent gentility. Etiquette was merely its outward sign, the cultural manifestation of an internal state of grace, a historical gift from the nobility to the commoners. When Lady Troubridge, in her peremptorily titled The Book of Etiquette (1926), declares that '"Etiquette" helps make life pleasanter, more attractive to people of every class',[24] she is promoting this paradoxical doctrine that the true spirit of democracy is embodied in upper-class privilege.

Etiquette at the turn of the century, then, should be seen as a means of social control, a way to retain social prestige in the face of real economic decline. As the town houses and country estates of the gentry were broken up, rented or bought by the industrial class, the nobility turned to promoting etiquette. In the 1880s The Queen magazine ran a series of articles entitled 'Au Fait' to instruct the newcomers on the social rules of the milieu they were entering and Burke's Peerage published a Book of Precedence.[25] And between 1900 and 1930, a period in which Lloyd George was waging legislative war against the upper house, etiquette books were being published at a rate of three a year.

But in publishing these books the aristocracy exposed itself to a new problem. In the nineteenth century, etiquette books reflected a belief that polite behaviour was a natural manifestation of good character and nothing could come between them. *The Spirit of Etiquette* (1855) denied categorically that 'a gentleman [can] ever be otherwise than a gentleman, nor can a man who is habitually vulgar assume the gentleman at will'.[26] Another book published the same year treats such matters as cultivating a repertoire of conversational gambits, or wearing suitable clothes, as quite uncontroversial emanations of one's superior nature.[27] As Andrew St George writes, 'The Victorians emphasised the steady link between conduct and character.'[28]

But only fifty years later, having staked its cultural authority on its unique manners, and setting these manners out in a series of guidebooks, the nobility made this cultural elevation into something which could be bought, adopted, *performed*. The paradox of trying both to impose your behaviour on everyone else and keep it as your own exclusive property is witnessed in Lady Troubridge's book. She begins by comparing the acquisition of good manners with learning dance steps:

> These rules and suggestions should be read with a view to instructing oneself upon the whole subject, and getting such a knowledge of its inner meaning (of which these outward observances are but a reflection) that, as in dancing, the formal steps once learned, the dancer can merge them at will into the rhythm of the whole.[29]

This passage characteristically insists on etiquette being tied holistically to inner virtue, the latter being reflected in the former. But it is the integrity of this social dancer that is called into question as every precept is laid down on the page. Elsewhere, she speculates that 'fine character may to a certain extent be an inherited possession' (p. 4). But what does 'to a certain extent' mean? After all, if it were true, if etiquette were merely the outward reflex of inherited character, the book would not be worth writing. The statement is true precisely to the extent that the book is valueless. Her Ladyship ploughs on:

'Refinement lies in the heart and the spirit rather than in outward appearance,' she insists, 'but it is by what we do and say that we prove that it exists within us' (p. 5). If proof is only to be judged by externals, however, and if externals can be learned, as the publishing of her book suggests, then the special authority of the nobility looks less and less plausible.

In short, this strategy backfired spectacularly. A guidebook published in 1923 censured the modern age: 'In these strenuous, bustling days, people rarely take the trouble to probe below the surface, and they are apt to accept individuals, like material things, at their face value.'[30] The passage is revealing; the words 'strenuous, bustling' obviously imply the world of business (as opposed to the world of gentrified leisure, which moved at a less urgent, perhaps less vulgar, pace). In this materialistic world, it seems that the spiritual virtue of the upper class has been ignored. People are only interested in surfaces and etiquette is now being adopted like any other material acquisition, without the inner refinement that was supposed to be its necessary counterpart. The same book laments, 'In general society, the quality of the heart matters little, so long as the surface is, at the same time, genial and polished' (p. 10).

Throughout the 1920s the aristocracy was losing confidence in the stability of its speech acts. The possibility of forgery which they, in writing these guides, had opened up had impaired the integrity of these original behavioural codes. Detaching the inner from the outer is urgently censured: Constance Burleigh, in *Etiquette Up to Date* (1925), writes of 'Party manners' (adopting good manners only for public show) that they 'cannot hide the awkwardness and ill-breeding beneath the poor veneer. Indeed, the assumption of manners for special occasions only may be likened to the daubing over of a common metal disc to simulate a golden sovereign.'[31] In so saying, Burleigh is both denigrating New Money for usurping civilised manners and engaging in wish-fulfilment by claiming that the truth will out. But the gold-coin analogy reminds us that forgers can be successful and counterfeiting may devalue the currency it counterfeits.

The counterfeits multiplied. In his polemical introduction to

Three Plays (1925), Noël Coward bemoaned the 'insidious
blight' of society's intermixing with the theatre.[32] There had
indeed been a sea change in relations between these worlds,
marking the new semi-respectability of the stage in general and
actresses in particular. In 1884 the future Marquess of
Aylesbury's high-profile marriage to Dolly Tester opened the
floodgates, as Pamela Horn writes: 'Overall there were twenty-
one marriages between peers and players over the period
1879–1914, with seven of the brides being American. Many
were Gaiety or Gibson girls, who had been carefully groomed not
only in their speech and deportment but in their dress sense as
well.'[33] It was the skilled deportment and designed respectability
of George Edwardes's 'Gaiety Girls' that explains their easy
entrance into 'good society'. Eileen Terry, in *Etiquette for All*
(1925), writes: 'Notice the easy way in which the Stage has
joined with the Peerage – obviously because the essential Stage
training teaches good manners, correct speech, and social
actions, and also a careful toilet and a graceful walk.'[34]

However, this too was dangerous. To associate noble manners
with acting was tantamount to admitting that these manners
were nothing but a performance, that forgery was their natural
condition. And it was this that gave Coward a lever to open the
aristocracy of manners to impish satire. After all, his indignation
was not at the diluting of noble blood with low-grade actresses'
stock, which some feared, but rather at the diluting of the stage
with nobility. *Operette* is a back-stage musical, set in the very
Edwardian milieu in which the worlds of society and stage
mingled so promiscuously. In the opening chorus of *The Model
Maid*, the pastiche musical comedy around which the action of
the play takes place, several Lords and Ladies sing, 'If it wasn't for
the Chorus / Dancing about where would the Peerage be?'[35]

Throughout *Operette*, this steady decline of the aristocratic
certainties is theatrically exploited, specifically by showing the
theatricalisation of the aristocracy. It parallels *The Model Maid* on
stage with the back-stage drama of a peer's inopportune love affair
with a chorus girl. That the lives of the nobility could so easily
take a musical comedy form is comment enough, but Coward goes

further. In one back-stage sequence, we witness three actors in their dressing room, waiting to go on. Decima Drury is dressed as 'The Duchess of Trenton', Edgar Fawcett as 'The Duke of Trenton' and Paul Trevor as 'The Marquis of Fairfield' (p.208). They look like aristocrats, but talk like actors, blurring the lines of demarcation between the two worlds, an effect enhanced by the fact that all characters, whether actor or peer, are, of course, played by actors. Coward frequently has fun with the interchangeability of these worlds and the main scenes of high social entertaining are hosted entirely by actresses.

Several of Coward's early plays artfully confuse players and peers. *Hay Fever* is set in a country house but the Lady of the Manor, Judith Bliss, is an actor. As her son and daughter observe, she seems to see the life of a gentlewoman more as an opportunity to get into character than a patrician responsibility:

SOREL: Where's mother?
SIMON: In the garden, practising.
SOREL: Practising?
SIMON (*stops drawing and looks at Sorel*): She's learning the names of the flowers by heart. I *always* distrust her when she becomes the Squire's lady.[36]

In *Easy Virtue*, Larita is the unwelcome intruder into the family home, and not least of the deprecations directed at her by Mrs Whittaker is the observation that her name would be 'excellent for musical comedy'.[37]

But it is on the level of etiquette that Coward's plays are most profoundly subversive. His early ones stage numerous offences against good manners. In *The Young Idea* (1923), Sholto and Gerda, children from George's first marriage, join in the drawing-room discussion with enthusiasm. Julia, a friend of the family, is quick to criticise their overeagerness to 'push themselves forward and monopolise the conversation'.[38] Her understanding of the etiquette is faultless; Lady Troubridge reminds us in a substantial summary of 'Conduct Which Is Incorrect' for young men and girls, that it includes specifically 'to be too pressing of attention'.[39]

Rudeness is the main motif of *Hay Fever* in which the Bliss family frequently reflect on their haphazard adoption of formalities. Sorel tells her brother that she has invited a friend for the weekend: 'I warned him not to expect good manners, but I hope you'll be as pleasant to him as you can,' admitting 'we're so awfully bad-mannered'.[40] At the end of the play, noticing that weekend guests have quietly left rather than endure any more bewildering rudeness, Judith Bliss remarks ironically, 'How rude' and her husband, David, agrees: 'People really do behave in the most extraordinary manner these days' (p. 93).

All this pales alongside the sensational scene created by Larita in *Easy Virtue*. The Whittaker family have confronted her with the truth about her past and she is quite unpenitent. Since there is due to be a party, the family do not want to make a scene and therefore ask her to remain upstairs, while they circulate a story that she is feeling unwell. But in the great *coup de théâtre* of the play, she appears at the top of the stairs:

> *Her dress is dead-white and cut extremely low; she is wearing three ropes of pearls and another long string twined round her right wrist. Her face is as white as her dress and her lips vivid scarlet. Her left arm positively glitters with diamond; ruby and emerald bracelets; her small tiara of rubies and diamonds matches her enormous ear-rings; she also displays a diamond anklet over her cobweb fine flesh-coloured stocking. She is carrying a tremendous scarlet ostrich-feather fan.*[41]

One can only speculate what Mary Woodman, author of *Correct Conduct*, might have thought, having cautioned so firmly: 'Avoid being daring in dress. It is a great mistake.'[42]

However, impoliteness does not undermine etiquette as such. Etiquette prepares a place for rudeness, assigns to certain actions the value of 'impoliteness', as events comprehended by the system. Rudeness is, in this sense, a function of etiquette. When Cicely, in *The Young Idea*, decides to snub the children of her husband's first marriage, she is making a deliberate calculation within the codes, using etiquette to make her point.[43] But what

Coward's more anarchic heroes and heroines do is produce a second kind of rudeness, one which suspends and erases etiquette. Key here is the linguistic self-consciousness of Coward's characters, their tendency to comment on what they say and how they are saying it. If the ideological force of etiquette lay in the rule which insisted that it should be adopted invisibly, when Coward's characters contravene this master rule and *talk about etiquette* the structure collapses. As Larita glides down the stairs, she publicly warns Mrs Whittaker, 'If you have been building up a few neat social lies on my account, it is very unwise of you – I don't live according to your social system.'[44] The remark, by revealing the operations of etiquette, throws into crisis the system it is supposed to be supporting.

Gerda's and Sholto's conduct works in much the same way. If they had only offended against the rules they could be dismissed. What is far more unsettling is their insistence on commenting on the rules as they try to stick to them:

> GERDA: It's all, naturally, new and thrilling to us here. You can't imagine how funny it is, everything being grey instead of brightly coloured, and everyone talking English, and not waving their arms much and –
>
> SHOLTO: Gerda, we're talking too much. Remember what father said!
>
> GERDA (*cheerfully*):   Sorry, everybody![45]

For the nobility, etiquette was a means of preserving a class system which allowed the landed interest to maintain their power and prestige. With etiquette undermined, the social system itself is under threat. This is certainly what the gentry believed: Ursula Mary Lyon asserted that etiquette is a means to ensure that 'social intercourse can be maintained and prevented from degenerating into chaos'.[46] As we have seen, these authors characteristically disguise concern for their own class as regard for the common good, but the author of *Complete Etiquette for Ladies and Gentlemen* is more candid: 'Society – good Society, that is – is a complicated machine, and, like such machines, will not work

smoothly and pleasantly unless every wheel and component part
gears with its surroundings.'[47] Coward's characters don't just
throw a spanner in the works, they dismantle the whole machine.

In part, Coward's satire unmasks etiquette's role in obscuring
the changing moral values of the 1920s. At the very opening of
The Young Idea, we discover that Cicely is engaged in an affair.
Even so, she is concerned with manners, telling her lover, 'I do
wish you wouldn't despise my husband so, Roddy. It isn't good
form.'[48] Within minutes, though, Coward has turned the
situation on its head, as her husband reveals that he knows all
about it and chides her for underestimating his intelligence.
When he compares Cicely unfavourably with his first wife,
Jennifer, she absurdly rounds on him for his lapse in decorum:
'How dare you talk to me of Jennifer' (p. 188). In *Private Lives*
(1930), Victor seems less concerned with Elyot's shameless
elopement with Amanda than to reiterate the advice laid down
three-quarters of a century earlier in *The Spirit of Etiquette*: 'Never
let your conversation be wholly frivolous.'[49]

> VICTOR: If you don't stop your damned flippancy, I'll
> knock your head off. In a situation such as this, it's in
> extremely bad taste.
> ELYOT: No worse than bluster and invective. As a matter
> of fact, as far as I know, this situation is entirely without
> precedent. We have no prescribed etiquette to fall back
> upon. I shall continue to be flippant.[50]

Elyot's reply exposes the inadequacy of etiquette to negotiate the
mercurial sexual relations we are witnessing.

But the target of this playfulness is class as much as morality.
Taking delight in exposing the rules on which Society works
involves placing them in inverted commas, theatricalising them.
In *Hay Fever* the moments at which the unmannerly Bliss family
launch into extracts from Judith's stage triumphs are parodic of
the formality of etiquette which elsewhere has been so lacking.
That the trigger for these performances is the line 'is this a game?',
is a sly acknowledgement that manners have become so detached

from any moral or cultural authority that they seem as artificial as the Bliss family's beloved parlour games. Gerda and Sholto in *The Young Idea* greet their father and his new wife by enacting theatrical sequences, placing the meetings in the same ironic inverted commas.

By putting these events on stage, Coward reveals their absurd performativity. The gentrified characters in *The Young Idea* are all obsessed with not making a scene. Cicely (wrongly) imagines the consequences of her husband discovering her affair: 'He'd do something dreadful: shoot himself or divorce me, or – anyhow, there'd be a terrible scandal,' implying that the serious personal consequences take second place to the horror of making a scene.[51] Off-stage characters are subjects of scandalous comment and speculation: Bessie Clifton and Jack Mostyn (p.210), Beryl at the 'Graymore Ball' (p.205) and as for Lady Churchington, 'Everyone was talking about it' (p.199). When Cicely and Roddy decide to elope, Gerda and Sholto have hidden behind the curtains, framing the secret within a kind of proscenium, turning it into theatre.

By placing these secrets on stage, by making a scene out of not making a scene, Coward reveals the rules of etiquette as little more than scripts, guidelines for performance. There need be nothing behind them and the cherished link between good manners and good character promoted by the Lords is broken apart. In this sense Coward's characters, with their charm, their elegance, their quixotic eloquence, are part of a sustained ghostly parody of the rules that society had been living by. In *Hay Fever* Sorel commends the diplomat, Richard Greatham, for his fine manners: 'You *always* say the right thing, and no one knows a bit what you're really thinking. That's what I adore.'[52] In *Private Lives* Elyot, momentarily anxious about their vulnerability, asks, 'What shall we do if they suddenly walk in on us?' Amanda beautifully captures the loss of etiquette's moral authority in a perfect answer: 'Behave exquisitely.'[53]

The accusation of snobbery and social climbing must be reconsidered in this light. John Pick's claim that Coward 'viewed the working classes distantly, and with a certain revulsion'[54] can be tested against a number of parallel scenes between middle-class and working-class characters in Coward's early work. *Some Other Private Lives* (1930), for example, is a pastiche of the second act of *Private Lives*, in which Amanda and Elyot have become Fred and Floss, whose tempers flare far more quickly and are expressed much more directly than their middle-class counterparts. *Class* (1924) is a revue sketch-as-thought-experiment, in which the story of a family shocked by their daughter's elopement is played twice, by middle-class characters in a working-class household and vice versa. Scene Two of *Cavalcade* depicts troops leaving for the Boer War. A middle-class woman's farewell to her husband is parallelled with a similar scene between their servants. The outpouring of emotion between the working-class couple is in sharp contrast to Robert's elaborate scheme for preventing an emotional farewell: 'I'm going to kiss you once more now, and then I want you to turn away and go on talking, so that you won't see me actually leave you.'[55]

Do these pieces suggest scornful snobbery? In fact, as David Edgar writes, 'Coward demonstrates time and again in his sketches that he can write effective and funny working-class dialogue.'[56] But more than this, Coward's attitude should be set alongside the verdict of contemporary authorities on verbal manners, one of whom described 'the lower classes discussing any topic at the corners of the streets' and shudderingly recalled 'their coarseness and rudeness in expression, but also the loudness and harshness of their voices'.[57] Given Coward's delight in exposing the absurd and baseless rules of the dying class, it is hard to imagine him approving such sentiments. The emotional reticence of the middle-class characters may better be seen as their burden than their glory.

As the real material basis of their power receded the aristocracy staked everything on their social forms and, like a sixteenth earl trying to attract paying customers to his country house, they invented a civilised ghost to support it. Unseating Their Lordships meant exposing this ghost for the tatty theatrical trick it always was. By the end of the 1930s the aristocracy's decline was sealed and, as David Cannadine argues, they had become baubles, designed to meet 'the increased demand for pomp and circumstance', an adornment to public ceremony, their original purpose, such as it ever was, long forgotten.[58] In 1938 Lady Londonderry mourned, 'Society as such now means nothing and it represents nothing.'[59] In this, the aristocracy had finally caught up with Coward, since this is exactly the state of affairs celebrated by Sorel in *Hay Fever*: 'We none of us ever mean *anything*.'[60] After the war, Coward would indeed be adopted by the social circle that he so mocked, although their power was now so vastly diminished that Coward's inclusion among them can only have added to their sense of flamboyant emptiness. Through the Twenties and Thirties Coward had played his part in prising their fingers from the reins of power, unsettling their claims to prestige and authority, until in the same year that Lady Londonderry was lamenting the decline of high society, he could present six titled gentlemen admitting what his plays already knew:

> We are quite prepared to fight – for our principles,
> Tho' none of us know so far
> What they really are.[61]

NOTES

1. John Pick, *The West End: Mismanagement and Snobbery* (Eastbourne: John Offord, 1983), Chapter 10.
2. *The Noël Coward Diaries,* edited by Graham Payn and Sheridan Morley (London: Weidenfeld & Nicolson, 1982), p.435.
3. Noël Coward, *'Peace in Our Time'* in *Plays: Seven* (London: Methuen, 1999), p.149.
4. Cole Lesley, *The Life of Noël Coward* (London: Jonathan Cape, 1976), p.33.
5. Philip Hoare, *Noël Coward* (London: Sinclair-Stevenson, 1995), p.43.
6. *Etiquette for Gentlemen: A Guide to the Rules and Observances of Good Society* (London: Ward, Lock & Co., 1923), p.7.
7. Ursula Mary Lyon, *Etiquette: A Guide to Public and Social Life* (London: Cassell, 1927), p.3.
8. David Cannadine, *The Decline and Fall of the British Aristocracy* (New Haven: Yale University Press, 1990), pp.74–82.
9. Noël Coward, *Easy Virtue* in *Plays: One* (London Methuen, 1999), p.256.
10. Cannadine, p.16.

11. Oscar Wilde, *The Importance of Being Earnest* (London: Nick Hern Books, 1995), p.19.

12. Quoted in Keith Middlemas, *Pursuit of Pleasure: High Society in the 1900s* (London: Gordon & Cremonesi, 1977), p.73.

13. Angela Lambert, *Unquiet Souls: The Indian Summer of the British Aristocracy 1880–1918* (London: Macmillan, 1984), p.8.

14. Cannadine, p.342.

15. *Etiquette for Gentlemen*, p.7.

16. G. R. M. Devereux, *Etiquette for Men: A Book of Modern Manners and Customs* (London: C. Arthur Pearson, 1902), p.12.

17. *Complete Etiquette for Ladies and Gentlemen: A Guide to the Rules and Observances of Good Society* (London: Ward, Lock & Co., 1900), Vol. 2, p.7.

18. Andrew St George, *The Descent of Manners: Etiquette, Rules and the Victorians* (London: Chatto & Windus, 1993), p.xiv.

19. *Etiquette for Gentlemen*, p.7.

20. Mary Woodman, *Correct Conduct: or, Etiquette for Everybody* (London: W. Foulsham, 1922), p.v.

21. *Complete Etiquette for Ladies and Gentlemen*, Vol.1, p.12.

22. Devereux, p.12.

23. Quoted in Cannadine, p.50.

24. Laura Troubridge, *The Book of Etiquette*, 2 Vols (London: Associated Booklovers' Company, 1926), Vol.1, p.2.

25. Cannadine, p.345.

26. *The Spirit of Etiquette and Guide to Polite Society for Ladies and Gentlemen* (London: Ward and Lock, 1855), p.5.

27. 'A Gentleman', *The Gentlemen's Guide to Etiquette, and Rules of True Politeness, as Observed by the Middle and Upper Classes of Society; with Instructions in the Art of Dress, Conversation, Letter Writing, Visiting, &c* (London: H. Elliot, 1855), p.5.

28. St George, p.33.

29. Troubridge, Vol.1, p.v.

30. *Etiquette for Gentlemen*, p.8.

31. Constance Burleigh, *Etiquette Up to Date* (London: T. Werner Laurie, 1925), p.xiii.

32. Noël Coward, *Three Plays* (London: Ernest Benn, 1925), p.x.

33. Pamela Horn, *High Society: The English Social Élite, 1880–1914* (Stroud: Alan Sutton, 1992), p.90.

34. Eileen Terry, *Etiquette for All: Man, Woman or Child* (London: W. Foulsham, 1925), p.11.

35. Noël Coward, *Operette* in *Play Parade: Two* (London: Heinemann, 1939), p.200.

36. Noël Coward, *Hay Fever* in *Plays: One* (London: Methuen, 1999), p.4.

37. *Easy Virtue*, p.267.

38. Noël Coward, *The Young Idea* in *Play Parade: Three* (London: Heinemann, 1950), p.202.
39. Troubridge, Vol.2, pp.222–3.
40. *Hay Fever*, p.6.
41. *Easy Virtue*, p.343.
42. Woodman, p.42.
43. *The Young Idea*, p.190.
44. *Easy Virtue*, p.344.
45. *The Young Idea*, p.204.
46. Lyon, p.1.
47. *Complete Etiquette for Ladies and Gentlemen*, p.15.
48. *The Young Idea*, p.185.
49. *The Spirit of Etiquette*, p.8.
50. Noël Coward, *Private Lives* in *Plays: Two* (London: Methuen, 1999), p.70.
51. *The Young Idea*, p.185.
52. *Hay Fever*, pp.38–39.
53. *Private Lives*, p.55.
54. Pick, p.136.
55. Noël Coward, *Cavalcade* in *Plays: Three* (London: Methuen, 1999), p.135.
56. David Edgar, 'Be Flippant', *London Review of Books*, 9 December 1999, p.27, reprinted in a revised form as Chapter 1 in the present volume.
57. Quoted in St George, p.70.
58. Cannadine, p.604.
59. Quoted in Cannadine, p.355.
60. *Operette*, p.305. Cannadino
61. *Hay Fever*, p.61.

The Excitement of Being English

Russell Jackson

At Drury Lane Theatre on 13 October 1931, after the first performance of *Cavalcade*, Noël Coward made one of his most famous public speeches: 'I hope this play has made you feel that, in spite of the troublous times we are living in, it is still a pretty exciting thing to be English.'[1] On 10 July 1941 Coward was in Plymouth, the centre of which had been devastated by bombing. After drinks with the hotel barmaid, Dorothy Gilbert, he wrote in his diary: 'She told me stories of the blitzes here. Quite without conscious drama, therefore infinitely more touching. It certainly is a pretty exciting thing to be English.'[2] The key phrase in the diary entry is 'quite without conscious drama' – it sums up Coward's feelings about what he identified as the core virtues of the English. He rarely referred to 'the British': like many of his compatriots at the time he seems to have regarded the other inhabitants of the islands as more or less amusing and picturesque variations on the definitive Anglo-Saxon qualities.

Coward harboured many of the commonplace prejudices of his time and country. His work contains a few slighting references to Jews (for example in 'The Stately Homes of England') and he was capable of admiring a Haitian chauffeur as 'a stalwart buck-nigger', but Coward was by no means a conscious racist – he seems to have been genuinely shocked to encounter thorough-going anti-Semitism during his visit to Poland in 1939.[3] Like radical political movements, systematic racism was among the features of foreign life he regarded as distinctively unEnglish. I would not argue that this makes such common attitudes unexceptionable, but simply that they are a subsidiary dimension of the dominant element in Coward's construction of English identity, his desire to locate and be enrolled in a national family with shared values. (It seems likely that the qualities of tact and reticence he identified with this 'English' character also reflect his attitude to the expression of his sexuality, but that is not my immediate concern in this essay.)

By the late 1930s the definition of Englishness had been a preoccupation of the press and the intelligentsia for some time, perhaps in response to the social upheaval of the First World War. Such popular (and frequently left-wing) forays into social analysis as J. B. Priestley's *English Journey* (1934) and the work of George Orwell were supplemented by the more scientific studies of the Mass Observation team, whose 'Penguin Special' *Britain by Mass Observation* (1939) offered an account of public opinion at the time of the Munich crisis.[4] National characteristics were in any case a mainstay of humorous journalism: between April 1939 and April 1940 *Punch* ran a famous series of cartoons by 'Pont' (Graham Laidler) illustrating such aspects of the middle-class 'British Character' as incomprehension of European languages and not knowing what meals to order from one's cook.[5] In the cinema short films by predominantly left-wing documentary makers, particularly those associated with the GPO Film Unit (subsequently the Crown Film Unit), concentrated on the dignity and rigours of 'ordinary' working lives. Underlying all this was an anxiety to distinguish 'real' national characteristics from those promoted by commerce and to particularise the 'mass' that was becoming such a potent political force. Priestley distinguished three Englands: 'Old England', largely a nostalgic construct of the tourist trade; 'Nineteenth-Century England', a source of wealth but also of social injustice and squalor; and 'post-war England'. He listed some of its features:

This is the England of arterial and by-pass roads, of filling stations and factories that look like exhibition buildings, of giant cinemas and dance-halls and cafés, bungalows with tiny garages, cocktail bars, Woolworths, motor-coaches, wireless, hiking, factory girls looking like actresses, greyhound racing and dirt tracks, swimming pools, and everything given away for cigarette coupons.

This England, Priestley admitted, belonged 'far more to the age itself than to this particular island. America, I supposed, was its real birthplace.'[6]

In the early days of the Second World War, with privation and danger likely to be visited more immediately than in 1914 on a wider range of the population, the need to identify a national spirit became more urgent. Like many others, Orwell and Priestley contributed to the war effort with patriotic essays, pamphlets and broadcasts defining what we were fighting for and how. The consensus was that the English were defiant but quietly so, in contrast to the belligerence of the nations swayed by loud-mouthed dictators and seduced by their appeals to an explicit ideology of state and nation. (Ideology was something other nationals had and talked about – usually loudly.) 'We have no use for extreme ways of thinking,' wrote Osbert Sitwell in 1939, 'and recognize at last that the traditional English love of compromise is more than a way of living: it is an aim in itself, the golden middle road which avoids the lies and bloodshed and torture on each side.'[7] In the aftermath of the war, explaining the political situation to American readers, Orwell emphasised 'the British preference for doing things slowly and not stirring up class hatred'.[8]

These virtues could be located in the homespun detail of national life and in the English landscape. Thus John Betjeman, in a BBC broadcast of 1943, significantly eliding 'British' and 'English', demonstrated variety by creating a series of vignettes, none of them of the kind to be found alongside the 'arterial roads' of Priestley's post-war England: cow parsley strewn on a village church altar, a Women's Institute meeting continuing while the Battle of Britain raged overhead and other rural images. His conclusion was that people who talked about 'the British' as though they were all the same 'have never lived in England': 'I know how useless it is to explain to them about cow parsley on the altar, villages, Women's Institutes, life in English towns. One cannot explain anything at once so kind and so complicated.'[9]

To foster solidarity among city dwellers it was probably wiser to stick to more general terms. Coward himself, broadcasting to the people of Australia in 1940, proclaimed: 'There is one thing I do know, not only with my mind and experience but with my roots and my instincts and my heart, and that is the spirit of the ordinary people of England: steadfast humour in the face of continual strain and horror, courage, determination and a quality of endurance that is beyond praise and almost beyond belief.'[10] One suspects that Betjemanesque catalogues of rural idiosyncrasies would have been beyond an urban playwright. Like Judith Bliss in *Hay Fever*, he would most likely have gone out into the garden to learn the names of the flowers.

Coward's regard for the complex of quietly expressed (and, ideally, almost unconscious) patriotic sentiments never wavered, but his confidence in the survival of 'Englishness' among its rightful heirs took some violent knocks. His absences abroad – particularly in the USA – on official and semi-official business could not be openly explained in a way that would satisfy his enemies in the press and elsewhere, and his court appearances in 1942 for currency violations were a bitter experience. Whether or not this was truly a 'People's War', it was widely perceived and propagandised as such. The dismissal of Winston Churchill in the 1945 election and the return of a Labour government depressed Coward as a sign that the 'wrong' set of popular values had prevailed.[11] Some right-wing authors expressed similar disillusion in specifically political terms. Evelyn Waugh, determinedly patrician in a manner never attempted by Coward, listed in 1946 his reasons for wanting to leave the country: 'The certainty that England as a great power is done for, that the loss of possessions, the claim of the English proletariat to be a privileged race, sloth and envy, must produce increasing poverty; that this time the cutting down will start at the top until only a proletariat and a bureaucracy survive.'[12]

By the late 1940s, disillusioned by the direction social change was taking and (perhaps a sign of it) the reception afforded his work, Coward had begun to sound like a Shaftesbury Avenue Coriolanus – at least in the privacy of his diary. In September 1947 he was in the United States when he learned about the unfavourable press reactions to *'Peace in Our Time'*: 'If that play turns out to be a flop I shall be forced to the reluctant and pompous conclusion that England does not deserve my work.' He tried to come to terms with this 'sick at heart feeling about England'. A few days later he 'found [him]self talking about England so very proudly' to his hosts, but explained this by reflecting that he was referring to 'England in the war years when her gallantry and common sense were married by emergency'. He hoped to resolve this 'confusion' by working on his second volume of autobiography, *Future Indefinite*.[13]

It is significant that Coward should be having these home thoughts from abroad in North America. He had always found America in general, and New York City in particular, a stimulating if slightly absurd source of refreshment, both before and during the war. By the late 1950s, however, he was appalled by the new-found dominance of world affairs by a nation so 'maddeningly volatile ... and so god-damned naïve ... It is terrifying to think that the future of Western civilization is in the hands of a lot of well-disposed, hysterical, neurotic children.'[14] In 1962 Coward is horrified by the effect of 'American progress' on Honolulu: 'It is not only that they have loud, ugly voices and too much money, it is that their basic sense of values is dead wrong. Nothing is any good unless it is big and expensive.'[15] With these, as with other bilious and reactionary entries in the diaries, it is only fair (or at least good manners) to remind oneself that Coward is writing to let off steam rather than persuade a public audience, but the attitudes expressed are of a piece with others explicitly or implicitly present in works intended for publication.

There was, of course, an immediately material reason for disenchantment with England: Coward's sufferings at the hands of the Inland Revenue, which led to his controversial decision to become a 'tax exile'. Nevertheless, at the heart of Coward's quarrel with post-war social change is the perception of decay in the English community of good feeling, reticence and kindness. What the stoically reticent Plymouth barmaid and the crass and noisy American tourists in Honolulu respectively exemplify and destroy is good manners. The opportunity to identify and celebrate essential Englishness allowed Coward to have (in the parlance of the time) 'a good war', entertaining the troops and producing two enduring icons of national sensibility: the films *In Which We Serve* (1941) and *Brief Encounter* (1945). When *This Happy Breed* proved only to have a temporary success, *Pacific, 1860* failed to open Drury Lane with the hoped-for *éclat*, and *'Peace in Our Time'* failed, Coward was faced with his own particular version of post-war disillusion: a falling-out with his public.

Time and again Coward insisted that his work was written and composed for 'the public', whose essentially favourable disposition towards him was frequently prejudiced by critics. This public consisted not of experts, but of 'ordinary' playgoers. In the later post-war years, when play after play failed to win critical approval, his denunciations became more and more strident. *South Sea Bubble* (1956) had been scorned by 'that small galaxy of scruffy critics and pretentious *savants* who know little and do less'.[16] After the Dublin try-out of *Waiting in the Wings* (1960), Coward was braced against the 'patronizing and beastly' London critics by 'having seen the reaction of ordinary playgoers to the play'. Unfortunately, when it opened in London, reading the notices 'was like being repeatedly slashed in the face'. The author felt especially sorry for his cast of veteran actresses, receiving a 'ghastly cold douche' after the 'heart-warming triumph' of the first-night reception.[17] Shortly after this Coward wrote a series of articles in the *Sunday Times* attacking the new playwrights sponsored by the unholy journalistic coterie, long a target of his private scorn. His sense of the differences between his work and that of younger authors became acute. Consoling himself for the poor critical reception of *Sail Away* in London (1961), he recorded receiving 'a large number of letters from strangers thanking me extravagantly for providing a light, cheerful entertainment without emphasis on squalor and devoid of message and social significance'.[18] Diary entries for the years coinciding with the Suez crisis and its aftermath and the success of Look Back in Anger reflect deepening disillusion about the state of the country and the theatre. As if in response to Osborne, Coward insists in his dairies that the Empire was 'a great and wonderful social, economic and even spiritual experiment'. This he contrasts with the 'woolly-headed, muddled "all men are equal" humanitarianism which has lost us [i.e. the English] so much pride and dignity in the modern world'.[19] Even the streets of the West End have lost their elegance and 'acquired a curious "welfare state" squalor which reminds me of Moscow'.[20]

What price London Pride now? In 1941 Coward's song had celebrated the sights and sounds of London to evoke and invoke a population united in resistance 'from the Ritz to the Anchor and Crown'. This was a time when 'we [could] feel our living past in our shadowed present' by conjuring up a historical sense. This imaginative faculty transcended class distinction, but was especially strong among the ordinary people: 'Cockney feet mark the beat of history.' Cockneys – and working-class Londoners in general – continued to provide a rare and dependable source of the 'English' virtues Coward associated with 'his' public, uncontaminated either by the Welfare State or the London theatre critics. These were genuine working people, not to be confused with 'the workers', a self-conscious and militant body exemplified by the factory hands he had found unresponsive and loutish during an early attempt to entertain at a Liverpool canteen concert in 1942.[21] In Coward's work, Cockneys are never associated with production-line work and even less with politically organised labour, but are seen in terms of assertive, common-sense individualism and independent tradesmanship. The heroes of This Happy Breed and 'Peace in Our Time', Frank Gibbons and Fred Shattock (the former played by Coward himself), are fantasies of the thinking but uneducated common man. Their politics are those of the popular right-wing press and, of course, are essentially kindly. In This Happy Breed a son's espousal of communism is a passing phase, strike-breaking in

1926 is a 'normal' and also social activity, and such events as the Abdication and the Munich agreement are taken philosophically. Frank's objection to plans for social reform is that they are too impulsive:

> We don't like doing things quickly in this country. It's like gardening, someone once said we was a nation of gardeners, and they weren't far out. We're used to planting things and watching them grow and looking out for changes in the weather . . . We've got our own way of settling things, it may be slow and it may be a bit dull, but it suits us all right and it always will.[22]

There is no analysis of how such opinions and attitudes are formed or are effective – that is far beyond Coward's ken or his inclinations. Men like Frank Gibbons are sociable, decent beings. They cope with news of world events much as they manage a tiresome mother-in-law, an elopement and even a death.[23] Sylvia, the play's supporter of appeasement, provides a contrast. Her credibility is damaged by being a Christian Scientist (one of Coward's pet hates and, significantly, American in origin) and she represents an unacceptable giving-in to fear. Frank is disgusted by public jubilation over Chamberlain's pact with Hitler – the Munich accord, agreed in the autumn of 1938 – and he describes 'something [. . .] that I wouldn't have believed could happen in this country. I've seen thousands of people, English people, mark you! Carrying on like maniacs, shouting and cheering with relief, for no other reason but that they'd been thoroughly frightened, and it made me sick and that's a fact!'.[24] Appeasement, it seems, has produced off stage a scene from a continuation of *Cavalcade*, this time exemplifying a temporary failure of English courage. From the perspective of 1942, when the play was first produced, appeasement was clearly a discredited policy, and the message of the scene is that Frank's attitude, endorsed by events, was truer to the real English spirit. As for the earlier conflict, Coward characterises it as apolitical: at the end of Act One Frank tells his erring, would-be socialist son that his own generation of men, who fought in the trenches 'all did the same thing for the same reason, no matter what we thought about politics'. Typically, Frank's way of referring to the men's sacrifice is laconic: 'a generation of men, most of which aren't here any more'.[25]

In 1959 Coward's diary records that he and Graham Payn had 'taken a great shine' to the East End pubs, where he encountered 'true Cockneys', distinguishable from their counterparts in kitchen-sink drama by being 'impeccably dressed', cheerful, friendly and disinclined to grumble. He would like to write 'an intimate, completely Cockney musical without any sordid overtones' and reflects that although the critics and 'left-wing highbrows' wouldn't like it, the public would.[26] In 1966 a pub crawl in the East End proved 'a completely enchanting outing' and also provided a textbook example of the ideal Noël Coward public, with its tactful combination of recognition and reserve:

> I was recognized wherever we went, but never once intruded upon or asked for autographs. The instinctive good manners of the true Cockney never ceases [sic] to impress me. It seems to me a simpler and much happier world. Nobody got roaring drunk, a great many of both sexes were extremely attractive, and nearby was the river and the docks and freight boats lit up and the feel of the sea.[27]

Another location where 'true' Englishness might be found was in the outposts of the Empire – or what was left of it. The stiff-backed maintenance of decorum in foreign climes had long been a staple of popular humorists. Pont's 'British Character' series in *Punch* had begun with a drawing of a bridge party in the jungle, and J. B. Morton's 'Beachcomber' column in the *Daily Express* often featured the exploits of the ruthless Empire builder and stickler for etiquette, 'Great White Carstairs'. The wry but affectionate celebration of unwavering national behaviour is present in Coward's song 'Mad Dogs and Englishmen', but it also has its serious counterpart in the title characters of the short story 'Mr and Mrs Edgehill' (1944). Despite their relatively humble origins, close to Coward's own roots, the couple have found themselves promoted to quasi-diplomatic rank on a remote Pacific island, where Mr Edgehill has been appointed British resident. In the late 1930s the atoll is developed as a staging post for flying-boats by an American airline and a luxury hotel is built, but despite the virtual redundancy of their office the English couple maintain their independence and devotion to king and country. Every morning the Union Jack is run up and every sunset it is ceremonially lowered. During this ceremony Mrs Edgehill has a 'London Pride' epiphany of patriotic nostalgia: 'Thoughts of home dropped into her mind. The soft wet green of Romney Marshes; the brightly coloured traffic in Piccadilly on a spring morning; the crowded pavements of Oxford Street; the bargain basement at Selfridge's and the Changing of the Guard.'[28]

At the end of the story war has broken out in the Pacific, and it seems that the Resident and his wife will have to be rescued by American warships. They accept this affront to their patriotism stoically, but then, to their immense pride, a Royal Navy ship arrives. The flag is still flying by the 'residence' built by Mr Edgehill, as his wife sits in the boat clutching the signed photograph of the King and Queen, which a thoughtful visitor has arranged for them to be sent.[29] In Coward's verse narrative 'Not Yet the Dodo' (published in 1967) the elderly couple who struggle to cope with the revelation of their son's bohemian lifestyle, modern tastes in drama and homosexuality are retired colonials: 'alien climates and tropical suns / Had sallowed their English faces'. Coward salutes the quietness of the couple's fortitude, their unwavering but undemonstrative decency in the face of disillusion and the climactic moment of the poem is 'Lady B's' generosity in adding a postscript to the letter she writes her son:

Please give our love to Danny and remember
That we expect you *both* in mid-September.[30]

The source of their anguish is a falling-off of standards on the part of a family member, which is explicitly emblematic of a decline in society at large.

Quiet resilience is also celebrated in the short stories dealing
with theatrical life, notably 'Aunt Tittie' (1939) and 'Ashes of
Roses' (1951) and in the remarkable 'Me and the Girls' (1964),
in which a camp, queer dancer is dying in a Swiss clinic. It is of
course at the very centre of *Still Life* (from *Tonight at 8.30*), which
ends with Laura's implicit determination to endure the
heartbreak she must never admit rather than succumb to the
temptation of suicide that is implied by her leaving the
refreshment room just before the boat train rushes through. The
film based on this play, *Brief Encounter*, makes this more explicit,
and adds the framing narrative in which Laura remembers her
affair and we are allowed to see the stolid decency and whole-
someness of the husband and the home life she has put at risk. As
well as the class implications of the play and the film, which Peter
Holland discusses elsewhere in this volume, the film – even more
than the play – contains an implicit celebration of 'Britishness'
reinforced by the loving accumulation of the details of home
counties' suburban life.[31]

It was in the services, and specifically in the Royal Navy, that
Coward found the most authentic version of his ideal community
of English virtues. During the Great War Coward's own
experience of military service had been less than distinguished,
but he seems to have hankered after the fellowship and pride-in-
tradition of the mess room. This even surfaces in the romantic
musical comedy *Operette* (1937), where Nigel Vaynham explains
how he 'mind[s] deeply about little things':

> – things that seem unimportant and irrelevant like – dining
> in Mess and drinking the King on guest nights out of our
> special regimental silver mug – talking to the troops after
> musketry drill in that blazing heat and finding them still
> ready to make jokes and swear – that's sentimental, I'm sure
> – but it's somehow part of everything I've been brought up
> to believe in.[32]

It was the camaraderie and easy good manners of the Royal
Navy that appealed most strongly to Coward, both as an ideal

community of men and a symbol of the national virtues. Before the war his friendship with 'Dickie' Mountbatten had given him an entry to wardrooms of His Majesty's ships and he had enjoyed socialising with all ranks. In wartime this was fused with an active version of the gallantry he admired. He described a voyage to Gibraltar in HMS *Charybdis* in terms similar to the later celebrations of East End pub-crawling: 'I roamed the ship from stem to stern, talked to ordinary seamen, able seamen, leading seamen, stokers, torpedo-men, signal-men, gun ratings, engine-room artificers, petty-officers and ward-room officers.'[33] Coward's good fellowship is more relaxed than would be allowable to the captain he portrays in *In Which We Serve*, but it has something of the quality of a distinguished visitor passing like a royal personage with tactfully masked condescension among his troops – as 'twere 'a little touch of Noël in the night'. The ideal relationship between officers and men dominates the film's 'story of a ship' and is combined with a celebration of the comforts and vagaries of 'ordinary' family life on shore. Coward wrote that the story of the fictional HMS *Torrin*, based on Mountbatten's own experiences, represented 'all the sentiment, the comedy, the tragedy, the casual valiance, the unvaunted heroism, the sadness without tears and the pride without end' of the senior service.[34] A sad coda to Coward's romantic admiration for the gallantry of the wartime services was his experience of a dinner for Battle of Britain veterans in New York in 1963, 'a sedate, tired little occasion' that made him want to stand up and shout 'Shut up! Stop it! What's the use of this calculated nostalgia? The England we knew and loved was betrayed at Munich, revived for one short year in 1940 and was supreme in adversity, and now no longer exists.' Thoughts of the 'foolish, gallant young men' of 1940 made him rail all the more bitterly in his diary (and in a verse account of the same occasion) against 'young, who spit, with phoney, left-wing disdain, on all that we, as a race, have contributed to the living world'.[35] The poem, 'The Battle of Britain Dinner, New York, 1963' is more openly (and unusually) xenophobic. The angry young men 'are not angry, merely scared and ignorant':

> Many of them are not even English
> But humourless refugees from alien lands
> Seeking protection in our English sanity
> And spitting on the valiant centuries
> That made the sanity possible.[36]

Here, more than anywhere else, Coward's post-war invective sounds like that of the populist press at whose hands he himself had suffered.

What Coward seems really to have longed for was a sense of belonging, specifically admission to one of the families formed by a commonly held sense of decent values and good manners, whether based directly on class, or on the bond forged by the sharing of common dangers. It was this that constituted his patriotic regard for Englishness and it was identified variously with different manifestations of the ordinary people (Clapham or Cockney), with the English abroad, and with the armed forces in and out of combat. The principal virtues of these groups are undemonstrative stoicism, cheerfulness, moderation and a willingness to accept change only if it is gradual and painless. They may need reminding of these things from time to time. This might be achieved with patient good humour (as by Frank in *This Happy Breed*), valiantly (by the captain in *In Which We Serve*), by the setting of a good example (as when a bomb blew in the doors of the Savoy and Coward took the microphone and sang), or by bitter reproof (as by Fred in 'Peace in Our Time'). Unfortunately, Coward himself was not ideally placed to make public pronouncements about duty and suffering in common. This was a recurring theme of his many enemies both during and after the war, and explains the unremitting self-justification of *Future Indefinite*.

Coward's affection for individual members of the British royal family (especially Queen Elizabeth the Queen Mother) and for the institution of royalty as it had been reformed after the near-disaster of the Abdication crisis, suggests that it formed another exemplary community in his view of the world. Another Coward family was the theatre itself, with actors facing the consequences of a possible failure to amuse and ill-disposed critics undermining their unity with the 'genuine' public in the stalls. Within the plays themselves a recurrent comic situation is the resistance of a group of like-spirited individuals against a philistine and orthodox world, whose representatives they exclude by closing ranks – at least temporarily. Significantly, sexual unorthodoxy is admitted and defended in the 'family' of the theatre itself and in the on-stage 'families' of the Blisses, of Amanda and Elyot, or of Leo, Gilda and Otto. In *Present Laughter* Garry Essendine is like a harassed paterfamilias from a Victorian or Edwardian farce, transposed into the hectic world of the theatrical 'family' surrounding Coward. The recurrent critical accusation (with Agate and others) had been that Coward's comic plays lacked heart, and his characters were shallow and one-dimensional, but when C. A. Lejeune reviewed *In Which We Serve* she reflected that 'Some way or another, whether through the infection of his fellow-actors, whether from the public mood, or simply because such things cannot be indefinitely delayed, his heart has sneaked up on Mr Coward. *In Which We Serve* never gushes, but there is a subtle warmth in the old astringency.'[37] When the King, the Queen and the Princesses visited Denham Studios and George VI took the salute from the crew of the sound-stage set of HMS *Torrin*, three of Coward's families were united in a moment of patriotic dignity. As director/captain/author, this was one of his finest hours.

Experience of post-war social change, press hostility and his gradual edging towards the controversial tax exile soured Coward's sense of being at home in England. The retrospective swipe at the appeasers in '*Peace in Our Time*' – which Harold Hobson described as a 'miniature of Armageddon . . . done in watercolours' – is effectively a lament for the destruction of the ideal family, here represented by a pub, with the 'real' family of the publican and the floating, virtual family of customers.[38] The German wartime occupation imagined in the play is in fact a metaphor for the post-war regime, which Coward found so destructive of true English self-respect. In the late Fifties and Sixties it took a visit to the East End pubs, or a well-conducted (and of course royal) public occasion to rekindle his faith. The wedding of Princess Elizabeth and Prince Philip in 1947 was 'most moving and beautifully done. English tradition at its best,' and after it he had a 'sharp argument' with Peter Quennell about the 'attack on the intellectuals in *"Peace in our Time"'*. The wedding of the daughter of the Duke of Buccleuch at Westminster Abbey in 1951 was 'absolutely exquisite – wonderful singing and impeccable style' and the royal family 'very, very grand and typically, indestructibly English'. Coward watched the television broadcast of Winston Churchill's funeral with members of his professional family (including Vivien Leigh, Graham Payn and Cole Lesley). He was 'in floods of tears most of the time' at the passing of a statesman whose attitude to him had often been, to say the least, equivocal, but who was now a symbol of national pride. 'No other race could have done so great a tribute with so little pomposity and so much dignity.' However, the wedding of Princess Margaret and Anthony Armstrong-Jones in 1960 did most to rekindle Coward's confidence in national virtues, and even prompted another memory of Drury Lane in 1931:

Nowhere in the world but England could such pomp and circumstance and pageantry be handled with such exquisite dignity. There wasn't one note of vulgarity or anything approaching it in the whole thing. In America such a balance between grandeur and jollity would be impossible; in France or Italy hysterical; in Germany heavy-handed, and in Russia ominous. But in dear London it was lusty, charming, romantic, splendid and conducted without a false note. It is *still* a pretty exciting thing to be English.[39]

NOTES

1. Cited by Sheridan Morley, *A Talent to Amuse. A Biography of Noël Coward* (London: Heinemann, 1969), p.159.
2. *The Noël Coward Diaries*, ed. Graham Payn and Sheridan Morley (London: Weidenfeld & Nicolson, 1979), p.7.

3. In 'The Stately Homes of England' the family's paintings have been disposed of 'with assistance from the Jews' – see *Operette* in *Play Parade: Two* (1939; enlarged edn, London: Heinemann, 1950), p.246; on the Haitian chauffeur, *Diaries*, p.255 (19 January 1955); on anti-Semitism in Poland, *Future Indefinite* (London: Heinemann, 1954), p.9.

4. *Britain by Mass Observation. Arranged and Written by Tom Harrison and Charles Madge.* New Introduction by Angus Calder (1939; new edn, London: Century Hutchinson, 1986). On the Mass Observation movement, and the 'masses' as a topic in British writing of the period, see Valentine Cunningham, *British Writers of the Thirties* (Oxford: OUP, 1988), Chapters 9 and 10.

5. See Bernard Hollowood, *Pont: The Life and Work of Graham Laidler, the Great 'Punch' Artist* (London: Collins, 1969), where a selection of these are reproduced.

6. J. B. Priestley, *English Journey* (1934; Harmondsworth: Penguin Books, 1977)

7. Osbert Sitwell, 'A War to End Class War,' (the *Spectator*, 17 November 1939) in *Articles of War. The Spectator Book of World War II*, edited by Fiona Glass and Philip Marsden-Smedley (London: Grafton Books, 1989), pp.67–69.

8. 'London Letter to *Partisan Review*' [early May 1946], *The Collected Essays, Journalism and Letters of George Orwell*, Vol.IV, *In Front of Your Nose 1945–1950*, ed. Sonia Orwell and Ian Angus (London, 1968; Harmondsworth: Penguin Books, 1970), pp.219–225. Orwell's wartime journalism and broadcasts are an invaluable source of information and opinion. For an informative overview, see also Robert Hewison, *Under Siege. Literary Life in London, 1939–1945* (London: Weidenfeld & Nicolson, 1977) and the same author's *Culture and Consensus. England, Art and Politics since 1940* (London: Methuen, 1995).

9. BBC broadcast, 'Coming Home', 1943, in *John Betjeman Coming Home. An Anthology of his Prose, 1920–1977*, ed. Candida Lycett Green (London: Methuen, 1998), pp.137–41.

10. Quoted by Jeffrey Richards, 'National Identity in British Wartime Films' in Philip M. Taylor, ed., *Britain and the Cinema in the Second World War*, (London: Macmillan, 1988), pp.42–61.

11. On the historical debate about the nature of the 'People's War' see Alan Munton, 'Fiction and the People's War' in *English Fiction of the Second World War* (London: Faber & Faber, 1989), pp. 6–33. The landmark account of the subject is Angus Calder's *The People's War: Britain 1939–1945* (London: Jonathan Cape, 1969). An invaluable study of post-war British politics is Peter Hennessy, *Never Again. Britain 1945–1951* (London: Jonathan Cape, 1993). A good sense of the 'Welfare State' world Coward escaped from in the late 1940s is given by the essays in *Age of*

Austerity 1945–1951, eds Michael Sissons and Philip French (London: Hodder & Stoughton, 1963), particularly important is Michael Frayn's essay 'Festival', on the significance of the 'Festival of Britain' in 1951.

12. Entry for 9 November 1946 in *The Diaries of Evelyn Waugh*, ed. Michael Davie (1976; revised edn, Harmondsworth: Penguin Books, 1979), p.661.

13. *Diaries*, p.92 (23 and 28 September 1947).

14. *Diaries*, p.351 (24 February 1957).

15. *Diaries*, p.498 (25 February 1962).

16. *Diaries*, p.318 (29 April 1956).

17. *Diaries*, pp.445, 447 (15 August and 11 September 1960).

18. *Diaries*, p.483 (29 October 1961).

19. *Diaries*, p.348 (3 February 1957). Compare p.342, a retrospect of the year 1956. Later Coward registers that his 'bewilderment' with John Osborne is 'because I am very old indeed and cannot understand why the younger generation, instead of knocking at the door, should bash the fuck out of it' (p.349: 17 February 1957).

20. *Diaries*, p.355 (5 June 1957). Coward's experience of Moscow is described in *Future Indefinite* (London: Heinemann, 1954).

21. *Diaries*, p.19 (6 June 1942).

22. *Plays: Four* (London: Methuen, 1999), p.280.

23. Another notable example of this character type was PC George Dixon, the wise, stoical, cheerful and thoroughly domesticated hero of *Dixon of Dock Green*, a long-running Fifties BBC television series created by Ted Willis. (The character first appeared in the film *The Blue Lamp*, in 1949.)

24. *Plays: Four*, pp.359–60

25. *Plays: Four*, p.298.

26. *Diaries*, p.412 (28 June 1959).

27. *Diaries*, p.633 (6 July 1966).

28. *Collected Short Stories* (London: Methuen, 1983), p.223.

29. Lady Cynthia Marchmont, the story's benefactress, is in fact a surrogate for Coward himself, who had performed the same act of kindness for a couple he encountered on Canton Island (see *Future Indefinite*, pp.189–90).

30. *Collected Verse*, (London: Methuen, 1984) p.38.

31. See Richard Dyer's study in the 'BFI Film Classics' series, *Brief Encounter* (London: British Film Institute, 1993), especially pp.41–65.

32. *Operette*, p.243.

33. *Future Indefinite*, p.246.

34. *Future Indefinite*, p.208.

35. *Diaries*, p.545 (14 September 1963).

36. *Collected Verse*, pp.151–2. Compare Coward's disgust at the behaviour of the workers at the Liverpool canteen concert in 1942: 'They grumble and strike and behave abominably while their very existence is made possible by

sailors and merchant seamen who get a quarter or less than a quarter what [*sic*] they do' (*Diaries*, p.19).

37. *Chestnuts in her Lap, 1936–1946* (London: Phoenix House, 1947), p.80.

38. Harold Hobson's phrase is in his reprinted review: *Theatre* (London: Longmans, Green and Co., 1948), p.113.

39. *Diaries*, pp.97 (20 June 1947); 173 (10 July 1951); 591 (4 February 1965) and 438 (8 May 1960).

A Class Act

Peter Holland

On the first page of *Present Indicative* (1937), the first volume of Coward's autobiography, after he has written briefly and wittily of his infancy and his much-loved woolly monkey called 'Doris', Coward turns to his mother's background:

> My mother came from what is known as 'Good Family', which means that she had been brought up in the tradition of being a gentlewoman, a difficult tradition to uphold with very little money in a small suburb, and liable to degenerate into refined gentility unless carefully watched.[1]

It is a difficult passage to read, densely packed with markers of a way of understanding status that is alien to our society a century later than the time Coward is describing and sixty-five years later than the time when Coward was describing it. 'Good Family' is both given initial capitals and offset by quotation marks, as if to attempt to ironise the dour threat out of its moral and status-conscious posture; that already old-fashioned word 'gentlewoman' suggests the awkward opposition to its implicit opposite, 'gentleman'; and the conjunction of 'degenerate' and 'refined gentility' reminds the reader that gentility is not a quality of which people, even the genteel, necessarily approve.

Though it is striking that Coward has nothing to say here – or later – about his father's family, he goes on to tell readers a substantial amount about his mother's, the Veitches. Philip Hoare, in his excellent biography, tells us a great deal more about them but the signs of social change are apparent: 'Good Family', when Hoare quotes this passage, no longer has its portentous initial capitals nor its off-setting and off-putting quotation marks.[2] In that punctuating change a social movement is defined, a world where the phrase 'good family' is rendered less equivocal, less disturbingly a sign of what Mrs Coward and her ancestors had lost. When Hoare speaks of Coward's mother's family as being of 'definite, if somewhat eroded, gentility',[3] the anxiety and the pejorative overtones captured in Coward's phrase, 'degenerate into refined gentility', are lost too; the concept of social placing becomes simpler, more reassuring, with stronger overtones of the benign image of distressed gentlefolk. Coward's phrasing, so carefully loaded with a precise 1930s sense of how these class-driven words carry meaning, is simplified into terms that are manageable in the differently driven but still class-aware terminology of the 1990s. The class standards of 1899 looked very different in 1937. Hoare's version is entirely accurate – as one would expect from so scrupulous a biographer – but he writes in a language of half a century later.

Now that the inhabitants of the United Kingdom have been reassuringly informed that the class war is over and that we live in a classless society, perhaps it will seem pointless to be worrying about Noël Coward's explorations of class. But, at a time when Judith Butler's argument that gender is a performative act[4] seems to be passing among too many critics as an accepted simple truth and when the argument from gender and sexuality has been effectively extended into ethnicity and nationality,[5] the senses in which class is or is not a performative act as well deserve a little further consideration. Strikingly, it is an American theory movement that has failed to consider class but the examination of class as performance is necessary, even if it is only to remind us how class used to function, something that supposedly we could not possibly observe today. Yet I perceive myself to be living in a culture where a conversation between two English people (and I would emphasise that I do, of course, mean English and not

British) is still so emphatically concerned to locate and place each, defining status through forms of socially shared vocabularies that rearticulate class in its late-twentieth-century formulation.

I am not going to be concerned with Coward's own performance of class, that sustained role that he worked on with such assiduity throughout his adult life, that strenuously controlled masking and rehearsing, redefining and revealing of how his social meaning might be perceived. But if we want to hear the degenerate tones of 'refined gentility' that Coward fears might be those of his mother, we ought to be listening to Myrtle Bagot, the 'buxom and imposing widow' whose 'expression [is] reasonably jaunty except on those occasions when her strong sense of refinement gets the better of her' as she controls the refreshment room of Milford Junction Station, that supposed haven from a world outside.[6] In the space between 'I don't see that there was anything to laugh at – a very natural request on a faine day' (pp.338–9) and 'Now look at me Banburys – all over the floor' (p.354) the different registers that define the aspiration to – and embarrassing failure to achieve – refined gentility are plainly marked.

I have quoted these examples of Myrtle's speech not from the film *Brief Encounter* but from *Still Life*, the play in *Tonight at 8.30* from which the film script developed. They are usually seen as being more or less the same, the film opening out the enclosed staging of the play in ways that magnify that 'doomed affair',[7] as the Rachmaninov swells, while maintaining the attitude of snobbish contempt that Hoare, who is far from alone in this, sees as 'endemic' to Coward. But in the very different balance between Alec and Laura against Myrtle and Albert, not to mention Beryl and Stanley, that *Still Life* establishes, I want to argue later that the affairs of the middle class are seen far less favourably, almost as if Coward's snobbery was directed first against Alec and Laura and only in the rewriting for the film redirected towards the employees of the railway, suggesting, surprisingly, that film was far more a space of assumed middle-class value than the theatre.

Coward's construction of class is seen at its comic and

magnificent best in a short sketch called *Class*, written for the Cochran revue *On With the Dance* (1925). The introductory speech establishes the parameters:

> [I]n the democratic England of to-day there is a good deal of discussion as to whether there are actual class differences or not. That all men are equal is undoubtedly a magnanimous theory, but strip the so-called 'upper classes' of their luxurious surroundings, and the usual trappings of gilded ease, and, I ask you, what happens?[8]

The answer is that the two extremes of social behaviour become effectively indistinguishable.

Class plays its scene out twice: the first time in 'an extremely squalid room in the East End' (p.42) where Alf, Ada and the rest of the family eat a high tea of shrimps and winkles, the second in 'a beautifully furnished dining-room in Mayfair' (p.46) with Alf now Alfred and Mr and Mrs Higgins metamorphosed into Sir Herbert and Lady Higgins. The events are the same, the language and circumstances are different. The joke is that the language registers are reversed so that it is Maud in the East End squalor who announces that 'I love Harry and he loves me, and we both love one another too much to marry' (p.45) while Maudie in Mayfair stuns the company with ''E loves me, and I love 'im, and we ain't the marrying sort neither' (p.48).

Between the two scenes the narratorial voice offers the contrast between 'an orthodox upper-class family in lower-class surroundings' and 'the reaction of the lower-class mind in higher-class surroundings' (p.46). But the voice is not necessarily accurate: it is never clear whether the characters we saw in the first half are an upper-class family at all, nor that the figures of the latter display 'lower-class mind[s]' as well as lower-class language since there is nothing to choose between them other than a linguistic style.

Class argues, insofar as a brief revue sketch argues anything, that there is no effectual difference between situation or reaction according to circumstance or social status.[9] Status is fixed and emblematised as an icon of order throughout Coward – an oddly self-disguising and socially reassuring argument for someone whose own social status changed so rapidly. But Barry Day's introductory note to *Class* seems to me to be at cross-purposes with the sketch. He is, of course, right to state that '[c]lass and the observation of its different manifestations was the bedrock on which much of Noël's work was based' (p.41) but when he observes that, at times, 'the affection was clearly felt, the touch was less sure and the result could appear patronising' it is not clear that *Class* displays any such patronising tones. Both classes are mocked equally; neither is patronised.

This characteristic Coward exploration of the indistinguish-ability of class is equally true of *Some Other Private Lives*, the parody of Act Two of *Private Lives* that Coward and Gertrude Lawrence performed at a gala matinée in December 1930 (on that occasion as a four-hander with Olivier and Adrianne Allen, although only the two-handed version performed in 1932 at Malvern has been published). Fred and Flossie, characters, Coward tells us, 'drawn from the poorer and less cultured sections of society',[10] enact what are essentially the same events as Amanda and Elyot, 'Sollocks' and all, with the language meta-morphosed as in *Class*: 'Is that the Grand Duchess Olga lying under the piano? / Yes, her husband died a few weeks ago, you know on his way back from Pulborough'[11] becomes ''Ere, ain't that the Grand Duchess Olga over there pickin' 'er nose? / Ow, yes, 'er old man got corpsed last Toosday comin' 'ome from the gasworks' (p.279). There is nothing patronising here and it is Amanda and Elyot as much as Flossie and Fred who are ridiculed by the comparison.

Day's observation is especially problematic since he offers as an example of when 'the notes [Coward] struck were true ones . . . the upstairs/downstairs Marryots and Bridges in *Cavalcade* (1931)'. *Cavalcade* belongs with *This Happy Breed* (written in 1939), the film script *In Which We Serve* (1942) and '*Peace in Our Time*' (written in 1946) as Coward's attempts to write history plays, vast pageant dramas whose model is explicitly Shakespearean in more than the title of *This Happy Breed*. While the recent tendency has been to see these plays as 'written in the Brechtian epic manner'[12] I cannot see much likelihood that Coward knew Brecht. Far more probable is that Coward and Brecht have a common source in Shakespeare's history plays, with Coward creating a tetralogy that is an analogy to the continuities and scale of Shakespeare's histories.

The Marryots are consistently offered to the audience of *Cavalcade* as the emblem of decency in the upper classes, a world of normative values epitomised by the opening stage direction, 'The drawing-room of a London house',[13] an indication of location that does not need to explain anything more about the status or geography of the house's position in London other than that it has a drawing room, that it is 'charmingly furnished in the taste of the period' and that it is thereby implicitly contrasted with a 'country house'. But the lot of the Bridges is much less sympathetically viewed: when they leave the Marryots' employ and take over a pub, Bridges becomes an embarrassing 'unkempt and unshaven' drunk who accuses the Marryots of being a 'lot of bloody shnobs' (p.162–3).

Even more troubling is the interview between Jane Marryot and Ellen Bridges after Joe Marryot has been having an affair with Fanny Bridges, now a singing star. Ellen believes the two should marry; Jane primly declares 'I never interfere with my son's affairs' (p.190), a phrase which allows a terrible pun on 'affairs' its full weight. When Ellen bursts out with 'I suppose you imagine my daughter isn't good enough to marry your son', a view which Ellen does not hold because '[t]hings aren't what they used to be, you know – it's all changing' (p.191), Jane can only say sympathetically, 'I'm so very, very sorry . . . Something seems to have gone out of all of us, and I'm not sure I like what's left.' In the event, as so often in *Cavalcade*, all is resolved by death, here by the convenient arrival of a telegram announcing Joe's death in the war. Coward appears, throughout *Cavalcade*, to offer Jane as the intelligent, feeling centre; her response to Joe's death, moving like a sleepwalker through the crowds that are celebrating the Armistice is, we ought to sense, the right response to the yelling euphoria. It is Jane, as well as Coward, who patronises Ellen.

The end of *Cavalcade*, that extraordinary depiction of chaos, is the most theatrically innovative and dramatically despairing moment that Coward ever wrote. Perhaps we ought to be reassured by its resolution into the sight of the Union Jack and the whole company singing the National Anthem, but Coward's final gesture seems a sop after the distress of the chaos. National pride is for Coward akin to religious faith but here it seems a fantasy against which the confusion of the twentieth century is awfully opposed. Class is itself the prime area in which the play is aware of a change it is obliged to document but unable to approve.

Cavalcade is unlike the other history plays in its unsure touch with the lower classes. Jane's attitude may be true as an accurate depiction of upper-class attitudes but Day's contrast of this with patronising elsewhere is mistaken. It is certainly there in *In Which We Serve*, especially in the contrasts of, for instance, Walter's awkwardly pretentious speech at his Christmas dinner table with Mrs Kinross's pained and sincere account of the lot of a naval wife at hers. But if we view the depiction of the Gibbons family in *This Happy Breed* as patronising that may be no more than our imposition of an irrelevant and ahistorical attitude. Coward's fundamental conservatism is apparent in the flippant attitude to the General Strike but the identification of Coward's politics will not in itself serve to prove him patronising.

The film of *This Happy Breed* was hugely successful. As C. A. Lejeune, reviewing it for *The Observer*, commented, 'This film about the suburbs has gone out into the suburbs, and the suburbs have taken it to their hearts. All the Gibbonses of Greater London have flocked to see themselves on screen. [. . .] It has gone straight to our address: or, as we say genteelly in our suburb, *Chez Nous*.'[14]

Frank Gibbons may be a cardboard icon of the salt-of-the-earth English middle class, a representation, as it were, of the class from which Coward came, but in Coward's ascription to him both of value and a rejection of appeasement, he shares a stance with Fred, the landlord of The Shy Gazelle in 'Peace in Our Time', especially in the latter's extraordinary dialogue with Alma on the virtues of defeat as the means of resisting that softness and smugness which, more even than snobbery, Coward sees as endemically English.[15] And it is not only a value system which the audiences were prepared to accept but also a rare recognisability. The Gibbons family and their problems are far less mocked and patronised by Coward than any other representation of lower-middle-class life that I know from the immediate post-war period. It is no less real and no more patronised than the world Osborne created in *Look Back in Anger* in 1956. Number 17 Sycamore Avenue, Clapham Common is a not unreasonable dramatic formulation of the houses of Sutton or Teddington that Coward knew.

If there is a smugness in *This Happy Breed* it is the assumption that the only correct attitude to one's social position is comfortable acquiescence. Queenie, Frank's dissatisfied daughter, runs off with a married man, unseen but carefully named by Coward as 'Major Blount' to indicate to the audience his social status.[16] Nearly destroyed by the experience in a sequence that reminds me of nothing so much as the account of Nina's experiences in the last act of Chekhov's *The Seagull*, Queenie returns a calmer and wiser person, much, perhaps, as Laura does to good old decent Fred and his crosswords in *Brief Encounter*.

There are, however, two crucial differences: the timescale and the details of the affair. Queenie runs off and it takes years before she returns, found by Billy running a tea shop in Menton, an image that I find almost irresistibly comic. Laura's passionate affair with Alec lasts only a few weeks, a tiny number of increasingly passionate meetings that end, unconsummated, when Stephen Lynn returns to his flat before Alec and Laura can get into bed. No wonder, then, that the reaction from the working-class audience at a preview screening in Rochester was laughter and mocking comment: 'Isn't 'e ever goin' to 'ave it orf with 'er?'[17] That reaction suggests the gap between assumptions of the audience that might be aligned with class and the different class values created by the moral codes institutionalised in the film industry.

Part of the force of *Brief Encounter* is precisely the compression of its timescale: the non-affair that turns Laura's world upside down and brings her to the edge, literally, of suicide is charted on successive Thursdays and the film shows us all of them. But *Still Life* does not. The five scenes of Coward's original playlet create a totally different time-frame for the events, something which commentators on play and film seem not to notice. The first scene is set in April and each successive scene is placed, explicitly in the head note for the scene, three months later, so that the time-span for the relationship between Alec and Laura is a complete year, not a few weeks.

Even more decisively, the scene in which Alec returns to the flat and Laura follows him and the scene where they are interrupted by the return of Stephen, are three months apart, where in *Brief Encounter* they are part of the same day. We are led to assume – and I fail to see how else we can read it – that Alec and Laura have been making love in the flat every Thursday afternoon for the intervening three months. A further three months pass between the interrupted lovemaking and the final parting. When Albert, in *Still Life* but not in *Brief Encounter*, refers to Alec and Laura as 'Romeo and Juliet' (p.373), there is an ironic gulf between the one night of passion that Shakespeare's young lovers are allowed and the regular weekly sex that these middle-aged lovers have been having, strictly controlled by the railway timetable. The Alec and Laura of *Brief Encounter* might be seen as a kind of illicit Romeo and Juliet without ridicule, precisely why it would appear Coward found no room in the film for Albert's comment. But the encounters of Alec and Laura in *Still Life* have not been brief at all.

The grand passion of the middle classes in the film makes the little fumbling relationships of the employees at Milford Junction petty by comparison, though there is just enough space for us to register that Laura's late return to the refreshment room, after the arrival of Stephen makes passion into sordid fumblings, prevents Beryl leaving for her date with Stanley, so that the self-interest of Laura, the assumption that she has a middle-class right to being allowed to keep the café open after hours, cuts into the entirely reasonable self-interest of Beryl after her working day is over.[18] In

Still Life the very longevity of the affair invites us to re-valuate its
pretensions, setting it as a regular event, as regular as the train
service on which it is dependent, against the growing though
gently mocked relationship between Albert and Myrtle or Beryl
and Stanley. *Brief Encounter*, in ways that George Eliot would
have recognised, finds tragedy in the disruptive though hardly
exceptional passion of the middle classes, allowing them an
intensity of feeling that bubbles away largely unsuspected
beneath the sensible clothes, the library book from Boots and the
weekly visit to the cinema. *Still Life* finds the same characters to
be magnifying an event which precisely through its duration
seems both more sordid, furtive and demeaning.

If we still choose to see Coward as patronising the working-
class characters, they seem, in *Still Life*, to occupy an unexpected
position, not humility but a moral high ground. What had
appeared indistinguishable in *Class* or *Some Other Private Lives*,
now proves to be only too easy to separate in its forms of
behaviour. From Coward's vantage point, the middle class of *Still
Life* do not appear to be performing their expected social role at
all well. Their class act is full of a suppression of furtive sexuality
that Coward at times shared, certainly understood and, in his
own manifestations of the ambiguities of his class status,
controlled with the elegance he brought to all his performances.
His is a hard class act to follow.

NOTES

1. Noël Coward, *Autobiography* (London: Methuen, 1999), p.5.
2. Philip Hoare, *Noël Coward* (London: Sinclair-Stevenson, 1995), p.2.
3. Ibid., p.2.
4. See, for example, Judith P. Butler, *Gender Trouble* (London: Routledge, 1990); Sue-Ellen Case, ed., *Performing Feminisms* (Baltimore: Johns Hopkins UP, 1990); Judith P. Butler and Joan W. Scott, eds, *Feminists Theorize the Political* (London: Routledge, 1992).
5. See, in particular, Sue-Ellen Case et al., eds, *Cruising the Performative* (Bloomington: Indiana UP, 1995).
6. *Still Life* in Noël Coward, *Plays: Three* (London: Methuen, 1979), pp.337–8. I take the station's location to be a deliberate pun on Milford Haven.
7. Hoare, p.269.

8. *Class* in Noël Coward, *Collected Revue Sketches and Parodies*, ed. Barry Day (London: Methuen, 1999), p.42.

9. Compare David Edgar's comment on the sketch's making 'an argument about the equivalence of family attitudes across classes that relies on the essentially theatrical device of placing them one after the other' (David Edgar, 'Be Flippant', *London Review of Books*, 9 December 1999, pp.27–9, reprinted in a revised form as chapter 1 in the present volume.

10. *Some Other Private Lives* in *Collected Revue Sketches and Parodies*, p.278.

11. *Private Lives* in Noël Coward, *Plays: Two* (London: Methuen, 1979), p.46.

12. Edgar, p.27.

13. *Cavalcade* in Noël Coward, *Plays: Three*, p.127.

14. C. A. Lejeune, *Chestnuts in Her Lap 1936–1946* (London: Phoenix House Ltd, 1947), p.117.

15. See *'Peace in Our Time'* in Noël Coward, *Plays: Seven* (London: Methuen, 1999), pp.143–4.

16. *This Happy Breed* in Noël Coward, *Plays: Four* (London: Methuen, 1979), p.353.

17. Quoted Hoare, p.361.

18. See also Richard Dyer, *Brief Encounter* (London: BFI Publishing, 1993; BFI Film Classics), pp.60–1.

Moving With Coward

Frances Gray

I want to begin with one of those instances in which, politically speaking, Coward seems to be going out of his way to shoot himself in the foot. In his series of *Sunday Times* articles responding to the *Look Back in Anger* generation, he writes:

> Some years ago [I] was giving alternate performances of *Present Laughter* and *This Happy Breed* at the Haymarket theatre. I can remember to this day the relief I used to feel when, after a matinée of the former, with its tension and tempo and concentrated timing, I returned in the evening to play Frank Gibbons ... to wander about in shirt-sleeves, take off my boots, pick my nose and drink cups of tea was so infinitely less demanding.[1]

This impressively manages to insult writers – apparently incapable of any sense of rhythm or style in portraying the working class; actors of working-class origin – incapable of playing anything but themselves; and, especially, the working class – so limited in its expressivity that it can be imitated by any actor capable of picking his nose and talking at the same time. One obvious conclusion is that Coward was incapable of understanding the idea of class struggle in any meaningfully physical terms. *This Happy Breed* considers the impact of the General Strike not in terms of miners starved out or bodies brutalised in clashes with the police, nor the painful efforts of women between the wars to achieve sexual self-determination, but in terms of ditsy Reg, 'enjoying [him]self tip-top . . . running about the streets and throwing stones and yelling [his] head off;[2] and the equally ditsy Queenie whose fate is to be 'stranded in a sort of boarding-house in Brussels' (p.353).

However, a more rewarding line of enquiry is also possible. In his description of playing Frank, Coward puts his finger on an aspect of the play shared by relatively few others in his output, one that marks it out as both politically reactionary and dramatically problematic: that of stasis. In *This Happy Breed* people stand and talk or sit and talk. All the action – stone-throwing, seduction, death or DIY – takes place off stage. And most of that action leads directly back to stasis. Reg gives up politics for respectable patriotism, Queenie marries the boy next door. Nobody *moves*.

This springs directly from the original circumstances of composition. In 1939 stasis could be seen as holding on, as positive action. Frank's speech to his infant grandson is about the energy involved in not changing. 'We 'aven't lived and died and struggled all these hundreds of years to get decency and justice and freedom for ourselves without being prepared to fight fifty wars if need be – to keep 'em' (p.372). But even by *This Happy Breed*'s deferred first performance in 1942 the idea of stasis as dynamic was no longer strong enough as a subject, as Coward later acknowledged. 'Wandering around' was the antithesis of the posture of alertness implicitly demanded by every propaganda poster about saving, vigilance or recruiting, and Frank would have seemed unacceptable even without the political upheavals of 1945.

The same difficulty occurs in the area of sexual politics with *Still Life*. Like Frank, Laura is rooted to the set. Trains move, the staff of the refreshment room have a vigorous off-stage life, but she sits – and meets a man, and falls in love, and fails to say a proper goodbye. Love, as she points out, is transformative, but what it transforms is not her body or mind but the objects around her: 'the dining-room curtains, and the wooden tub with a silver top that holds biscuits, and a water-colour of San Remo that my mother painted'.[3] All these look different; for them to *be* different, however, would require Laura to reposition herself in relation to these props of middle-class existence: to re-imagine morality so that it is grounded either in sacrifice, or in desire, both of them dynamic impulses. What she does is to group herself with the biscuit barrel etc. and stigmatise herself as 'cheap'. In the filmed version, *Brief Encounter*, the shakiness of this moral premise becomes more apparent as the doomed lovers move through landscapes full of possibilities – sexy films, rural seclusion, even austerity as they dry off after a boating mishap in a simple hut, stripped of their fussier pieces of clothing. The ending, with Celia Johnson back in a stuffy room and the arms of the man Kenneth Tynan has forever designated 'that-admirable-actor-Cyril-Raymond', is so grim that despite all the lovers' moral debate we can't help seeing it as a judgement on timidity. On stage, however, the moment when Laura abandons her dreary neighbour in the buffet as the express train roars through contrasts so sharply with the overall stasis that, for a moment, it offers up the possibility of transformation – perhaps into a Karenina who dies for love, perhaps into a Nora who slams the door of the dolls' house on the old life. When Laura comes staggering back to the Bath buns and biscuit barrels, she brings with her the need to question the exact nature of the morality they stand for, the question Coward has been dodging throughout and which he continues to avoid as the audience admires the technical virtuosity of his use of the single set.

While in both *This Happy Breed* and *Still Life* stasis starts with a set and traps the body in political stalemate, other plays assume a sexual or social mobility within stasis and the result is a tension that almost pulls them apart. *Easy Virtue* is, as Coward acknowledged, an *hommage* to the Edwardian well-made play and what he called its 'vanished moral attitudes'.[4] Specifically, of course, he meant sexual attitudes; but what is interesting as he impacts the three-act structure, the woman with a past and the compromising document on to a post-Freudian world is that he also has to navigate shifts in the other code the Edwardians took for granted, that of money. It was easy for a Pinero audience to read the whole *mise-en-scène*: clothes, props and bodily posture told you the social position, income and credit rating of each character as well as his or her sexual history, and there were a limited number of ways in which the relationship between these would work out.

In *Easy Virtue* Larita's body moves with fluid ease throughout, resisting all demands that she charge about on the tennis court or dance with the graceless young men who lay bets on her willingness to do so. This is not the relaxation of stasis, however, but of subversion. The society into which she has married is used to mapping its moral judgements on the bodies of class outsiders like Rose Jenkins, the sexually active maid whose dismissal Mrs Whittaker organises so briskly. Larita appears at different times as new wife, divorcée, friend, flirt and object of gutter press scandal, but while she may change her clothes occasionally her body does not alter. An Edwardian adventuress would here be required alternately to brazen it out with corsets at full power or to collapse in moral meltdown, perhaps passing society's judgement on herself with a revolver in a locked room.

While Larita's challenge on the most intimate bodily level is clear, the struggle also exists at the level of other material signifiers in a more puzzling way. The Whittakers feel, like good Edwardians, that they would be more comfortable if they could nail down the source of her income – marriage, inheritance, or the fruits of vice? They get it wrong because the codes offered by the well-made play to indicate old money or new brass are no longer quite reliable. Instead, they have to struggle on another playing field, that of style. They drink claret cup; Larita asks for champagne. They play tennis; she reads Proust. They like statuettes of the Venus de Milo; she smashes one in a rare departure from her relaxed mode.

As Coward was beginning his writing career in the Twenties, a volume was published which became the bible of good manners for Americans who wanted to give the impression of old money, Emily Post's *Etiquette*. Post decrees that 'It should be unnecessary to [say] that none but vulgarians would employ a butler . . . who wears a mustache'.[5] This is not a rule: it is the patch on the medieval map that reads 'Here be dragons'. For if this goes without saying, what remains unsaid? It's too late to take a razor to Jeeves now. The immediate signifier of vulgarity, his hairy upper lip, has been replaced by another, your ignorance of its signification. You wear that ignorance as signifier of your status as nouveau riche. Old money doesn't have to ask.

Hence Larita's opening question, 'Can your butler speak French?,'[6] is a tricky one. If the Whittakers have struggled to surround themselves with what they hope are the trappings of a well-born family, they are on the edge of an abyss. If they are secure in their social status there is a clear suggestion here that it is no longer enough.

What, however, does 'not enough' mean? How should the actress who plays Larita inflect the question? Is the challenge of the multilingual butler posed with destructive intent – like asking Rumpelstiltskin his name – with a view to exposing the whole system of social signifiers as arbitrary and absurd? Or is Coward simply replacing one set of arbitrary codes with another, more chic but equally divisive in class terms? The play never manages to make up its mind on that point, as is made clear by the stylistic differences between the spoken text and the stage directions. While there are real arguments about religion, repression and morality between Larita and the Whittakers, there is a gap between them on the bodily level. Larita is never ridiculous; even when she loads herself with jewellery for the party in Act Three she is operating at the level of conscious parody, enjoying her own performance as Edwardian vamp. But – rarely for Coward – Whittaker society is the subject of relentlessly satirical stage directions: 'She is the type of woman who has the reputation of "having been quite lovely" as a girl'; 'He has had the forethought to wear white gloves which have wrinkled up slightly, displaying a mercifully brief expanse of blood-red wrists.' Or – a running gag – 'her dress is awfully pretty – yellow, with stockings to match . . .' (pp.284, 334, 336). The supporting cast seem to be expected to adopt almost cartoonish bodies, against which Larita, at ease in her own skin, is seen as sexually and socially authentic; but what that authenticity might involve in political terms is hard to guess.

This double attitude to social signifiers and the body is also

present in *Relative Values* a quarter of a century later. Here there
are two outsiders who challenge the aristocratic family: Miranda,
the film star who wants to marry the son of the house, and her
sister Moxie, the maid they allow to borrow the status of family
friend for the duration of Miranda's visit. Coward is too sensitive
to post-war change to attempt to treat the situation of a maid
posing as lady as intrinsically funny, although he recoups the
laughs he has lost in this direction by inserting a butler nostalgic
for just such a socially rigid past, thus putting the jokes, as it were,
into inverted commas. The bulk of the humour, however, arises
out of Miranda's attempts to manipulate the signifiers of the
landed gentry – knitting bags, horn-rimmed glasses (for reading
Country Life, perhaps) – to show how well she can cope, while
simultaneously operating another set – Bow Bells, drunken
parents – to offer them the pleasures of patronising a working-
class Cinderella. Meanwhile Moxie, secure in her Sidcup origins,
performs her own part better than her actress sister; she may lapse
into deference, but at no point does she betray ignorance of the
code. Are we in the territory of *Pygmalion,* which undermines
class division by showing how far it depends on arbitrary codes
which any intelligent person can learn, or is the butler's final
toast to the downfall of social equality something we are expected
to endorse? We can't, perhaps, afford to ask this question until
we've left the theatre and, wisely, Coward has Moxie tell the
butler to shut up.

Both *Relative Values* and *Easy Virtue* contain major characters
who are preoccupied with the business of self-presentation, and it
has long been acknowledged that Coward is at his most assured
and most poignant when showing the relationship between the
performed self and the performer. 'Watching myself go by' is the
phrase used for this by both Larita and Coward's alter ego, Garry
Essendine, in *Present Laughter*. It is interesting that when this
element enters into a play, even one with a potentially
conservative agenda, stasis is always disrupted and it becomes
impossible to envisage a continuation of the status quo or
unequivocally to regret its passing. I want to go on to explore the
relationship between the self, the body which performs the self,

and the economic and sexual systems within which it moves in more detail.

An alternative title I briefly considered for this paper was culled not from a theatrical or critical text but from a note from a harassed colleague trying to co-ordinate resit exams: 'Have you marked the resubmitted Deviant Body?' 'The resubmitted deviant body: Coward and some aspects of cultural inscription reconsidered' sounded so postmodern that it was hard to resist. However, it also reflected an irritating aspect of postmodern somatics, the sense that the body on which culture performs its inscriptions is stylised into abstraction. Coward's presentation is an acknowledgement of the mechanics of the process, the relationship of the body to economic survival both in terms of the pains work can inflict on it and the necessity to maintain it in a marketable state. While all Coward's self-dramatisers tend to hypochondria, it is those who market themselves who are the most eloquent on the subjects of neuralgia, glands, or painful feet (Design for Living), failing memory (Waiting in the Wings) or even piles (Coward in Present Indicative).

In Song at Twilight, designed as a swansong for himself in 1966, Coward interrogated the relationship between self-image, marketing and sexuality in a play that was poignantly autobiographical. In typically sardonic vein he introduces his theme in a parody of the well-made play stock situation: former lovers reunite and secrets are revealed. As they flirt over dinner, Carlotta, once mistress of the successful writer Sir Hugo Latymer, attacks her chocolate soufflé while describing in detail the final days of her career and her last remaining tooth; this insistent, practical physicality is the key to her mission: to strip the heterosexual mask from Sir Hugo. As the play progresses, the relationship between sexuality, success and compromise becomes more and more apparent. Hugo's refusal to be sexually authentic has provided him with a comfortable life, the best of medical care in old age and respectability: but he has impoverished his work, deprived his wife of sexual happiness and severely damaged the life of his lover Perry. Throughout the action he remains in one room, with his books, his pills and his telephone. However, it is not the telephone but the active Carlotta who tells him of Perry's death; her narrative is unspecific but painful in its detail, hinting at the ravages of alcohol and promiscuity. But at the revival in the West End in 1999 the shadow of AIDS was inevitably present. Has Hugo pushed Perry into a lifestyle that has had terrible consequences? If so, where does his responsibility lie? While the characters in the play have differing perspectives on the question, the agonised grief of Corin Redgrave's Hugo in the final moments of the play gave it a sharp timeliness, one that Coward's critics in the Sixties could not have anticipated.

This close attention to body disorders and marketing suggests a possible language in which to examine Coward's disruption of stasis, that of dance. Throughout the Twenties and Thirties substantial changes took place in the way dance was understood as discipline and spectacle. In particular, certain distinctions became blurred. One was that between theatrical and social dance. While Edwardian spectators might watch a cancan or *Swan Lake* according to taste and means, it was unlikely that they themselves would attempt either. However, it would be entirely possible to watch the Charleston and do it yourself, to see an exhibition dancer perform a tango in imitation of Valentino and take tango lessons or even hire a partner. As this distinction eroded so too did other barriers – between ballet and jazz dance, for example, in the American musical. This blurring has visible consequences in revue and musicals, and especially in the work of Fred Astaire, whose dance vocabulary considerably illuminates Coward's work.

The distinguishing mark of Astaire's choreography is self-consciousness; we never lose sight of the intelligence creating the dance as it occurs. In a classical ballet there is no reality beyond the impelling music: we should not be able to tell the dancer from the dance. With Astaire – frequently cast as a professional dancer or showman – we see him thinking as he dances. He may start from an emotional situation like loneliness and express it through movements which become more energetic and complex as the choreography takes over: or by trying out steps which become an exuberant statement of his delight in energy. Or he may dance as a form of sexual challenge – frequently an irate Ginger Rogers finds him rhythmically circling her while making it clear that he is dancing solely to annoy her, or placate her, or just please himself; he is dancing because dance is what he does. There is no sexual motive – until a point at which every dance finally arrives, a tiny, but always magical, pause before the *pas de deux* switches into a different gear and Fred and Ginger are unmistakably together – performing because they are dancers, performing because this is the way they speak to one another; the distinctions between language and choreography, between theatrical and social, are irretrievably shattered.

This tiny and magical pause could be deemed the unit that Barthes proposed in his Sadian grammar, an *erotème*, the smallest unit of erotic communication, and our recognition of it as such is perhaps part of the pleasure.[7] Coward, I believe, makes use of the grammar of this kind of dance in his comedies of performance. The rhythms of the exchange on the balcony between Elyot and Amanda in *Private Lives* are precisely those of an Astaire tap-dance, brisk alternating lines about chopsticks and the Taj Mahal superimposed on a 'nasty insistent little tune' until the real issue, that of desire, cannot be deferred and the magical pause takes place:

> AMANDA: And it didn't look like a biscuit box, did it? I've always felt that it might.
> ELYOT: Darling, darling, I love you so.[8]

Coward described *Private Lives* as originating in a vision 'of Gertie ... in a white Molyneux dress on a terrace in the South of France'.[9] Instead of imagined characters, he begins with two specific performing bodies: Noël Coward and Gertrude Lawrence. Even before the written text is acted, the reader has been constructed as part of a paying audience. Instead of a private scene at which we peek through the fourth wall like voyeurs, we are watching a conscious performance only complete when we are there. *Private Lives* is the only one of the flagship comedies Coward identified in his preface to *Play Parade: Five* – the others being *Hay Fever*, *Blithe Spirit*, *Design for Living* and *Present*

Laughter – in which major characters are not involved in performing or marketing themselves, and this insertion of Lawrence into the text seems designed to rectify the omission. In all these comedies we are alerted to the particular conditions of the performing self.

Every erotic encounter parallels the new language of dance with its blurring of social and theatrical: for instance, there is the several times repeated latchkey ritual in *Present Laughter*, increasingly fanciful in its dialogue of sexual challenge and deferral until the 'magic pause' takes place on the line when Garry and Joanna stop arguing long enough to kiss: 'I won't hear a word against the Albert Hall.'[10] Our relationship to the erotic presence of Garry is shot through with our awareness of him as an object of consumption. The plot deals precisely with the relationship between his enjoyably improvisatory philandering like this and his career as matinée idol, a balance carefully managed by a motley group who control the words he speaks, the spaces in which he speaks them and the going rates of pay. Paradoxically, he is easier to tame on the erotic front, abandoning a lover the moment one of his management team exploits his Pavlovian reaction to the words 'Forum Theatre'. Artistically, he has to be channelled: he wants to play Peer Gynt, the man who discovers the nothingness at the core of his being, and this has to be stopped at all costs. For Garry is exactly what we see: an object of desire who can only create himself by linguistic dance, who can only attain the magical pause if there is a theatre in which a pause *is* a pause, a unit of erotic exchange and not just an awkward hiatus in the conversation. Hence we do not simply consume him as object: by interpreting his show-off tirades as units in an erotic grammar, we are partners in the dance. We are, of course, sitting this particular one out. But our status empowers us to permit him to select substitute partners and when his peacock display of language on the subject of the Theatre of Tomorrow transforms Roland Maule into a love-struck groupie, new possibilities open up.

Naturally these are not spelt out, any more than the rhythms of the exchange between Leo and Otto in *Design for Living* concerning the word 'wimple' are overtly followed through. But the fact that they have arisen in a situation simultaneously private and self-consciously performative acts as a kind of guarantee: not that the emotions are especially sincere, or lasting, or morally praiseworthy, but that they have a certain authenticity. Someone says of the self-consciously outrageous queens in *Semi-Monde*: 'They are not even real of their kind.' When one of Coward's performers erodes the boundary between watching a dance and dancing it, between the performing body for which we pay and the performing body performing for its own pleasure, it is real of its kind. Whoever the participants in the dance may be, their acknowledgement of the erotic grammar which shapes their performance suspends, for a moment, other kinds of relations. Agnes de Mille, pioneer of the new dance, wrote of the woman dancer: 'Never at any moment is she threatened . . . her privacy can never be usurped . . . The very physical stresses, the strengthening and bracing and tautening of her back and leg supply such a sense of driving power as to give the illusion of male potency.'[11]

Gender or sexual orientation and the power struggles contingent upon them break down in the very fact of performance. If Coward's stasis plays are conservative, those which set the body in self-conscious motion have too radical a sense of possibility to be so.

I should like to conclude with an image which has often been seen as a tribute to the status quo and all things static, the closing tableau of *Cavalcade*. While we see the aristocratic family shorn of its sons and at odds with former servants, and the chaos of a joyless post-war world dancing around them, we also have a single figure placed above them and articulating what it means to be part of the twentieth century. Fanny, the servant's daughter, is a performer and both sexually and socially mobile. Her mother assumes that this mobility is of the same kind we have seen in the chorus girls from *Mirabelle*, the show-within-the-show interrupted with news of the relief of Mafeking, for whom the unspoken question is: 'Whom do I sleep with to get out of show business and into the aristocracy?' Joe's mother, with frigid distaste, refuses to discuss the subject. Briefly, there is the possibility of an overt confrontation between classes, which is neatly avoided by a *coup de théâtre*: a telegram announces Joe's death at the Front.

But if the class conflict is avoided, that of sexual politics is not. While Joe's death silences the older generation, it confirms Fanny in a single status she may already have chosen. Her goodbye to Joe is full of sexual tenderness but when he asks her if she loves him she replies only, 'Yes, I think so.' As the 1930s begin, she presides over the chaos, singing. The opening night of *Cavalcade* shared the front page of the Daily Mail with the news that 'The Reichstag re-opened – it is significant that nearly 150 National Socialist and Nationalist members absented themselves yesterday, and that the Reichstag building was guarded like a fortress'.[12] Coward's curtain speech, to the effect that it was 'still a pretty exciting thing to be English', might have celebrated stasis, but only in the beleaguered style of Frank Gibbons, and only in fleeting contrast to the 'Twentieth Century Blues' sung by the most mobile figure in the play. *Cavalcade* may be both nostalgic and conservative, but the presence of the performer offers the possibility of asking questions about sexual and social change; as such, its closing moments offer an image that sums up the forces which energise Coward's plays and also suggest that the theatre is the best place in which to come to grips with them.

NOTES

1. Noël Coward, *Sunday Times*, 22 January 1961.
2. Noël Coward, *Plays: Four* (London: Methuen, 1983), p.298.
3. Noël Coward, *Plays: Three* (London: Methuen, 1979), p.353.
4. Noël Coward, *Plays: One* (London: Methuen, 1982), introduction.
5. Emily Post, *Etiquette: the Blue Book of Social Usage* (New York: Funk and Wagnall, 1924), p.295.
6. Noël Coward, *Plays: One*, p.266.
7. Roland Barthes, *Sade, Fourier, Loyola*, tr. R. Miller (London: Cape 1977), p.77.
8. Noël Coward, *Plays: Two* (London: Methuen, 1979), p.34.
9. Noël Coward, *Present Indicative* (London: Heinemann, 1937), p.373.
10. Noël Coward, *Plays: Four* (London: Methuen, 1983), p.196.
11. Agnes de Mille, *Dance to the Piper* (London: Columbus, 1987), p.66.
12. *Daily Mail*, 14 October 1931.

Playing with the Audience

Jean Chothia

In 1895 Bernard Shaw wrote of Oscar Wilde in the *Saturday Review*: 'In a certain sense Mr Wilde is our only thorough playwright. He plays with everything: with wit, with philosophy, with drama, with actors and audience, with the whole theatre. Such a feat scandalises the Englishman, who can no more play with wit than he can with a football or a cricket bat. He works at both.'[1]

Shaw's recognition of 'play' in playwriting – play with ideas, with the audience and with 'the whole theatre' – goes to the heart of Wilde's writing but is as appropriate to Noël Coward as it is to Wilde or Shaw himself. Like Wilde, Coward wrote for performance in mainstream theatre and, presenting himself as an entertainer, he, too, necessarily wore a mask. Like Wilde, he was also a remaker, borrowing from and writing variations on other people's works with immense facility.[2] All three share a tendency to use and subvert traditional mores and theatrical structures; the necessary comic distance possessed, perhaps, because each was – whether for reasons of class, nationality, sexuality, or a combination of these – an outsider, as Shaw suggests when he distinguishes Wilde from the scandalised 'Englishman'. And each made one or more of the enduring comedies of the English repertory.

In this paper I want to look at some of the ways in which Coward plays and to suggest that his dramatic method invites the audience to join the game, while always reserving to himself the right to startle with previously undisclosed rules. He overcomes the potentially scandalised Englishman in each of us by leading us, as audience, to feel ourselves 'insiders', not so much with the characters as with the dramatist. He makes us conscious of the shaping consciousness behind the action. A simple example from an early play illustrates this.

In the first act of *Fallen Angels* (1925) it is revealed that Julia and Jane, respectable married women, have both, with typical Coward symmetry, kept secret from their husbands the existence of a former lover, the same former lover, Maurice, with whom each is again in contact. In Act Two, the women anticipate his imminent arrival with mounting excitement. When the maid enters, Julia, in a frantic attempt to signal to Jane the need for discretion, abruptly changes the subject with:

> JULIA: Yes, naturally depressing in November because of the fog.

Jane's reception of the signal is evident when she counters with the even more bizarre:

> JANE: But only if you pay your subscription in advance.[3]

While the non sequitur serves to indicate their panic, our fleeting recognition of it *as* a non sequitur lets us, the audience, into the game. On the replay, at the maid's next entrance, when thoughts of Maurice have become more fevered, we recognise the diversionary tactics:

> JULIA: And those hands –
> JANE: And teeth –
> JULIA: And legs! Oh, Jane!
> JANE: Oh, Julia!
>   (*Re-enter Saunders . . .*)
> JULIA: The cushions of the carriages are always so dusty.
> JANE: She ought never to have been burnt at the stake because she was such a nice girl.

JULIA: I can hardly wait until strawberries come in again.
(p.205)

The wonderful absurdity of the diversions, moreover, is itself
diverting.

The behaviour of Coward's characters is frequently labelled
'appalling' by commentators – but there is usually glee in the
description. The discourteous frankness, the Strindbergian
directness, of both male and female characters is invigorating.
While it is hard to forgive any writer the line, and possibly the
sentiment, 'certain women should be struck regularly, like
gongs',[4] it is quickly apparent that women in a Coward comedy
are as self-assertive, self-possessed or self-deceived as men and,
like Jane and Julia, as likely to seethe with sudden desire, so that
courtship and the battle of the sexes are waged on strictly equal
terms. (Fallen Angels ends with the husbands' sinking recognition
of the manoeuvre by which they have been led to send their wives
off upstairs with the former lover.) Similarly, if the minor figures
are stooges, they are drawn equally from both sexes: the feeble
flapper, Jackie, in Hay Fever is matched by the stuffed-shirt
diplomat, Richard; the excessively womanly woman, Sibyl, in
Private Lives, by the manly man, Victor. Sorel Bliss holds hold her
own against brother Simon as effectively as Judith fights with
husband David. Elizabeth Robins, the English theatre's first
Hedda Gabler, later declared that it was not the message that
inspired the 'wholehearted, enchanted devotion' she and her
fellow actresses gave to the promotion and interpretation of Ibsen
in the 1890s but 'the joy of having in our hands . . . such glorious
actable stuff'.[5] I can't believe but that after the first surprised
recognition, the women, if not the men, in the audience aren't as
cheered by the creation of Sorel or Amanda as they are by Hedda,
by Rosalind and Millamant, or by Molière's Célimène.

Having taken the point that there is more dramatic energy,
more theatrical originality, in the Bliss family than in their
sycophantic guests, more fun and feeling in Amanda and Elyot in
Private Lives than in the convention-bound spouses they betray,
we want Coward to go further, to make them even more vividly

outspoken, more daring or more monstrous in their behaviour. This isn't a matter of condoning – we may at times feel sympathy, at others be appalled. What we are responding to is dramatic energy, as we respond, for instance (to take a very different work), to Macbeth and Lady Macbeth, without condoning their deeds. We sit forward in our seats when these characters are on the stage.

Coward's characters perform, and we are led to recognise performance, and to relish it. As Garry Essendine says in *Present Laughter*, 'I'm always acting – watching myself go by'[6] and, thus prompted, we too begin to watch for his next piece of role play. Making Judith Bliss an actress and David Bliss a romantic novelist in *Hay Fever* gives Coward immediate access to convincing fictive invention. Some of the theatrical jokes in that play are directly between dramatist and audience – obvious, in Judith's promise to attend the 'first night' of Sandy's boxing match;[7] more covert when her star vehicle, *Love's Whirlwind*, shares its title with one of Arkadina's in *The Seagull*,[8] or when the end of the supposed extract from *Love's Whirlwind* that closes Act Two, 'Don't strike! he is your father!!!!' (p.75), echoes the closing lines of Act Three of Wilde's *A Woman of No Importance*. Others derive from the shared language and experience of the Bliss family, notably their propensity to switch into melodramatic confession – or renunciation – mode. The tropes and clichéd registers of popular fiction and drama are reworked deliberately by the family for their own amusement and that of the audience, who understand, and the horror of the guests, who do not. Such quotation is acknowledged in Act One:

> JUDITH: Be Victor a minute, Sorel –
> SOREL (*rising*):   Do you mean when he comes in at the end of the act?
> JUDITH: Yes. You know – 'Is this a game?' (p. 21)

They then run through Judith's scene so that when, towards the end of Act Two, one of the tormented guests, Richard, enters during a hysterical argument and innocently asks 'Is this a game?'

(p.74), the audience is well ahead of the bemused guests as the family take the cue and rerun the sequence *we*, but not the house guests, encountered earlier.

As this suggests, if he is in his own way a feminist, Coward is also a sort of modernist in his tendency to present his audiences with the artifice of theatre. Probably the most striking moments of meta-theatrical awareness come in *Present Laughter*, with, for example:

> MORRIS: Anyhow, if it hadn't been for our restraining influence you'd be in the provinces by now.
> GARRY: And what's the matter with the provinces, may I ask? They've often proved to be a great deal more intelligent than London.
> HENRY: Be careful! Someone might hear![9]

– a sequence calculated to play equally well in London *and* the Provinces. Again, having encountered in Act Three the increasingly pressing and risqué advances on Garry, first of a young woman, then a young man, each swearing absolute devotion, then of the vamp, Joanna, proposing a relationship based not on love but on sex, the audience is in a position to appreciate the exchange that follows the *fourth* ring on the doorbell:

> JOANNA: Who's that?
> GARRY: With any luck it's the Lord Chamberlain. (p.237)

Energy in comedy comes in part from activity. The action in Coward's comedies, although it can seem frenetic, takes place largely in the dialogue, leading to successive permutations in relationships which, while they may be increasingly forbidden, are, we can hardly deny, increasingly appropriate. Characters are continually moving on: they are met while dressing to go out; they find themselves sleeping in unexpected places; ill-equipped, they have to borrow pyjamas; suitcases wait in the hall. Just arrived at a French coastal resort for their respective honey-

moons, Amanda and Elyot must decamp to Paris. Pursued by
their respective spouses, they must make another hasty exit.
Arguments erupt; couples fall into embraces or, equally readily,
into physical fighting. The impression is of impulsive reactions, of
imminent revelation or collapse. What is distinctive is the
panache with which these elements are combined and the
control Coward exerts over the proliferating complications. The
security for the audience that is brought by the incorporation of
traditional farce elements is undercut by an untraditional
directness of statement that cuts through the subterfuges of polite
discourse. The pressures of desire and promiscuous or adulterous
activity, for example, are spoken with startling openness.

Already in *The Vortex* (1924) the characteristic square-dance
pattern of the action was present: by the end of the play the
characters had changed partners. What Peter Holland has called
Coward's 'comic geometry'[10] is there to be recognised in the
texture as well as the structure of the writing. The repetitions and
mirroring of activity and of dialogue lead us into, invite us to be
ahead of, the action. They also invite us to appreciate the artifice
and ingenuity of theatre. In *Present Laughter*, one ring on the door
bell is followed by two more; one oath of undying devotion by
another and then another. Daphne's explanation of her presence
in Garry's flat and dressing gown at the opening of Act One is
told to three people in succession. When, at the opening of Act
Two, Scene One Joanna, too, claims to have lost her latchkey *we*
share Garry's response of 'Oh Joanna!'[11] and it might equally well
be 'Oh Noël!' *Private Lives*, opening on to identical balconies on
to which two newly married couples emerge from identical
French windows with identical cocktails, leads on to a direct
partner swap. The echoes, repetition-with-variation and pattern-
ing of the dialogue all contribute to the comedy of anticipation
and pressurise the audience to recognise Elyot and Amanda as
natural partners before ever they do themselves. Not only is there
evident generosity with regard to the past:

> SIBYL: She was a fool to lose you.
> ELYOT: We lost each other;[12]

but each new spouse is wrong-footed as each attempts to impose conventional values in consecutive opening exchanges. Amanda's 'thank you, Victor, that's most encouraging' in response to his calling her 'so sweet' (p.17) is as sardonic as Elyot's calling Sibyl a 'completely feminine little creature' (p.7), while Elyot's claim to love 'more wisely' now (p.6) is closely echoed by Amanda's 'more calmly' (p.14). Sibyl's sense of feminine propriety in the matter of sunburn – 'I mustn't get sunburnt', 'Why not?', 'I hate it on women' (p.7) – becomes an even more effective marker and gains in comic value when directly echoed in Victor's 'I hate sunburnt women ... It's somehow, well, unsuitable' and is further undermined in Amanda's response, 'It's awfully suitable to me darling' (p.12). Coward drives the play forward by putting information in the audience's way; giving clues that encourage anticipation of the subsequent action.

Coward's dialogue is no more Wildean than it is Shavian, he has neither the epigrammatic texture of the former nor the disconcerting sharpshooting[13] of the latter, yet we are at least as satisfactorily startled and rewarded by his as by either of theirs. His own comments on this are astute. In his autobiography he describes having found the newly typed-up Hay Fever 'a little tedious':

I think that the reason for this was that I was passing through a transition stage as a writer; my dialogue was becoming more natural and less elaborate, and I was beginning to concentrate more on the comedy values of situation rather than the comedy values of actual lines. I expect that when I read through Hay Fever that first time, I was subconsciously bemoaning its lack of snappy epigrams.[14]

Mannered as Coward's public performance could be, polished as his dialogue evidently is, that claim to its 'becoming more natural' is fair, as is that idea of 'comedy values of situation' rather than 'actual lines'. Without doing anything as dull as reproducing everyday speech, he taps into our capacity to recognise our own habits, subterfuges and misunderstandings in speech. Accompanying gesture and manner of speech, as well as silences between, and the very direction of the words themselves, work to shape our interpretation.

The dialogue is compelling for the audience because of the remarkable way it dramatises pragmatics: the recognition that we often speak words which substitute for what we are actually thinking; that the primary function of conversation is often not the exchange of information; that what is *understood* in conversation differs from the paraphraseable meaning. Coward presents the gaps and inconsequentialities of normal conversation in intensified, more staccato, form. In this, as in the meta-theatricality, he takes us into the world of post-Second World War drama. (The various breakfast table sequences – in *Fallen Angels*, in *Private Lives* – are notable forerunners of the opening of Pinter's *The Birthday Party*.) We are required to supply the feeling behind the lines but also the implication the characters are avoiding *by means of* their lines. So, in *Present Laughter*:

> GARRY: How was the Toscanni concert?
> JOANNA: Glorious. (*She sits down*) He played the Eighth and the Seventh.
> GARRY: Personally I prefer the Fifth.
> JOANNA: I like the Ninth best of all.
> GARRY (*casually sitting beside her on the sofa*):   There's nothing like the dear old Ninth.
> JOANNA: I love the Queen's Hall, don't you? It's so uncompromising.
> GARRY (*taking her hand*):   I love the Albert Hall much more.
> JOANNA: (*leaning against him*): I wonder why. I always find it depressing.

until:

> GARRY (*his mouth on hers*):   I won't hear a word against the Albert Hall.[15]

'Comedy values of situation', indeed; which is not to say that at times, even while seeing the absurdity of a situation, we can't also be touched by it as, for example, in *Private Lives*:

> AMANDA: You're in love with yours aren't you?
> ELYOT: Certainly.
> AMANDA: There you are then.
> ELYOT: There we both are, then.[16]

so that when strong feeling is expressed, as in Elyot's response to Amanda's 'How was the Taj Mahal?', 'Unbelievable, a sort of dream' (p.34), the audience is in a position to recognise the intensity behind the oblique utterance.

The surface inconsequentiality of the dialogue can (as with the subterfuge absurdities in *Fallen Angels*) become surreal. It frequently does in the long exchange between Elyot and Amanda that is Act Two of *Private Lives*:

> AMANDA: Have you ever crossed the Sahara on a camel?
> ELYOT: Frequently. When I was a boy we used to do it all the time. My Grandmother had a wonderful seat on a camel. (p.41)

What we hear there, as well as the banter, is a willingness to follow on, mutual harmony. Elsewhere, coolness, or distance, is signalled, often by one character's taking literally the loose or exaggerated statement of another, as when, in response to her new husband's jovial, 'You know I feel rather scared of you at close quarters', Amanda in Act One drily replies, 'That promises to be very embarrassing' (p.15). Similarly when, in Act Two, to Elyot's self-righteous claim, 'I have only had three minute liqueur glasses of brandy the whole evening long. A child of two couldn't get drunk on that', Amanda's response is the literal, 'On the contrary, a child of two could get violently drunk on only *one* glass of brandy' (p. 61), the atmosphere is more effectively cooled than it would have been by a straightforward rebuttal of his untrue claim about how much he had drunk.

The *Observer* critic who wrote dismissively in 1930 of *Private Lives* 'their style is mainly in their clothes; as conversationalists they are mere back-chatterers'[17] could not have been more wrong. Although, of course, their style is *also* in their clothes. Coward was well aware of the erotic power of beautiful and beautifully dressed actors displaying themselves and, even as we register this, we probably find ourselves succumbing, lured, as he claimed to have been himself, by the image of the woman 'in a white Molyneux dress on a terrace in the South of France',[18] but if so, the image endures because, not in spite of, the control of the writing in which it is set.

One further point about Coward's play with dramatic form, which goes to the core of his major comedies, is worth noting. *Traditionally*, English comic plots are resolved in marriage, in a reassertion, however ironically shadowed, of belief in the institution with its bonds and promises, rather than in impulse and anarchy. This is as true of *The Importance of Being Earnest* as it is of *Much Ado About Nothing* or *The Way of the World*. Coward does not allow his audience such an escape. Not only does he put the idea of divorce and separation firmly on to the stage but, at the end of his plays the betrayals, the topsy-turvy events, the continual changing of partners in the dance, look set to continue indefinitely. (And lest the safer option might seem better, *Private Lives* ends with Victor and Sibyl engaged in vicious argument.) *Private Lives* just pre-dates, and in its 1931 film version must surely have been influential on, the crop of comedies of remarriage, including *Philadelphia Story* and *Adam's Rib* identified by Stanley Cavell as a Hollywood genre that flourished between 1934 and 1941.[19] Coward's comedy differs from them in its refusal to work through to complete reconciliation and new harmony. His audience is asked to see marriage not as the answer but as part of the chaos. The common-sense ties in *Private Lives* are dissolved in favour of the earlier but evidently unsustainable one. Garry Essendine's philandering will continue; the formal bond in *Design for Living* has no power against the desires and jealousies of the troilism that defies society's code. This may be an inevitable result of Coward's positing social, personal and economic equality of sexual partners; it may derive from covert treatment of homosexual attachment, or it may simply be the invasion of comic form by a clear-sightedness that resists the shaping comfort of tradition. But while the implications of the endings of Coward's comedies may be disconcerting and his view of relationships bleak, I don't think we resist them. We have been too fully participant in the unfolding for that. Although problems are not solved, which of us is not smiling conspiratorially at the endings he produces, as the guests in *Hay Fever* make their escape, or the central couples of *Private Lives* and *Present Laughter* tiptoe off in mutual, if temporary, alliance.

Coward's own famously low-key acknowledgement of his major comedies – 'on rereading them, I find them both un-pretentious and well-constructed'[20] – is very much to the point in any discussion of his dramatic craftsmanship and his associated capacity to draw in his audience. At his best, the audience can't but delight in 'the achieve of, the mastery of the thing'. In his much-quoted *Sunday Times* article, Coward gave advice not entirely different from that which Garry Essendine offers the hopeful playwright-of-the-future in *Present Laughter*. In 1961 Coward wrote (my italics): 'Consider the public. Treat it with tact and courtesy. It will accept much from you *if you are clever enough to win it to your side* . . . Coax it, charm it, stimulate it, shock it now and then if you must, make it laugh, make it cry and *make it think*, but above all dear pioneers . . . never, never, never bore the living hell out of it.'[21]

It is the winning us to his side that Coward does so con-vincingly in his most achieved comedies of manners.

NOTES

1. George Bernard Shaw, *Saturday Review*, 12 January 1895.
2. Wilde's remaking is discussed at length in Kerry Powell, *Oscar Wilde and the Theatre of the 1890s* (Cambridge: CUP, 1990) and see, for example, Frances Gray's discussion of Coward's reworking of O'Neill's *Strange Interlude* in *Design for Living*, in *Noël Coward* (London: Macmillan, 1987), p.160.
3. *Fallen Angels*, in Noël Coward, *Plays: One* (London: Methuen, 1989), p.204.

4. *Private Lives*, in Noël Coward, *Plays: Two* (London: Methuen, 1986), p.72.
5. Elizabeth Robins, *Ibsen and the Actress* (London: Hogarth Press, 1928), p.20.
6. *Present Laughter*, in Noël Coward, *Plays: Four* (London: Methuen, 1990), p.148.
7. *Hay Fever*, in Noël Coward, *Plays: One* (London: Methuen, 1989), p.24.
8. Chekhov's play was performed by the Moscow Art Theatre during Coward's visit to New York in 1922, as Christopher Innes points out in *Modern British Drama* (Cambridge: CUP, 1992), p. 250.
9. *Plays: Four*, p.243.
10. Peter Holland, 'Noël Coward and Comic Geometry', in M. Cordner, P. D. Holland and J. Kerrigan (eds), *English Comedy* (Cambridge: CUP, 1994), pp.267–87.
11. *Plays: Four*, p.186.
12. *Plays: Two*, p.5.
13. See Shaw's account of Ibsen 'sharpshooting at the audience', *The Quintessence of Ibsenism* (London: Constable, 1913), p.145.
14. Coward, *Present Indicative* (1937), reprinted in *The Autobiography of Noël Coward* (London: Methuen, 1986), p.124.
15. *Plays: Four*, p.196.
16. *Plays: Two*, p.29.
17. *Observer*, 29 September 1930.
18. Coward, *Present Indicative*, p.217.
19. See Stanley Cavell, *Pursuits of Happiness: the Hollywood Comedy of Remarriage* (Cambridge, Mass.: Harvard UP, 1981).
20. Coward, introduction, *Play Parade, Vol. 5* (London: Heinemann, 1958), p.xxxiii.
21. *Sunday Times*, 15 January 1961.

Le printemps du théâtre:
Coward's France

John Stokes

DAVID (*reading*):   'Paris in spring, with the Champs Elysées
alive and dancing in the sunlight; lightly-dressed children
like gay painted butterflies . . . the streets were thronged
with hurrying vehicles, the thin peek-peek of taxi-
hooters –'

SOREL: I love peek-peek.

DAVID (*ignoring her*):   '– seemed to merge in with the other
vivid noises, weaving a vast pattern of sound which was
Paris –'

JUDITH: What was Paris, dear?

DAVID: *Which* was Paris.

JUDITH: What was Paris?

DAVID: You can't say a vast pattern of sound what was
Paris.

A slight pause.

JUDITH: Yes, but – What was Paris?[1]

Hay Fever ends with David Bliss continuing to read from his
novel: 'Jane Sefton, in her scarlet Hispano, swept out of the Rue
St. Honoré into the Place de la Concorde . . .' – but even this is
controversial, prompting corrections from both Judith and Sorel.
'Do you think I don't know Paris as well as you do?' David
protests, though, in fact, as Judith correctly points out, the rue St
Honoré doesn't run directly into the Place de la Concorde and

David is certainly wrong to claim that the rue Boissy d'Anglas is parallel to the rue de Rivoli.

This may be Noël Coward's final knowing joke against the Parisian pretensions of a self-obsessed character since from his very first hit – 'Parisian Pierrot' sung by Gertrude Lawrence in *London Calling* in 1923 – to Otto's shabby Paris flat (specifically contrasted with Leo's suite at the Georges V) in *Design for Living* ten years later, Coward makes it clear that he knows his Paris, the city of *hôtels de luxe*, of *grands boulevards*, very well indeed.[2]

In the Twenties, though, there were several versions of the city on offer, several 'patterns of sound'. There's a passage in the published diaries of Maurice Sachs for the years 1919 to 1929 entitled *Au Temps du Boeuf sur le Toit* after the famous avant-garde night club, in which Sachs describes two contrasting friends, each representing his own view of Paris. One is called Blaise and he likes: Cocteau, jazz, Picasso, Juan Gris, the *Nouvelle Revue Française*, negro art, Matisse, popular dance halls, circuses and fairs. The other is called Antoine and he thinks that this is all populist nonsense. Antoine admires writers like Anatole France, composers like Reynaldo Hahn, playwrights like Sacha Guitry and he prefers restaurants like le Fouquet's, tea at Claridge's, horse-riding followed by dinner at Paillard with a mannequin. The only thing that Blaise and Antoine have in common is that they both admire the great music-hall star Mistinguett.[3]

It's fairly clear, I think, whose side history has been on in this debate: Blaise, the Left Bank modernist – his are the tastes that have survived. On the other hand, drawing the line at horse-riding, Noël Coward would surely, on the whole, have preferred to be with Antoine, the Right Bank sophisticate. Even Coward's 'Parisian Pierrot' is a socialite who haunts neither the traditional fairground nor the moonlit woodland of Watteau's paintings, but rather the *boîtes* and *boutiques* of the rue de la Paix. Burnt out with high-class modern living, he's a poor little rich boy, a characteristically world-weary contribution to the cult of Pierrot that runs from Beardsley to Picasso, from Verlaine to Laforgue, from the silent mime play *L'Enfant Prodigue* that played with

immense success in London in the 1890s, to Stravinsky's
Petrouchka (1911) and Schoenberg's *Pierrot lunaire* (1912).[4]

Coward's song begins by admitting distant tradition:

> Fantasy in olden days
> In varying and different ways
> Was very much in vogue
> Columbine and Pantaloon
> A wistful Pierrot 'neath the moon,
> And Harlequin a rogue

but each of its three verses points up a contrast with the present
and the lyric as a whole ends with today, the music comple-
menting the words with a hint of ragtime in the piano break
which enlivens the *thé-dansant* good manners of the strings, and
a harp-like sound in the background that hints at ancient
melancholy.

> Parisian Pierrot,
> Society's hero,
> The lord of a day,
> The rue de la Paix
> Is under your sway,
> The world may flatter
> But what does that matter,
> They'll never shatter
> Your gloom profound,
> Parisian Pierrot,
> Your spirit's at zero,
> Divinely forlorn,
> With exquisite scorn
> From sunset to dawn,
> The limbo is calling,
> Your star will be falling,
> As soon as the clock goes round.[5]

Coward's version of the fashionable *commedia* figure is a good example of his extraordinary knack of connecting, in often unacknowledged ways, with artistic trends. This Parisian Pierrot might be a society model for the music-hall performer in Colette's early novel of theatrical life *La Vagabonde* whose speciality is a *Pierrot neurasthénique*[6] or, allowing for the ambiguity of gender encouraged by Gertrude Lawrence's rendition, the mysterious woman glimpsed in a Paris restaurant by the heroine of Jean Rhys's *Quartet* (1928): 'a lady with a pale face, crimson lips, a close-fitting black hat and eyebrows like half moons. She was indeed exactly like Pierrot and every now and then she would turn and look at her self in the glass approvingly.'[7]

'Decadent Paris' went on for a long time, right into the Twenties, and Coward capitalised on the surviving conventions. 'La flamme' in *This Year of Grace* (1928) calls for more drinks because 'This is what the world thinks / Is la Vie Parisienne' and tells her lover 'I want to smite you and beat you and bite you / And swoon and swoon and swoon' since 'Nothing suffices but decadent vices'. It is, after all, 'the Bohemian way'.[8] It was in Paris, of course, that Nicky Lancaster picked up his drug habit:

NICKY: If you'd seen me in Paris – studying, studying – all
          night long until the grey dawn put the guttering candle to
          shame – and my nerveless hands dropped from the keys.
HELEN: Candles gutter awfully quickly when they're burnt
          at both ends.[9]

And the Parisian motif is still at work in *Bitter Sweet* (1929), above all in the songs of Manon, who has '*une aventure dans les boîtes des boulevards*'.[10]

Also situated on the Right Bank was the theatre that Coward knew best: boulevard theatre, the theatre of Sacha Guitry, with whom, as a writer, he is frequently if not always helpfully compared, and of Guitry's wife (at least until 1934), the *soubrette*, singer, actress and dancer Yvonne Printemps, who often appeared in London as well. She starred in Coward's own *Conversation Piece* in 1934 and, in 1936, would have been in Ben Travers's *Oh*

Mistress Mine (songs by Vivian Ellis and Cole Porter) had not the similarity of the storyline to the Abdication crisis led to its being called off.

John Gielgud describes her as a kind of French Gertrude Lawrence, with 'trim elegant figure, appealing spaniel eyes and a broad turned-up nose'. Printemps' acting, says Gielgud, 'had something of the same inimitable brand of impish sentimental comedy' as Lawrence and, unlike Lawrence, 'whose singing voice, fascinating though it was, could be distinctly unreliable and wobbly, Printemps' tones were exquisitely delicate and true'.[11] That this was the case her recordings still tell us.

Printemps was, or rather she became, a star of operetta, that essentially nineteenth-century form into which Coward poured a good deal of his time and talent. The operetta (or as Coward preferred to call it, stressing the essential Frenchness of the form, the *opérette*) draws upon haute couture and high living, and a certain kind of sexuality – the old-fashioned 'sentimental' sexuality of middle-aged men and young girls, of chaperones and courtesans. It's a sexuality that is 'witty and naughty and pretty', and you can hear it, for instance, in another song from *London Calling*, 'Prenez garde, Lisette'.[12] Coward became a master of this flirtatious, opportunistic mode of lovemaking, with its underlying hard-headedness, and Yvonne Printemps helped him fix the register.

Born in 1894, she had started as a child performer by imitating Yvette Guilbert, making her début at the Folies Bergère in *Nue cocotte* while still in her teens. She stayed at the Folies for some four years, a contemporary there of Colette who much later was to speak of her 'incurable jeunesse' and who wrote about her rendition of 'Véronique' by Messager in *Revue de Paris* (1918): 'She has a voice that is exultant with joy – a joy that is intelligently applied. "Progess", someone cried. Call it progress if you like, but above all it's the use of her true nature and her natural abilities. She must sing: her voice is fetching and true, and it has the quality of warmth whilst retaining her "young-girl" sweetness.'[13]

At the Folies, along with Maurice Chevalier, Printemps was a

supporting act for Mistinguett; at the Olympia music hall she
sang, danced, did acrobatics, often cross-dressed. Her romantic
involvement and subsequent marriage with Guitry led to a more
dramatic, if more restrained, repertoire in which opulence played
an increasingly important part. When Coward visited Paris (he
went there for the very first time in the early 1920s) he would
often see her, usually in the latest offering from Guitry. She filled
precisely his own definition of a star: a unique being who 'had
made her name inseparable from the history of her time'.[14]

There are pictures and descriptions of Printemps from the
Twenties which invoke this versatility. In the Parisian *Revue de
Printemps* in 1924 she appeared as the Prince of Wales in the
uniform of a naval officer,[15] as Yvette Guilbert (a nod to her own
origins as well as to the mythology of the *café conc* in general), as
Diane de Poitiers and as several others, both male and female.
She was always at home *en travestie*, at various times playing
Debureau, the great mime, as well as the composer Mozart in a
celebrated Guitry play. Sometimes she dressed as a flapper,
showing plenty of leg, later she followed an older tradition and
appeared in the 'frou-frou' style of gown affected by Bernhardt
and the great stars of the Nineties (among her films was Abel
Gance's 1934 version of *La Dame aux Camélias*). Her dresses were
famous as, according to the conventions of a star, they were
required to be.[16] Costumed always by Lanvin, she perpetuated the
close artistic and commercial link between theatre and fashion,
between entertainment and consumption, that continued long
into the twentieth century. And, because Yvonne Printemps was
a star of the opulent boulevard and of *opérette*, she was ideally
equipped for one particular strand in Coward's art.

There was a problem: she couldn't speak English. Printemps'
London performances depended in large part on the purity of her
singing voice and the transparent legibility of those gestures –
those so-called 'moues, grins, pouts and grimaces'[17] – that the
English think to be essentially French. Coward's solution in
Conversation Piece was to cast her as a young Frenchwoman whose
English is still slightly halting and to make her learn her lines
parrot fashion. It was a device that Guitry had used previously

himself when he had Printemps take the part of an English entertainer in his play *L'Illusioniste*, which she performed in London in 1920.

Coward's device was a cunning variation on the time-honoured English theatrical trick of including some basic French dialogue in an English-language play (he offers the classic version with his French maid in *Private Lives*). The joke gains when it's a French person speaking English because the more English they speak the more ineradicably French they reveal themselves to be. This is generally thought to be funny, though attractive too. In Shakespeare's *Henry V* Katherine is tempted into saying naughty things under the cover of language. In today's Anglo-French pop culture – from Françoise Hardy in the Sixties to Antoine de Caunes and Jean-Paul Gaultier in the Nineties – we still love it when they get things slightly wrong, and they know it. Sex is generally involved. There's a song in *Conversation Piece* with the refrain 'there's always something fishy about the French'[18] – where 'fishy' probably really means filthy. 'Fish' was, I suspect, a period double entendre – Cole Porter undoubtedly gave the word a certain ring.[19]

The plot of *Conversation Piece* is taken from 'Dormer Creston's' prosy historical novel *The Regent and his Daughter*[20] and it's very slight, although there is a sexual undercurrent. Set in Regency Brighton in 1811 during the aftermath of the French Revolution, the play featured Coward himself in the part of Paul, Duc de Chaucigny-Varennes, an impoverished aristocrat, self-appointed guardian of the girl he claims to be his ward, in fact an orphan café entertainer, Melanie, whom he takes on a trip to England with the express purpose of finding her a rich husband. After an entanglement with a pleasant but unsatisfying young English aristocrat, Melanie confesses, to Paul's bewilderment, that it is Paul himself she loves. Wandering in despair around the gardens of the Royal Pavilion (a wordless mime scene, much praised at the time), he then realises that he has lost his heart to her, as well as any chance of making a fortune, and he rushes back to their lodging, only to find it full of her packed trunks. In fact, she is merely hiding away, awaiting his return.

Pictures of the production do make it look extraordinarily wooden. Coward is much worse in this respect than Printemps, although one probably needs to bear in mind that he was ill and was soon to withdraw from the show because of appendicitis, to be replaced by Printemps' lover, later her second husband, Pierre Fresnay. One has to shut one's eyes and listen to the music to see what audiences saw in Printemps' version of the classic ingénue. This is even true, surely, of the show's greatest hit, one of Coward's most popular songs at the time. 'I'll follow my secret heart' has a tricky lyric given that difficult jump on the word 'follow' in the first line, which Printemps apparently made even more challenging by singing the song in the key of A flat.

Yet, successfully negotiated, this little hurdle actually contributes to the dramatic situation because the point about ingénue roles is that they are always primed to learn about the world. They're ripe, and to convey that potential the performer must imply a certain prior ability. This can be 'charming' (a key word in Conversation Piece, which has a whole routine based on the word, and elsewhere in Coward), but can also become facile, nudging – as Coward certainly knew since he later complained that 'cuteness' had always been the danger in Printemps' stage personality.[21]

Even if honour was saved with a respectable run of five months, Conversation Piece was not, by Coward's highest standards, a success. Along with Bitter Sweet or a play like Marquise, it would surely be among the hardest of all the Coward works to revive, to appreciate even. And the reason is to do with what now seems a deadly combination of sentiment and sex: a readiness to weep at erotic yearning and frustration that looks like a trivial and indulgent response to drama. Yet when, together with Laurence Olivier and Vivien Leigh, Coward went in the early Fifties to see Printemps in Hyménée by Edouard Bourdet he was happy, even proud, to report that all three were stricken with floods of tears.[22] He also describes being incredibly moved by her ability to overcome extreme stage fright, particularly when this preceded her rendition of 'I'll follow my secret heart'.[23]

Of course, to make Coward appear more of a modernist, to put him on the winning side, we have to downplay this side of him, the writer who was infatuated with showbiz heroics, with the international upper class, with brand names and 'sentimental sex', and in contrast make much more of the raffish young things in the comedies who are stuck in the contemporary, who manage to be alternately casual and anguished in their pursuit of love. Yet the categories can sometimes overlap: there are undercurrents of difficulty in the most saccharine of operettas and even the modern lovers at least start out dewy-eyed.

Accustomed though we are to dividing Coward's pre-war work into two: the historical dramas where barriers are crossed, as in *Conversation Piece*, where romance succeeds and infinite happiness is achieved; and the contemporary plays where love is complicated, competitive, and unresolved.[24] Printemps, like Coward himself, had something of both in her theatrical make-up and in her career. *Conversation Piece* may be self-evidently escapist, but in her other performances – as in her far from private life – she offered a more demanding kind of freedom, the spontaneity that the composer Francis Poulenc had in mind when he said: 'Yvonne Printemps sings as she breathes, as she lives, which means that her voice can express joy as easily as sadness.'[25] Coward must have seen, and heard, that living quality in her even as he tried to catch it on the wing.

There undoubtedly was another, more practised Printemps in addition to the 'charming' *ingénue*. We hear that alternative Printemps most clearly in songs by composers other than Coward – in, for instance, the work of Messager, of Fauré, of Reynaldo Hahn, a repertoire that Coward knew well.[26] Long before Roland Barthes had defined the physical quality of great singers as 'the grain of the voice' ('the body in the voice as it sings, the hand as it writes, the limb as it performs'[27]) Printemps's muscular quality had been noted. A French admirer wrote how she 'leapt from that Olympia trapeze on to the stages of operetta and comedy. She left the music hall that she had made a more tuneful place. The music hall lost its marvel! But what an image of her it retained! The most gracious of creatures, a blue woman-bird, a magical being,

swinging in the air, poised, in tune with the rhythm of a song
which repeated to her how pretty she was . . .'[28]

Printemps' 'grain' is supple, limber – an inner spring inside the
song, an acrobatic element in her sound. Even in *Conversation
Piece* Coward tried to incorporate some of that past history by
having Printemps demonstrate the bent-double, walking-on-
your-hands routine that she seems to have enjoyed on and off the
stage. We can hear something of the same callisthenic quality in
Printemps's recording of what was apparently the first song
Coward ever heard her sing, '*J'ai deux amants*' from Guitry's
L'Amour Masqué in 1923:

> *J'ai deux amants . . .*
> *C'est beaucoup mieux,*
> *Car je fais croire à chacun d'eux*
> *Que l'autre est le monsieur sérieux.*
> *Mon Dieu, que c'est bête, les hommes! . . .*
> *Ils me donnent la même somme*
> *Exactement par mois . . .*
> *Et je fais croire à chacun d'eux*
> *Que l'autre m'a donné le double chaque fois*
> *Et, ma foi*
> *Ils me croirent*
> *Ils me croirent*
> *Tous les deux! . . .*
>
> *Un seul amant*
> *C'est ennuyeux,*
> *C'est monotone soupçonneux . . .*
> *Tandis que deux, c'est vraiment mieux!*[29]

In the version that she recorded in London in 1929 Printemps
ends the song with a musical high kick, a shriek or giggle of sheer
delight. It's the kind of Twenties sprightliness that looked so well
in a bathing suit; 'the body in the voice as it sings' can be seen
more clearly in some wonderful holiday photos of Printemps
taken by the great photographer Jacques-Henri Lartigue which
show her performing beach acrobatics, joining in swimming

games and, once or twice, laughingly nude.[30] Like all masters of his art Lartigue does with his camera what everyone else wants to do with theirs – he just does it better and has better, more professionally spontaneous models. Lartigue wasn't alone in saying that when Printemps sang it was as if she was inventing the words on the spot, but perhaps he knew more about that talent than most.[31] In the Twenties he had an affair with her and it took place largely by the sea. Here is a passage from his journal for 1926 (the setting is Royan on the south-west coast):

> Six o'clock in the evening. Light bathes my body. I am naked on my balcony. I await my SHE. She is prettying and perfuming herself with all her pleasure, painting herself ready to make love.
>
> The columns of the balcony are hallowed by the sun: not clear, unfocused and vague in my eyes. A scent of resin drifts in through the window.[32]

This is *'l'heure bleue'*, best savoured in a French seaside resort, the sweet early evening moment of sexual promise. Not for nothing did Guerlain introduce his perfume of that name in 1912, although it's largely thanks to Noël Coward that we think we know the moment so well. We've been here before and, perhaps, if we're lucky we'll be here again: a terrace by the sea, a view of the harbour, a first drink – 'an orchestra playing not very far off'.

In his memoirs Coward says that the inspiration for the opening of *Private Lives* came to him first as he lay sleepless in a Tokyo hotel and Gertrude Lawrence appeared in a kind of vision wearing a white Molyneux dress on a terrace in the South of France.[33] In fact, the text makes clear that the hotel needs to be in Deauville and not only to allow the convenient access to Paris that the plot demands.

In 1937 Deauville was still being described as 'the most Babylonian resort in the world'. Its appearance was deceptive. Essentially the town consisted of an enormous cream and white casino with two huge hotels on either side – the *Normandy*, which had wide eaves and looked like an inflated farmhouse, and the

Royal, with its mock-Regency air. There was a third luxury hotel a little further away, near the golf course, and clustered around the centre some four hundred villas – some of them with cute names, 'Pierrot Cottage', for instance, or the oddly Anglophile 'Darling Cottage' and 'Daisy Cottage'. They belonged to some of 'the richest men in France – the Aga Khan; R. B. Strasburger; Monsieur Weisweiller ... Monsieur Arples the jeweller; and several Rothschilds'.[34]

This could all look rather desolate out of season, but in high summer Deauville became quite 'erotically gay':

> You never know what you are going to see next. It may be a one-armed man bathing; it may be a chimpanzee scratching for fleas, perched on the shoulder of a film star; it may be Irish trainers and English jockeys; youths with medicine bottles; little men with the red ribbon of the Legion of Honour in sweat shirts; or widowers with a black eye patch over one eye and a white poodle on a lead; or English peeresses in blue silk pyjamas; or English sheep dogs; or debutantes in tight white flannel trousers; or millionaires in yachting caps; or hucksters selling smoked spectacles; or gigolos with wire-haired terriers so well bred as to be knock-kneed.[35]

It's not that Deauville didn't have style, in a way it was nothing *but* style – the fake Normandy thatch, those 'cottages' with their coy names, its taste for 'bathing cloaks' 'in which all the ingenuity of the Futurists, Dadaists, and Cubists has been called in ... strange semi-oriental designs are seen in gorgeous shades of red, orange, royal-blue, bright green, with touches of black and dark brown'.[36]

The theatrical *demi-monde*, Printemps and Guitry among them, decamped to this expensive stage set, although when Colette's imaginary Parisian showgirl, Mitsou, goes to Deauville she leaves unimpressed. 'I don't understand places where everyone stays outside like that during the day,' she tells her lover. 'I can see that you go into a casino or into a tea shop, but all those people outside as if they had nowhere to go.' When the man reminds her of Deauville's 'wide wild waves' she simply shakes her head: 'The country's not for me.'[37] Colette's joke, of course, is that Deauville is no more country than the rue de la Paix, the Place de la Concorde, are country – although if Deauville really had just been Paris by the sea there would, presumably, have been no point in going there.

With all this excitement going on around them it's not easy at first to see why Elyot and Amanda in *Private Lives* have opted for Deauville for their romantic honeymoon, let alone Sibyl and Victor. Unless they belong to a 'set', which seems unlikely. The Deauville regulars described in *The Sketch* of the early Twenties, for instance, are the likes of 'The Duchess of Sutherland, who was formerly Lady Eileen Butler . . . the daughter of the seventh Earl of Lanesborough . . . Captain Humphrey de Trafford MC, son of Sir Humphrey de Trafford, third Baronet of Trafford, Lancs'.[38] These are not the kind of people we actually see in a Coward play (the Duke of Westminster will never appear in *Private Lives*, despite the presence of his yacht in the harbour) even if, as a socialite himself, the author may well have known their kind personally. Who would be interested in *Private Lives* if it literally involved the dreary duchesses and chinless dukes who lounge on Normandy beaches in the pages of the society magazines of the Twenties? None of them comes close to the tense poise of Elyot and Amanda. Indeed, inter-war aristocracy, including royalty – Mountbatten, Edward VIII – often seem to resemble slack imitations of Coward himself.

But then, Coward's upper-class characters – and in this respect at least they are like those of Wilde or Wodehouse or Saki – are, fantasy puppets: a heavy dose of style and grace has been added to stiffen the unattractive reality. To say that a stylish aristocracy never existed, that it is indeed a contradiction in terms (since style is a construction, while aristocracy claims inheritance), is merely to state what is visibly obvious from the documentary record. It's more interesting to speculate why Coward should have thought, quite rightly, that his creations would strike a chord in the national psyche, might fulfil some mysterious need in his audiences. Middle-class aspirations are at work, obviously, a protest against the commuter's lot. A more theatrical explanation might be to see the consummate style of Coward's people as the revolt of a talented professional against affluent amateurs. To which the only defence of the rich – and it's unanswerable – is, as usual, money itself. Deauville, the more humble English visitors complain, is the place where 'they charge you two shillings for an orange juice',[39] where the taxi drivers try to exact 'ten francs for a mere hundred yards ... the orgy of expensiveness ... the paradise of the newly rich'.[40]

Coward's brilliant English couple are able to participate, unthinkingly, in that frenetic, costly axis of Paris and Deauville – stopping off at Rouen en route – in a double reversal of pastoral pattern whereby they make their now illegitimate love in the heart of the city, quite oblivious of the natives. And when love turns nasty, violent and bitter, then the streets of Paris are forgotten completely. As the TLS reviewer of the 1999 National Theatre production neatly put it: Private Lives is 'about Englishness displaced – Coward's couple live on an island of English manners in a sea of delightful foreign distractions: the casino, the beach, Paris, the Taj Mahal'.[41] It's also a play about the penalty and privilege of the thoughtlessly well-off who use places as backdrops. These people are not even proper Francophiles; like the bickering Blisses at the end of Hay Fever, they're too busy with themselves. Travel, especially perhaps when it's to France, always narrows the English mind. But then again, all Coward's romantic places are really only where we want them to be: wherever the blue is bluest and hotel bills (mentioned not once in Private Lives) need never be paid.

NOTES

1. Hay Fever in Noël Coward Plays: One (London: Methuen, 1999), p.89.
2. The 1999 Savoy Theatre production of Hay Fever confirmed the distant Parisian ambiance by having Judith Bliss (Geraldine McEwan) break into the 1940s hit 'Je suis seule ce soir' at the point in Act Two where Coward says 'She plays and sings a little French song' – an effective, if slightly

anachronistic touch, given the pianoless set. Information from Miss McEwan.

3. Maurice Sachs, *Au temps du Boeuf sur le Toit* (Paris: Nouvelle revue critique, 1948).

4. Martin Green, *Children of the Sun. A narrative of 'decadence' after 1918* (London: Constable, 1977), pp.50–61.

5. Noël Coward, *The Lyrics* (London: Heinemann, 1965), p.14.

6. Colette, *La Vagabonde* (Paris: Ollendorf, 1910), p.53.

7. Jean Rhys, *Quartet* (New York: Harper and Row, 1957), p.122.

8. *Lyrics*, pp.43–4.

9. *The Vortex* in Noël Coward, *Plays: One* (London: Methuen, 1979), p.141.

10. *Lyrics*, p.79.

11. *Backward Glances* (London: Sceptre, 1989), p.33.

12. *Lyrics*, pp.11–12.

13. *Yvonne Printemps ou L'Impromptu de Versailles* (Paris: La Table Ronde, 1953), p.160. This and all subsequent translations are my own. There are two other main sources for Printemps: Karine Ciupa, *Yvonne Printemps: l'heure bleu* (Paris: Robert Laffont, 1989) and Claude Dufresne, *Yvonne Printemps: le doux parfum du péché* (Paris: Librairie Académique Perrin, 1988). The British Library also has [Patrick O'Connor] *Yvonne Printemps 1894–1977* (Richmond, Surrey: Patrick O'Connor, 1978).

14. *L'Impromptu*, p.112.

15. This would seem to belong with the long-established cross-dressing tradition of women costumed as naval officers that Jacky Bratton has traced in 'Beating the bounds: gender play and role reversal in the Edwardian music hall', *The Edwardian Theatre: Essays on Performance and the Stage*, Michael R. Booth and Joel H. Kaplan (eds.) (Cambridge: CUP, 1996), pp.86–110.

16. See Joel H. Kaplan and Sheila Stowell, *Theatre and Fashion: Oscar Wilde to the Suffragettes* (Cambridge: CUP, 1994).

17. Unidentified cutting, Theatre Museum.

18. *Conversation Piece* (London: Heinemann, 1934), pp. 45–6.

19. Stephen Citron, *Noël and Cole: The Sophisticates* (London: Sinclair-Stevenson, 1992), p.76.

20. Dormer Creston [pseud. Dorothy Julia Baynes] (London: Thornton Butterworth, 1932).

21. *L'Impromptu*, p.113

22. *L'Impromptu*, p.113 and 177.

23. *L'Impromptu*, p. 115.

24. The distinction is made by Clive Fisher in *Noël Coward* (London: Weidenfeld & Nicolson, 1992).

25. *L'Impromptu*, p.46.

26. Compare Clara's 'One Gabriel Fauré, two Reynaldo Hahns and an Aria' in

The Vortex, p.101.

27. *Image Music Text* (London: Fontana, 1977), p.188.

28. Jean Barreyre, 'Yvonne Printemps et le Music-hall' in *L'Impromptu,* p.110.

29. Ciupa, p.103. 'I have two lovers,/It's much better that way,/For I make each of them believe/That the other is the main one./My God, how foolish men are!/Every month they give me/Exactly the same amount . . . /And every time I make each of them believe/That the other has given me twice as much/And believe it or not/They believe me . . . /A single love/Is boring,/It's monotonous and suspicious . . . /Whereas two – that's altogether better!'

30. See J.-H. Lartigue, *Les Femmes* (London: Studio Vista, 1974) and *Diary of a Century* (Harmondsworth: Penguin Books, 1978).

31. Jacques-Henri Lartigue, *L'Emerveillé écrit à mesure 1923–1931* (Paris: Editions Stock, 1981), p.18.

32. *L'Emerveillé*, pp.6–7.

33. *Present Indicative* (London: William Heinemann, 1937), p.373.

34. Description based on Charles Graves, *Deauville Taxi* (London: Ivor Nicholson and Watson, 1937), p.18.

35. *Deauville Taxi*, p.19.

36. *The Sketch*, 16 August 1922.

37. *Mitsou, ou Comment l'Esprit vient aux Filles* (Paris: Le Livre de Demain, Athème Fayard & Cie, 1923), p.65.

38. *The Sketch*, 23 August 1922. The paper ran a regular column throughout the season: 'Deauville diversions (Being the Musings of Miranda)'.

39. *Deauville Taxi*, p.25.

40. *The Sketch*, 2 August 1922.

41. Sylvia Brownrigg, *TLS*, 28 May 1999, p.20.

A Weekend in the Country: Coward, Wilde and Saki

Peter Raby

It is not difficult to sketch lines of connection between Oscar Wilde and Noël Coward, either as personalities or as writers, even if Coward had not undertaken his own, arguably redundant, tribute to Wilde with his musical version of *Lady Windermere's Fan*, *After the Ball*. Perhaps the superficial likeness grated on Coward. Certainly he had some scathing things to say about Wilde as a person: 'Poor Oscar Wilde, what a silly, conceited, inadequate creature he was and what a dreadful self-deceiver.' [1]

Coward, as a child actor, entered a world rich with 1890s and Wildean connections. He worked for Charles Hawtrey, the first Lord Goring and himself the author of a parody of Wilde. He met Robert Ross. He collaborated with Charles Cochrane, school contemporary of Aubrey Beardsley. Jackie's gauche confession in *Hay Fever* – 'Oh, yes: I went to Dieppe once – we had a house there for the summer.' Richard (*kindly*) – 'Dear little place – Dieppe' – seems to echo Wilde's put-down of Beardsley – 'Yes, dear Aubrey is almost too Parisian, he cannot forget that he has been to Dieppe – once.'[2] When Larita in *Easy Virtue* reads Proust's *Sodom and Gomorrah*, is there a glance at Beardsley's picture of Salome's favourite literature, Zola, Baudelaire and the Marquis de Sade?

These details and resonances are supported by broader-brushed correspondences. Like Wilde, Coward sometimes professed a nonchalance and facility about his writing, which masked meticulous attention to detail and sustained discipline. Like Wilde, he subscribed to a cult of youth. Like Wilde, he began with comparatively little, and created not only a style and a manner, but a whole world which included the creation of himself, in dress and speech and attitude. As Philip Hoare commented about Coward after the success of *The Vortex*, 'For the first time since Oscar Wilde, a writer's appearance seemed as important as what he wrote.'[3] Coward, by an act of self-invention, had effectively created himself. As did Wilde and, in a different mode, Beardsley, he defined a decade; and, again like Wilde, he enjoyed a huge popularity – although it was a fragile one, balanced precariously on a razor edge of taste and fashion.

When Coward went to stay with the Astley Coopers at Hambleton Hall, deep in the hunting country of Rutlandshire, in 1915 at the age of fifteen, he found a copy of Saki's latest volume of stories, *Beasts and Superbeasts*, on the hall table, and read it avidly.[4] This was the last book Saki – Hector Hugh Munro – published during his life. Saki's work was an acknowledged influence on Coward, both in terms of style and tone, and, in some cases, actual plot. In *Beasts and Superbeasts*, in its predecessors, *Reginald*, *Reginald in Russia* and *The Chronicles of Clovis* – and in the posthumous collection *The Toys of Peace*,[5] he created an extraordinary set of pictures of the English leisured classes, an Edwardian time warp in which the days, or the weekends, passed very slowly, a portrait of a society in which nobody worked, except at finding ways to occupy themselves before the next meal. In a number of respects he can be seen as a bridge between Wilde and Coward, an imitator and filter of certain aspects of Wilde's attitude and style, but also a writer who surveys a later generation from a Wildean perspective and takes us into territory Wilde seldom bothered to visit.

Munro acquired an early admiration for Wilde. Sent out in June 1893 to a post in the Burma police, he wrote long letters to his sister from his uncomfortable place of exile and duty: 'Owl and oaf thou art, not to see *Woman of no importance* and *Second Mrs*

T. *The* plays of the season; what would I not give to be able to see them.' Always as interested in fauna, wild and domestic, as in human beings, he described the details of his new pony Microbe: 'Poor little neglected beast, he looked on so modestly and wistfully when the mare was being given her corn and he was so charmed and thankful when he found he was going to have some too; and when he had a plantain brought him for dessert he began to think with "Mrs Erlynne" that the world was "an intensely amusing place".'[6]

Munro adopted Mrs Erlynne's attitude, perhaps as a way of surviving in a life that might otherwise have seemed unbearable – to use an adjective that he employed in a different sense in his novel *The Unbearable Bassington*,[7] a dark and bitter story of a golden, handsome, improvident youth, which has clear echoes of *The Picture of Dorian Gray*. Munro's first collection of stories, *Reginald*, features a young man as raconteur and entertainer: descended from Algernon Moncrieff, Reginald, like his successors in later collections, Clovis Sangrail or Bertie van Tahn, is a dandy in dress and manner, sharp of wit, crisp of tongue, egotistical, amoral, sardonic, self-assured, idle if possible, and relentless in the search for pleasure, preferably at someone else's expense. Cigarette in hand, carnation in buttonhole, he delivers his observations on life like a character from a society comedy.

Beasts and Superbeasts contains a number of distinctive features that would have commended themselves to their fifteen-year-old reader at Hambleton Hall, not least the fact that the world depicted was a mirror image, if a slightly distorted one, of the country house world to which he was having his first introduction. It was a world both eccentrically English and sophisticatedly European, at least in the cross-references and conversational flourishes of the odd assortment of characters gathered together by the various hostesses. Munro offered a portrait gallery of Edwardian England, titled, or wealthy, or aspiring to being both: of large houses in a lush landscape, usually Devon or Somerset rather than Shropshire; of leisured days punctuated by elaborate meals made possible by numerous servants, of whom by far the most important is the cook; of ingenious ways of passing the time – the garden party (for the women), the hunting (for everyone), the shooting (for the men – but Reginald does not stir himself to shoot, except once, in a mocking gesture of defiance, a peacock) – and, after dinner, music, bridge, or country house games. Practically no one has a profession – a little model farming, managed by an agent; a little light politics. Among the guests are the occasional painter, or, significantly, a writer of comedy sketches, Lucas Harrowcluff.

It is a world of exotic, resonant names, more outrageous than Wilde's, but never quite shifting so far from reality that they lose contact with their contemporary equivalents: Framton Nuttel, Sir Lulworth Quayne, Mrs Quabarl, Lady Blonze, Teresa Thropplestance, Mrs Nougat-Jones. And in their midst move precocious young men with mature tastes such as Clovis Sangrail, self-possessed young women of fifteen or sixteen like Vera Durmot: cool, ruthless, clear-eyed, inventing stories and scenarios, discomforting the elderly, the staid, the smug, the mean and the dull (while quite prepared to eat their food). The collections celebrate a cult of youth – and of youth, usually, triumphant.

Although Saki's stories and fables seem infinitely leisured, and present an urbane and polished veneer to the reader, they are not bland. Disruption, in various forms, stirs beneath the surface. The wits undertake elaborate teases, unsettle the serious with invented scenarios. Apparently innocent children exact sharp revenge. Flashes of cruelty appear from a seemingly clear sky. The title *Beasts and Superbeasts* would appear to refer both to humanity, and to the menagerie of birds and animals that range the pages – a cat that has been taught to speak, formidable prize boars, an ox in the morning room, tigers, wolves and Sredni Vashtar, the great polecat ferret who kills an odious aunt. In the woods of Edwardian England the savage survives. Death is present in Arcadia, as also, surprisingly, is socialism. 'The Byzantine Omelette', for example, records a weekend party that goes horribly wrong, when the household servants down tools because Sophie Chattel-Monkheim has employed a strike-breaking cook, the only man in England who knows how to make a Byzantine omelette – and when she dismisses Gaspare to appease her maid and so ensure that her hair is 'built into an elaborate reflection of the prevailing fashion', the kitchen staff strike in sympathy. Even the dinner rolls have to be returned behind the green baize door. Sophie is not seen in society for eighteen months and her doctors forbid her to attend anything too exciting, such as a drawing-room meeting or a Fabian conference. In Saki's construction of society, as with Wilde's sketch of Lord Henry Weston in *A Woman of No Importance*, the bottom line of social acceptance is predicated upon a good cook.

Just before the First World War Munro was working on a play in conjunction with Charles Maude (whose brother Cyril played Cayley Drummle in the first production of *The Second Mrs Tanqueray*). Maude's role, by his own account, was to shorten the script, give it incident, and generally adapt it for 'stage purposes'[8] – but the language, the style, the world it depicts is totally consistent with the rest of Munro's writing. Because of the war and Munro's death, the play was not produced until 1924 – at the Amateur Dramatic Club in Cambridge,[9] so in one sense it is post-Coward. But in manner, and matter, *The Watched Pot* is an imitation of Wilde and represents a curious no man's land between the playwriting of the 1890s and the style and atmosphere of the 1920s.

The Watched Pot, or *The Mistress of Briony*, has a familiar, even comforting, society-play structure: Act One, Briony Manor, the Breakfast Room. Act Two, the Hall, the next evening. Act Three, the Breakfast Room, the next morning. The curtain opens on two characters, Ludovic Bavvel, prospective Parliamentary candidate, fidgeting with papers at the escritoire; and Mrs Vulpy, a would-be fashionable lady of a certain age, glancing at the illustrated papers:

> BAVVEL: Excuse the question, Mrs Vulpy, are you a widow?
> MRS VULPY: I really can't say with any certainty.
> BAVVEL: You can't say?
> MRS VULPY: With any certainty.[10]

The plot is simple, if not trivial. Briony Manor is controlled by a formidable matriarch, Hortensia Bavvel, who will exercise power until the marriage of her son Trevor: the collective objective of everyone, in order to secure peace and enjoyment in place of tyranny, is to get Trevor married – and four women are present who intend to secure him, and Briony, for life. The house party schemes to provide a suitable context to encourage a proposal. Theatricals? A gymkhana? Either would be equally abhorrent to Hortensia, described (shades of Lady Bracknell) as a Gorgon and as a Catherine the Second of Russia without any of Catherine's redeeming vices. Taking advantage of Hortensia's temporary absence, the guests organise an impromptu dance.

For Act Two, Munro uses the occasion of an off-stage event to create a fluid sequence of encounters and dialogues, as characters seek privacy, escape from the dancing, plot, or observe (the model might be Act Two of *Lady Windermere's Fan*, and Munro's structure shares a number of features with the third act of Coward's *Easy Virtue*). The young people are dressed in sheets and pillow cases, with linen masks – a bizarre concept which veers between a romp in a boarding-school romance and a kind of Anglicised Dionysian revel. One character, named only as 'the Drummond boy', erupts three times into the proceedings, wearing a dog mask and howling like the Hound of the Baskervilles. The dandy, René St Gall, drinks wine, and feasts on grapes and peaches, while other characters gorge themselves on rice pudding and pickled walnuts. Order has dissolved, and the dancers weave in and out in a frenzied conga, to be stunned, naturally, by the early return of Hortensia. 'May I ask who has organized this abominable and indecent orgy in my house?' (p.268) She is particularly offended by what she describes as 'promiscuous dancing', to an accompaniment of French songs. The lame explanations tumble out – 'We were having games', 'Old English games', 'Charades'.

Wilde, of course, never allows his characters to become quite so boisterous or bacchanalian as Munro. Rice pudding and pickled walnuts seem more like Pinero. But the Wildean manner is pervasive in the tone, if not the content, of the dialogue. Mrs

Vulpy, for example: 'Other people's husbands are rather an overrated lot. I prefer unmarried men any day; they've so much more experience' (p.279). Mrs Vulpy has mislaid a husband; René St Gall, the young dandy, has mislaid his mother. When Clare Hennessey – who, it transpires, has been married secretly to Trevor for two months – announces the convenient death of her great-aunt, Mrs Packington, she explains that she had to keep her visits to Briony secret, since her aunt had a very special dislike of Hortensia. 'How very embarrassing,' comments a choric colonel. 'Not at all,' replies Clare. 'I like duplicity, when it's well done' (p.314). Mrs Packington's passing is no more disturbing than Bunbury's – as Hortensia observes, she was 'a great invalid' – or, at any rate, 'a great consumer of medicines' (p.313). Consuming is the keynote. Everyone celebrates the largesse that will flow from having a generous hostess as Mistress of Briony. The carriage waits at the door only for Hortensia, off to attend a serious conference at Exeter by the 4.15 down, and for Mrs Vulpy, whose nasturtium-coloured hair and too thinly concealed intentions debar her from the party. Four bottles of champagne are opened. Moselle is ordered for the servants' hall.

If the servants don't get to drink the champagne in this play, William the pageboy at least wins the sweepstake on the marriage contest and comments shrewdly on the Agathas and Sybils who inhabit the breakfast room:

> What I envy about you, miss, is your play-going way of taking things. You just sit and wait till things has been brought to a climax and then you put on your hat and gloves and walk outside. It's different for those who've got to go on living with the climax. (pp.282–31)

As William summarises, 'Home life is a different thing with you gentry, you're so comfortable and heathen' (p.265).

In *The Watched Pot*, Munro has put into dramatic form the world and the manner of his stories. He constructs images of a segment of society, seen from a slightly detached, ironic point of view – a masquerade, or cavalcade, of England, in this act of

social theatre, which begins ritually each Friday evening or
Saturday morning, when the dogcart or motor car meets the
London train. One by one the characters assemble, in search of –
love? A satisfactory marriage? An emerald tiepin? A sinecure? But
certainly good meals, free beds and entertainment. They talk,
manoeuvre, pose, change partners – and order of a sort is restored.
Theirs is, essentially, a comfortable and heathen life. As with
Wilde, the façade of respectability is maintained, even though
the foundations have stirred and shifted. Munro's humans have
the polish of high society and the appetites of the farmyard – and
there is always a ferret in a cage at the bottom of the garden, a
wild beast in the woods. Society is shifting. As Clare Hennessey
comments, echoing Mabel Chiltern, 'We shall keep up the model
dairy and the model pigsties, but we've decided that we won't be
a model couple' (p.316). Youth triumphs – but what does the
future hold? Another weekend – another dance? This is a play
written under the deepening shadow of approaching war.

   Coward's plays of 1923 and 1924, *Fallen Angels*, *The Vortex*,
Hay Fever and *Easy Virtue*, form an astonishingly assured portrait
of a certain kind of Englishness. In some respects Coward seems
to explore a continuum with Saki's manner and subject matter, at
least in his construction of a social pattern. *Hay Fever* follows the
classic, if compressed, structure of an English country house
weekend, or a parody of one, set in that conveniently public
space, the Hall, with the second act given over to progressively
destabilising games. Act Two of *The Vortex* takes place on the
Sunday evening of another weekend from hell, as the stricken
characters dance to the gramophone. *Fallen Angels*, too, is a
weekend play, this time with the men separated from the women:
the husbands depart to play golf (even more boring and
despicable than tennis in Coward's scale of values), while the
women remain, and dine and become seriously drunk together, as
they await their mutual French lover. *Easy Virtue*, another Hall
setting, covers a more extended period, but still employs three of
the linchpins of English upper-class country life – lunch, a tennis
party; and an evening dance – as the context for the action. The
overall impression is of boredom kept, with difficulty, at bay. This

post-war world remains one of leisure and wealth, not work. Certainly, with the exception of one category, no one is defined by his or her occupation. The characters' off-stage jobs, if they have them, do not seem very substantial. Richard Greatham is a diplomat, a vague and Wildean profession. Colonel Whittaker of *Easy Virtue* must once have been in the army, but his rank is used more as the label of a type than as a link with experience. From the perspective of a period dominated by the idea of work, a weekend, or a month, in the country offers scarcely imaginable idleness. The exceptions are 'the artists' – the Blisses, for example, who act, write, draw, sing, or Nicky Lancaster, the musician – self-appointed entertainers for the leisured classes. No one reads much in a Wilde play, or a Saki story. But to write, or compose, or to read *Sodom and Gomorrah*, as Larita Whittaker does, rather than the *Tatler*, forms an important indicator in Coward's world. His children of the sun are blessed with a talent to amuse.

In two respects, especially, Coward stretches out further than Wilde or Saki. Sex, or romance, is an essential ingredient of the country house visit. Wilde acknowledges this in *A Woman of No Importance*, in the exchanges between Lord Illingworth and Mrs Allonby, in the attentions paid by Pontefract and Kelvil to Lady Stutfield and in the stage-managed 'insult' on Hester. (Mrs Cheveley and her recollected encounter with old Lord Mortlock in the conservatory at Tenby offers another example of the motif in *An Ideal Husband*.) But these incidents are largely conventional. Saki's weekend world is a relatively sex-free zone, although full of arcane displacement activities, reflecting Munro's own make-up, half Puck, half Pan. In Coward's plays the reality of sex is far more prevalent. And whether the treatment is serious – as in *The Vortex* and *Easy Virtue* – or comic – as in *Hay Fever* and *Fallen Angels* – the overall impact seems much the same: sex is disruptive, compelling, even overwhelming, while sex and marriage are difficult, perhaps impossible, to reconcile. In that comedy of youth *The Young Idea*,[11] an everyday story of hunting folk that could serve as a sourcebook for a Jilly Cooper novel, the first embrace between wayward wife Cicely and

neighbour Roddy comes in the opening minute, swiftly followed
by a passionate kiss. Enter husband George: 'Hallo, Roddy! Why
aren't you hunting today?'[12] The night before, the whole house
party has been enjoying traditional English country house games
– 'Claud Eccles hid with Priscilla heaps of times' (p.7). As George
observes about his twin children Gerda and Sholto, shamelessly
borrowed from *You Never Can Tell*, 'It will be interesting for them
to come to an English hunting county, where immorality is
conducted by rules and regulations' (p.11). George (aged forty-
five or so) has to go to Italy to be reconciled with his first wife:
'The only thing in the world that matters is Youth. And I've got
it back again. I'm twenty-one, and I want to laugh and shout and
tear the house down! Come and kiss me!' The married men of
Fallen Angels listen 'with stricken faces' as Maurice sings *'Je
t'aime'* to their wives. Coward acknowledges the ever present fact
of sexual appetite, as well as the untameable nature of love.

   The weekend in the country has been explored by many
novelists as a way of dissecting England and Englishness: in Isobel
Colegate's *The Shooting Party*, for example, where the guns in the
coverts foretell the artillery of the trenches; or through the
increasingly arid rituals of *A Handful of Dust*. Firbank, in a more
louche and exotic manner, and P. G. Wodehouse, in a lighter
vein, extend the fictional boundaries of these social manoeuvres.
Coward, while exploiting the theatrical potential – and seeing
the country weekend as a kind of social theatre in itself – adds a
key dimension, that of self-awareness. Where Wilde's characters
tend to share a language, a heightened imitation which is
recognisably artificial – and where Saki's major characters imitate
Wilde – Coward's dialogue, polished, sophisticated, witty,
parodic, with its carefully constructed rhythms and music, is at
the same time a little looser, more fluent, more natural, less
continuously striving for effect. There seems rather more space
between the words, space for private thought – and for more
subtle and often surprisingly rapid shifts between the witty and
the serious. One particularly striking example is the conversation
between Larita Whittaker and Charles Burleigh in Act Three of
Easy Virtue, Coward's tribute to the well-made society play:

LARITA: You've been awfully nice to me.

CHARLES: Why not? We speak the same language.

LARITA: Yes – I suppose we do.

CHARLES: And naturally one feels instinctively drawn – particularly in this atmosphere.

LARITA: English country life. (*She smiles*)

CHARLES: Yes, English country life.

LARITA: I wonder if it's a handicap having our sort of minds?

CHARLES: In what way?

LARITA: Watching ourselves go by.[13]

(The two are sitting out the dance – and the exchange is heightened by Larita's deliberately overstated appearance: dead-white dress, cut extremely low, three ropes of pearls and another long string twined round her right wrist; dead-white face, vivid scarlet lips; diamond, ruby and emerald bracelets on her left arm; tiara, enormous earrings; diamond anklet over cobweb flesh-coloured stockings; tremendous scarlet ostrich-feather fan.) Larita leaves, in a scene that echoes Lady Windermere's departure from her own dance – but, unlike Lady Windermere, she will not return. Larita's model is Mrs Erlynne. She finds life immensely amusing, but her sharp-eyed analysis includes herself and embraces the pain of truth.

An audience is continuously challenged as to how to respond to Coward's version, or versions, of England. Does he explode it or, in a strange way, celebrate it? His achievement in these early plays seems to lie in his ability to do both things at once, rather as Chekhov does within the patterns of the not quite everlasting Russian summers. This finely tuned tension plays on an audience in a shifting pattern that alternately entertains and disconcerts, inviting us to enjoy the mockery, sometimes gentle, often fierce, and at other times to indulge in a kind of affirmative nostalgia. Wilde's last word on the subject was *The Importance of Being Earnest*, described by Shaw, accurately enough, as heartless – and Wilde had little reason thereafter to revise his attitude. But Hector Munro, who ruthlessly pinned out the Edwardians like specimens of exotic butterflies, died in the trenches, a convinced patriot, his last recorded words being 'put that bloody cigarette out'; and Coward, finding England an intensely amusing place, ends by securing a kind of affection not just for the customers of the Rose and Crown, but for the bourgeoisie of Tunbridge Wells and even for the decaying denizens of the stately homes of England, Lord Elderley, Lord Borrowmere, Lord Sickert and Lord Camp. As a child actor, Noël Coward played the role of Slightly in *Peter Pan*; he cannot have failed to notice that Barrie's villain, Captain Hook, has infinitely the best part – and that he enters the yawning cavity of the crocodile's mouth 'like one greeting a friend' and murmuring 'Floreat Etona'. Coward, like Wilde, offers his audiences the disconcerting, wry pleasure of watching ourselves go by.

NOTES

1. Coward's 1949 comment after reading *De Profundis*. Graham Payn and Sheridan Morley (eds), *The Noël Coward Diaries* (London: Weidenfeld & Nicolson, 1982), p.135.
2. Jean Paul Raymond and Charles Ricketts, *Oscar Wilde, Recollections* (Bloomsbury: The Nonesuch Press, 1933), p.52.
3. Philip Hoare, *Noël Coward* (London: Sinclair-Stevenson, 1995), p.140. One might add Shaw to the list of playwrights who invented themselves, although in his case in a sharply contrasting sartorial manner.
4. Philip Hoare, pp.39–43.
5. Saki's first two collections were *Reginald* (London: Methuen, 1904) and *Reginald in Russia* (London: Methuen, 1910). There followed *The Chronicles of Clovis* (London: John Lane, The Bodley Head, 1911); *Beasts and Superbeasts* (London: John Lane, The Bodley Head, 1914); and *The Toys of Peace* (London: John Lane, The Bodley Head, 1919).
6. Ethel M. Munro's biography of her brother appeared in *The Square Egg and Other Sketches* (London: John Lane, The Bodley Head, 1924). The letters of 26.7.1893 and 17.9.1893 are quoted on pp.40 and 45.
7. *The Unbearable Bassington* (London: John Lane, The Bodley Head, 1914).
8. Maude's comments preface *The Watched Pot* in the *Square Egg and Other Sketches*, p. 162.
9. *The Watched Pot*'s stage life, in addition to the ADC performance, November 1924, includes productions at the Arts Theatre, London, August 1943; and, in the United States, the Harvard Dramatic Club in 1933 and at the Cherry Lane Theatre, New York, 1947.

10. *The Watched Pot* in *The Square Egg and Other Sketches* (London: John Lane, The Bodley Head, 1924), p.192.
11. *The Young Idea* opened at the Savoy Theatre, London, 1 February 1923.
12. Noël Coward, *The Young Idea* (London and New York: Samuel French Ltd), p.7.
13. *Easy Virtue* in Noël Coward, *Plays: One* (London: Methuen 1979), p.351.

The Potency of Cheap Music

Dominic Vlasto

I t has been said often enough that Noël Coward was a unique creative writer, who displayed a combination of skills which were seen together in no other artist of the twentieth century. Yet there is still a tendency for critics and commentators to shrug their shoulders at Coward's musical output, as if it were a comparatively minor area of his creativity largely superfluous to his more mainstream literary work. Coward's music, however, and his own presentation of it, form a large part of any popular conception of his art, and it is surely crucial to remember that Coward was not *also* a writer of music and lyrics, but that his output in this particular area is strongly influenced by and often completely integral to his dramatic work.

Nearly fifty years ago Coward himself bemoaned a lack of critical discrimination in this area: 'The critics are quite incapable of distinguishing between good light music and bad light music, and the public are so saturated with the cheaper outpourings of Tin Pan Alley . . . that their natural taste will soon die a horribly unnatural death.'[1] Perhaps a general feeling that it is difficult to make distinctions of quality in light music – or perhaps because it is *only* light music – explains why no musicological or analytical approach to the subject has been thought necessary.

Indeed, one often questions whether such an approach ever works terribly well. It is notable that almost all of the scores of books which have been published on the work of the great songwriters of the twentieth century are orientated biograph-ically and, where they touch on the subject of musical skills at all, are presented in terms of lyrics rather than music. As far as Coward is concerned, the closest anyone has yet come to presenting musical analysis is in the closing sections of Stephen Citron's *Noël and Cole*.[2] Yet because the work is an overall comparison of Porter and Coward it is limited in scope, with only around a dozen songs of each composer receiving any analysis of musical structure. Moreover, Citron's choice of material for analysis is puzzling on account of what was *not* chosen. The work of George Gershwin, perhaps the most literate, original and influential of all such composers, has recently been treated thoroughly by Deena Rosenberg in her book on George and Ira Gershwin's songwriting partnership,[3] but here the language of musical analysis tends to interrupt any sense of coherent textual narrative, and one is often left wondering about the significance of harmonic and melodic elements which are analysed and whether a musicological approach is even desirable in such a context.

We can start to understand this unease by recognising an important difference between music and the printed word. Once a play script, story or piece of verse is written down it becomes defined, and even allowing for differences in interpretation in performance will remain fixed in that form. Light music, however, is not defined in the same way by publication. The publishers of such music are quite deliberately trying to present the work in a form that will appeal to the broadest possible market, and will tend to print material which is not too technically demanding and therefore approachable by the pianist of average ability. This is a fact of life recognised by composers of light music, who also naturally want the benefit of the highest possible sales of hard copies of their work. When one comes to preparing work for *performance*, any bonds to definitive musical content get looser still. Even such a careful and thoughtful tran-scriber as Norman Hackforth said: 'There simply is *no* sacrosanct Authorised Version: the only constant is the melody and the broad scheme of harmonic progressions.'[4]

In fact, Coward's music, like the vast majority of similar work, was often in the hands of musical directors, orchestrators, accompanists or arrangers almost as soon as it was composed. At a straightforward practical level, this often leads to performance versions of songs being amplified from a simpler original, or to a situation in which later performance of a particular piece defines the work in a slightly different form from its original presentation in (say) the score of a musical. This is true, for example, of Coward's 'I Like America' (*Ace of Clubs*, 1950), where the entire thirty-six-bar introductory section of musically scripted banter between Harry and the Ace Girls, although preserved in the sheet music printed in *The Noël Coward Song Book*, is entirely absent from either of Coward's own recordings of the piece.* A similar chopping away of sections originally scored for chorus, and a degree of lyric rewriting, characterised all performances and publications of 'Uncle Harry' subsequent to its stage and score presentation in *Pacific 1860* (1946), which had itself been an amplification of a simpler original song.

Coward was surprisingly candid about his lack of ability to read music or write it down himself. He did make a youthful gesture to train himself to these skills, but flounced out from his tuition when confronted with a classically trained harmony tutor's traditional prohibition against using consecutive fifths. 'Had I intended', he wrote later:

> at the outset of my career to devote all my energies to music I would have endured the necessary training cheerfully enough, but . . . I was willing to allow the musical side of my creative talent to take care of itself . . . I have often been irritated in later years by my inability to write music down effectively and by my complete lack of knowledge of orchestration except by ear, but . . . I have never been unduly depressed by the fact that all my music has to be dictated.[5]

Such lack of training in technical musicianship is actually surprisingly common among light music composers, and Coward at least had the armour of unorthodox but thoroughly adequate piano-playing skills. In fact, he was more candid about his musical shortcomings and played the piano with more competence than Irving Berlin. The musicians who, in different times and places, worked most closely with him all noted his exceptionally good musical ear (for period style as well as for melody and harmony) and there was no suggestion from them of any lack of creative originality or musical incompetence on Coward's part, although they recognised his limitations. Of Coward's accompanists, Peter Matz noted that 'musically, he was not as literate as he was verbally . . . he could play the piano – he played okay, he played nice, he didn't play wrong notes or anything; but he was limited harmonically,[6] while Norman Hackforth emphasised his sense of determination despite his technical limitations: 'His chord-structure was often rather unorthodox, but never false . . . [and] he always knew precisely what he wanted, even though there were times when he found this more difficult to convey.'[7]

Hackforth and Matz made significant contributions to the presentation of Coward's music, along with an earlier accompanist, Carroll Gibbons, and Coward acknowledged his lasting debt to them by specifying bequests to Hackforth and Matz in his will. The work of all three was largely sequential: Gibbons (who recorded over twenty pieces with Coward) was responsible for the detail of a series of sessions which largely defined Coward's public musical style between 1928 and 1941; Hackforth (fourteen recordings) performed at once the twin roles of sensitive live cabaret accompanist and careful amanuensis between 1941 and 1958, and Matz (well over forty pieces recorded) provided new orchestrations and accompaniments for the re-presentation of the Coward musical catalogue (originally to American audiences) between 1955 and 1961.

Coward came to know Gibbons well enough to refer to him throughout his diaries only ever as 'Carroll'. As one of the leading dance-band leaders and syncopated swing pianists of his day, not to mention his filling the role of Director of Light Music for HMV, Gibbons' musical reputation was unassailable and his

talent rather greater than his self-deprecatory manner might have
suggested. His personal piano-playing style was polished, light,
artful and intelligent. There are strong comparisons between his
work and that of the pianist/composer Billy Mayerl (the pianist at
the first UK performance of Gershwin's *Rhapsody in Blue*), who
was one of the few light musicians to work seriously hard at
writing down swing piano style on paper. Gibbons was as
musically literate as Mayerl – he had in fact come to England
from America in the early 1920s to go to music college and stayed
– and had himself written down and published some of his own
swing piano *brilliantes*, such as 'Moonbeams Dance' (1930) and
'Bubbling Over' (1937).

Coward was to show his respect for Gibbons' talents by
recording one of his compositions, 'It's Only You', along with his
own 'Imagine the Duchess's Feelings' in the same 1941 session.*
Both are good displays of Gibbons' deceptively light touch with
syncopated right-hand chords over a firm rhythmic swung bass.
Indeed, the latter is remarkable for an accompaniment in which
for almost all of the refrain not a hint of the melody can be heard,
and for a clear demonstration of another favourite Gibbons
pianistic trick of picking out a sort of harmonic counter-melody
in the middle of the piano texture with his right thumb. Gibbons
also provided an exceptionally delicately balanced rubato swing
accompaniment for the 1934 recording of 'I Travel Alone';* but
for an extraordinary combination of Coward and Gibbons listen
to his 'Poor Little Rich Girl' (of March 1938).* In its mood and
pacing, and in its contrast between the simplistic melodic
meandering of the tune and the breakneck restlessness of the
accompaniment, it surely presents something close to a definitive
interpretation of this song. It is also musically a very clever,
integrated and satisfying accompaniment, despite the fact that it
almost certainly never left Gibbons' head. The normal 'spaces' in
songs which present accompanists and orchestrators with the
opportunity to enjoy themselves come at the melodic pause
between the conclusion of one lyric line and the start of the next,
and in 'Poor Little Rich Girl' these melodic spaces are lengthened
by the fact that most of the lyric lines end on a long held note.

So, five times during each refrain there are a clear four bars' worth of time for Gibbons to indulge himself – and us – with his pianistic scintillations. Each of these kingfisher-like flashes of rhythmic brilliance, often including extended syncopations in the right hand, shares the same melodic motif.

Ex. 1 'Poor Little Rich Girl'
($\downarrow$ =180!)

As a performance blueprint this is *infinitely* better than the now rather dated and pedestrian printed sheet music version; but one accepts that publishing an accompaniment like this for standard sheet music editions is not feasible, even if it might be desirable.

Norman Hackforth first worked with Coward in 1941 and clearly very quickly made his mark: when contemplating a forthcoming concert tour to South Africa in 1944, Coward rejoiced in securing Hackforth's services with the comment that 'apart from being a first-rate musician, he has accompanied me so much in the past and knows all my tricks'.[8] Their subsequent punishing schedule of wartime fund-raising and troop concerts tours, in conditions of close proximity and sometimes acute discomfort, formed the backbone of a working relationship stretching over seventeen years. Immediately after the war Coward placed two of Hackforth's own songs, 'Music Hath Charms' and 'Loch

Lomond', in his revue *Sigh No More* (there was to have been a third, but it was dropped and replaced by 'Matelot'); further proof of the high regard in which Hackforth was held is evident in the fact that even after the fiasco of *After the Ball*, which Coward saw for the first time in Manchester in April 1954 and which prompted him to fire Hackforth from the musical directorship, he was unhesitatingly brought back as accompanist for the fourth season of Café de Paris cabaret performances the same autumn and for all of Coward's subsequent London cabaret appearances till 1958.

In later life, Hackforth was proud to maintain that he knew as much about Coward's performance style as anyone then alive, and was careful to pass on many performance tips, mostly to do with how to approach delivery of the lyrics. He also made tapes of his accompaniments to much of the Coward cabaret repertoire and paper transcriptions of a few. It is revealing that his accompaniment tracks for many of the comedy songs only fleetingly register anything approaching the song melody (rather similarly to what can be seen in bars 5–8 of the quoted Gibbons accompaniment to 'Poor Little Rich Girl'). One of Hackforth's most interesting transcriptions is his original accompaniment for 'Nina', which he said 'the publishers undoubtedly would have found far too detailed and pianistically difficult'.[9] They would probably have thrown up their hands in horror at the crossing hands rhumba/beguine figurations, which figure sporadically throughout the original, although what they actually printed is in many ways no less difficult. They could have made life so much easier for themselves and the wider world of putative interpreters of the material if they had *not* chosen (quite unnecessarily and inappropriately) to reproduce the melody in the right hand of the accompaniment from start to finish of the song. (See examples 2 and 3.)

It is odd that the publishers chose to reproduce the most difficult bar of all – the second-time bar leading into the coda – almost unaltered, which merely illustrates a profound lack of thoughtful consistency on their part. Thoughtlessness no doubt also accounts for the fact that the only known recording of Noël

Ex. 2 The original accompaniment for the end of 'Nina'

and Norman performing 'Nina', made in Calcutta in 1944, was unaccountably omitted from a recent CD issue which included all the other Coward songs recorded in the same session.*

There is of course a danger of becoming too wedded to the idea that even an archival performance version of a song, however interestingly different, should be regarded as definitive. Even Hackforth, the most careful writer down of Coward's material, made the point that in rehearsal songs were 'subject to a process of constant improvement, particularly where chord progressions were concerned . . . [I considered this] a normal part of my ability to make the final result.'[10] Hackforth thought that he himself was

Ex. 3 The sheet music version for the end of 'Nina'

less willing to be intimidated by Coward's brusque approach to
dictation ('This is what I want – write it down!') than he
suspected some of his predecessors such as Elsie April may have
been. In fact, there is some evidence that transcriptions made
during the April era include specific elements of Coward's own
piano playing. Hackforth remembered his habit of playing as
many notes in the right hand as could be fitted in without altering
the basic harmonic outline, which may account for the precise
form in which 'Half-Caste Woman' was published. The
contention is that no amanuensis or publisher's arranger would
have invented the precise figuration of clumps of right-hand

notes off their own bat and that this is therefore likely to be a
literal transcription of Coward's own playing. (See example 4.)

Ex. 4 'Half Caste Woman' (1931)

A harmonic element, so much used by Coward that it becomes
characteristic of his music, is a dominant seventh chord with a
sharpened fifth, used mostly at cadences. It is such a noticeable
characteristic that Vivian Ellis said that he 'could recognise
[Coward's music] a mile away with both eyes shut. Indeed, I'd
tease him about his exclusive patent, a chord of the dominant
five-and-a-half.'[11] Most of the time its use does not intrude –

Ex. 5 'You Were There' (*Noël Coward Song Book*)

indeed, it provides a cadence of some considerable forward motion, particularly useful for linking the end of a verse section with the refrain that follows; but there are a couple of very odd uses of the progression, most notably in 'You Were There' (1936):

This surely has to be a literal transcription of Coward's own playing, since no publisher or arranger would invent the resultant harmonic muddle caused by using such a progression twice in close succession. The contemporaneous recording of 'You Were There'* preserves this idiosyncratic unorthodoxy, as does the sheet music (transcribed by Elsie April); but by the time the piece was included in the opening medley for the Café de Paris cabaret performances in 1951,* Hackforth had found a more elegant solution:

Ex. 6 'You Were There' (Hackforth Accompaniment)

Hackforth also made quiet amendments to some original sheet music versions of songs which were subsequently reprinted in the 1953 *Noël Coward Song Book*. These can all be considered as 'better' than the originals in their improved sense of harmonic direction or chordal figuration. One obvious example is 'Someday I'll Find You', where an improved cadence at the end of the first melodic phrase had clearly (from many recordings) become Coward's own choice: (See examples 7 and 8.)

Ex. 7 Original sheet music accompaniment for 'Some Day I'll Find You'

Ex. 8 *Noël Coward Song Book* accompaniment for 'Some Day I'll Find You'

There are always going to be inconsistencies deriving from this 'loose' approach to light music and it is clear that where Coward's music is concerned even the harmonic underlay is not always completely sacrosanct. There is even one example, when Coward was no longer around to voice any opinion in the matter, of the publishers themselves taking the initiative to make an 'improvement'. The posthumously published song 'There Will Always Be' had been held with affection in Hackforth's memory from 1944 till 1977, when he discovered that there was no trace of it in Coward's estate. He then wrote it out exactly as he remembered it being dictated:

Ex. 9 'There Will Always Be' – original dictation

Tho' the fates de - ceive me, I'll al - ways know, deep down in - side me, Love...

However, the publishers considered the chord underlying the word 'know' (basically a weak inversion of the tonic E♭) unsatisfactory and replaced it with the quite differently-feeling Dmaj7, which imparts a strong forward progression to the music.

Ex. 10 'There Will Always Be' – accompaniment as published (1978)

It is certainly debatable that the harmonic stasis of the original is exactly what Coward required for the song and that it should have been retained. He would, at any event, have been capable of recognising and realising the difference.[12]

Coward's work was certainly changed by Peter Matz, but mostly on the level of new, often invigorating accompaniments and band arrangements. In the euphoria of his astonishing reception at Las Vegas, Coward wrote that Matz's 'orchestral arrangements and variations are incredible – vital and imaginative. Sometimes they go too far for my personal taste, but I cannot fail to be impressed by the expert knowledge of instrumentation. [He] knows more about the range of various instruments and the potentialities of various combinations than anyone of any age that I have *ever* met in England.'[13] However, even the imaginative Matz remembered being put firmly in his place by Coward when getting ready for Las Vegas: 'He made me learn, very forcefully, that this was about comedy. A couple of times he screamed, "Don't play when I am making a joke!", [and] I gradually saw that this was a whole other kind of music.'[14] Nevertheless, the Las Vegas recordings display Matz's sensitive approach to orchestral accompaniment for what was essentially a theatrical performance. He realised that writing accompaniments for Coward songs which were to be played by a 'kind of a hot dance band, a typical Las Vegas show band with saxophones and many trumpets and trombones' needed finesse and much discretion, and that 'what it boiled down to was . . . the orchestra would play an introduction and get the thing started, and then mostly it would be just the piano and the drum and the bass, maybe. And then the orchestra would play maybe an interlude and then an ending.'[15]

This sort of structure, where short orchestral intros and endings sandwich a performance that is effectively accompanied by piano alone, was used for most of the comedy numbers performed at Las Vegas. Hackforth's 'Loch Lomond'* (by now firmly part of Coward's performance repertoire) has just ten seconds of orchestra as it builds to a climax at the very end of the piece, while the orchestral instruments in 'Nina'* are heard only in the declamatory introduction and in the (quite long) coda. But sometimes Matz's writing for instruments is a little more in evidence, and more inventive, than his statement might suggest. In the case of 'A Bar on the Piccola Marina'* there's a deft and unobtrusive use of instruments during the refrains, where muted trumpets and clarinets in close harmony first point up the 'fills' between lyric lines, and then sustain chords and support the harmony in the section which starts, 'She'd just sit there, knocking back the gin', leaving the piano at this point to flash in and out with jazzy decorations. The string bass is present throughout, but only comes to the fore, along with a *quiet* snare drum, in the '*Viva, viva!* and *che ragazza!*' interlude – and thus only *just* when most effective. The more lyrical the song, the more free is Matz's use of instruments, but you have to listen hard to a number such as 'World Weary'* to discern exactly what it is he has done, as it is sometimes so discreet – a single quiet clarinet moving on minims, perhaps – as to slip by almost without being noticeable. Paradoxically, in this context this is perhaps the greatest accolade one can pay to such musical craftsmanship.

However, it is probably in the studio recordings for the following year's album *Noël Coward in New York** that Matz's expertise as arranger and accompanist can be heard to best advantage. In one respect this work also marks Coward's own recording apogee, in that the quality of recorded sound as well as the timbre, tuning and control of his own voice are all superior to anything that had come before or that was to follow. At the time, Coward thought that the last recording session, where four songs were accompanied just by Matz and a small group of expert individual instrumentalists on double bass, trumpet, guitar and drums, had gone 'fairly triumphantly' and wrote in his diary of the 'exciting' results. The recordings of 'Half-Caste Woman' and 'Twentieth Century Blues' have a lot in common in their mood and tempo – pure nightclub jazz at a strictly controlled ninety-six beats a minute – and both feature the exciting little touch of surprising doublings in the tempo for the space of one bar in their second refrains. 'Sail Away' manages to produce a surprising lyricism from such a limited combination of accompanying instruments, with good use of richly chordal piano figurations, while 'Time and Again' amounts to a completely new interpretation of a superbly well-crafted song which without this recording might have been almost unknown. The earlier recording of the song in 1952* marks its brief appearance in the Café de Paris cabaret shows, in which context Hackforth remembered that it 'didn't ever really work' and from which it was soon dropped. In 1952 the verse section is something of a scramble and the orchestrations rather intrusively clumsy; few, however, could fail to be convinced that the number finds its true voice and definitive tempo with Matz's jazz combo accompaniment, which sets the whole song to the same beat from the start, very slightly slower than originally performed and much more sparsely pointed in the accompaniment. Matz's shafts of jazz piano improvisation add a level of both rhythmic and harmonic interest which is almost worthy of Gibbons, and the whole is delivered in a deliciously laid-back swing jazz style which offers maximum enjoyment of the clever cross-rhythmic stresses at the end of the 'middle eight' passages. It is beyond question a great accompaniment for a great song and a realisation of its potential which might otherwise not have occurred.

Given the number of variables in how the material is actually written down, printed, accompanied or orchestrated, it will be clear that light music is a hugely flexible art form which can be as dependent on its supporting musicians as on its star singers for its impact and success. Some contemporary interpreters find it implicitly intimidating that most well-known Coward material is still well-known today principally on account of his own extensively marketed recorded legacy; but the fact that he himself presented such varied interpretations does at least mean that no single performance can be regarded as wholly definitive. New interpretations of Coward's music tend to be successful when performers remember that, with the comedy material, it makes theatrical as much as musical demands on the singer, that Coward's range of compositional styles (from Viennese operetta to the blues) requires thought and sensitivity in interpretation, and that clarity of text is paramount in all styles. Coward knew that the intrinsic quality of the voice itself is perhaps the least important element, commenting, 'I can't sing, but I know how to, which is quite different.'[16] He was certainly not slow, however, to criticise what he considered to be inappropriate interpretations. In 1945, for example, at the time of *Sigh No More*, he had 'a temperamental outburst of rage as a result of accidentally hearing on the radio a vocal rendering of "Matelot" at a tempo to which he took exception ... he picked up the telephone, called [the director of light music at Chappell's], pulverized him for several minutes ... and ended by saying: "I wish to make myself perfectly clear. I absolutely forbid any further performance on the radio of my songs from the revue, without my express permission." '[17] One should hardly be surprised to find that Coward cared deeply about the standard of presentation of his work, and the musicians who worked with him all noted his capacity for sheer effort and his meticulous preparation of every note of every phrase. The only legacy that this should leave is an aspirational one: if nothing else, the existing library of thoughtful and imaginative accompaniments (as well as vocal lines in the hands of an expert lyricist) provides very good examples to follow.

It is interesting to speculate upon what Coward would have made of the 1998 release of fifteen new interpretations of his songs by Robbie Williams, Marianne Faithfull, Elton John and Paul McCartney among others, on the album *Twentieth Century Blues*.* The album may have helped to prove that Coward is still cool, but in terms of sales it was rather a disappointment, and one may edge towards a conclusion as to why this was so by trying to listen to the lyrics on some of these tracks. However, successful new performances, even of numbers which Coward made quint-essentially his own, are always possible. Kenneth Williams's version of 'Mad Dogs and Englishmen'* is a case in point: Williams's idiosyncratic, drawling voice is very different indeed from Coward's, but he recognised the absolute need with this song for a rhythmically precise and clear lyric, and because this is his first concern, the performance is extremely effective despite some needlessly fussy orchestration.

The art is that of natural clarity, and one can do no better than

heed Coward's own dictats on the matter: 'I wonder why it is,' he
wrote, 'that . . . my lyrics are [such traps] for singers. Nobody
seems capable of leaving well enough alone and allowing the
words to take care of themselves. Neither my lyrics nor my
dialogue require decoration; all they do require are clarity, diction
and intention and a minimum of gesture and business.'[18] Armed
with that proviso, and as long as accompanying musicians don't
over-accompany, performers may at least start off on the right
foot towards getting satisfactory interpretations of this most
potentially potent of musical forms.

ACKNOWLEDGEMENTS
To Warner/Chappell Music Ltd (owners of the copyrights) and
IMP Ltd, for kind permission to reproduce extracts of the songs
'Poor Little Rich Girl', 'Nina', 'Half-Caste Woman', 'You Were
There', 'Some Day I'll Find You' and 'There Will Always Be'; to
the Norman Hackforth Estate for permission to quote from
unpublished documents; to Alan Farley (KALW Radio, San
Francisco) for access to the transcripts of his collection of
interviews, *Conversations About Coward*.

NOTES
1. *The Noël Coward Song Book* (London: Michael Joseph, 1953), pp.16–17.
2. Stephen Citron, *Noël and Cole: the Sophisticates* (London: Sinclair-Stephenson, 1992).
3. Deena Rosenberg, *Fascinating Rhythm* (London: Octopus Publishing Group, 1992).
4. Norman Hackforth, letter to author, 4 March 1978.
5. *The Noël Coward Song Book* (London: Michael Joseph, 1953), p.13. This
   lack of technical knowledge may have lent force to rumours that Coward
   plagiarised, but in this respect he suffered no worse than many other light
   music composers, notably including Cole Porter who successfully defended
   court actions brought against him for plagiarism. In Coward's case there
   were persistent rumours that his amanuensis from 1923 till the war years,
   Elsie April, actually wrote bits of his scores and that he cannibalised the
   work of other musicians with whom he worked. But such innuendoes can
   usually be traced back to people he 'left behind' as his career moved
   onwards and may have more to do with simple envy than having any
   substance in fact. The sole directly traceable plagiarism, the melody at the
   start of the refrain of 'Dance Little Lady' (which goes back to 'Ah Moon of

My Deight' from Liza Lehmann's 'In a Persian Garden' of 1896) was later willingly admitted to by Coward, although he maintained that he 'didn't realise it when it came into my head [which it did, according to *Present Indicative*, at the end of a meeting with C. B. Cochran at his office] and now it's too late to do anything about it' (quoted in Philip Hoare, *Noël Coward* (London: Sinclair-Stephenson, 1995, p.192).

6. *Conversations About Coward*, unpublished transcript of radio interview with Peter Matz, 23 May 1986.
7. Norman Hackforth; letter to author, 8 January 1978.
8. Noël Coward, *Middle East Diary* (London: Heinemann, 1944) p.91.
9. Norman Hackforth, letter to author, 8 January 1978.
10. Norman Hackforth, interview with author, 3 November 1996.
11. Vivian Ellis, *Sir Noël – the Man and his Music* in *Performing Right*, No.60, October 1973 [PRS, London].
12. Musicologists may be interested to note that Coward reused the seven opening notes of the melody of 'There Will Always Be' in 'Go, I Beg You Go' from *After the Ball* in 1954.
13. *The Noël Coward Diaries*, ed. Graham Payn and Sheridan Morley (London: Weidenfeld & Nicolson, 1979) entry for 12 June 1955.
14. *Conversations About Coward*: unpublished transcript of radio interview with Peter Matz, 23 May 1986.
15. Ibid.
16. Quoted by John Heilpern in the *Observer* (1969).
17. Norman Hackforth, *And the Next Object* (autobiography) (London: Angus & Robertson, 1975).
18. *The Diaries*, entry for 27 September 1956.

*Recordings referred to in the text (available on HMV 4 CD set *The Master's Voice*: EMI 0777 7 80580 2 1 unless otherwise specified):

'I Like America': Café de Paris Orchestra, conductor Simone, piano accompaniment Hackforth; London, 14 December 1951.

'I Like America': orchestra, conductor and piano accompaniment Matz; New York, 1 November 1956 (Sony CD MDK47253).

'Imagine the Duchess's Feelings' and 'It's Only You' (Gibbons): piano accompaniment Gibbons; London, 28 July 1941.

'I Travel Alone': piano accompaniment Gibbons; London, 29 October 1934.

'Poor Little Rich Girl': piano accompaniment Gibbons;

London, 24 March 1938.

'There Have Been Songs in England', 'Uncle Harry' and 'I Wonder What Happened to Him?': piano accompaniment Hackforth; Calcutta, 10 July 1944 (Harbinger CD HCD 1701).

'You Were There': (with Gertrude Lawrence) Phoenix Theatre Orchestra, conductor Greenwood; London, 15 January 1936.

'Cabaret Medley': Café de Paris Orchestra, conductor Simone, piano accompaniment Hackforth; London, 14 December 1951.

'Loch Lomond', 'Nina', 'A Bar on the Piccola Marina' and 'World Weary': Carlton Hayes Orchestra, piano accompaniment Matz; Las Vegas, 28 June 1955 (Sony CD MDK 47253).

Noël Coward in New York:(all recordings): orchestra arranged, conducted and piano accompaniment Matz; New York, 1–2 Nov 1956 (Sony CD MDK 47253).

'Time and Again': Café de Paris Orchestra, conductor Simone, piano accompaniment Hackforth; London, 9 June 1952.

Twentieth Century Blues: (various artists) London, 1998 (EMI 7243 49463127).

'Mad Dogs and Englishmen': Kenneth Williams and Brian Fahey orchestra; London, 1965 (EMI CD 7243 5 20727 2 9).

Cowardice, Decadence and the Contemporary Theatre

Michael Coveney

Oscar Wilde and Noël Coward, arch hedonists both. The first was destroyed by the hypocrisy of the age, with only the slightest element of his own vanity and folly intruding. The second aged happily into harmless hypocrisy. Having denounced, for instance, the abdicating King Edward VIII, Coward lost no time hobnobbing with the former monarch and the Duchess of Windsor the minute the war was over. Indeed, the Duke of Windsor became a rival example to Coward of a high-living, hard-drinking sexually ambivalent totem of privilege in an age of austerity. That age, unlike our own, needed the remote, unobtainable glamour of others to gawp at, on the whole non-enviously.

Nonetheless, during his own lifetime many British subjects looked askance at Coward's effusive avowals of royalty-struck patriotism while he went out of his way not to pay taxes by living abroad. I first heard of an antipathy towards him when, as a child, my parents talked of going to see *Present Laughter* just after the war and my grandfather greeted their enthusiasm for the play with the jaundiced remark, 'When is he ever going to take off that bloody dressing gown?'

Although my parents found Coward a bit sophisticated – their word, probably, for camp or outré – he was a fixture in their lives in a way no playwright is today. During the war, my mother now

says, he and 'the other bloke' – Ivor Novello, also a bit
sophisticated, I fear – kept them entertained on stage and screen.

Coward, for all his posturing, touched the lives, in a peculiar
way, of the man in the street. My parents were typical London
Irish working class with white-collar, lower-middle-class
aspirations. Coward for them was the raffish epitome of style and
grace in the theatre. The rumpus over the Bad Boy of the 1920s,
the author of *The Vortex*, had levelled out into a projection of
witty elitism and admirable high spirits.

Garry Essendine was the embodiment of Coward and the
manipulation of his own myth at the centre of everyone else's
attention. No one before or since in the British theatre has ever
made such an unremitting exhibition of himself. The result was a
penetration of the cultural consciousness unmatched, probably,
by any other British artist, certainly playwright, this century.
John Osborne said Coward was his own greatest invention and
contribution to the twentieth century. And Kenneth Tynan
averred in 1953 that, in fifty years time, everyone would still
know what precisely was meant by 'a very Noël Coward sort of
person'.

Cigarette on the go, smart attire, even when casual, a pocket
handkerchief, a quizzical gaze, an unruffled calm, a lightness of
movement, a sharpness of wit – and also a discreet but active
sexuality.

That is the kind of chap we mean and the first such I ever knew
ran an amateur dramatic company in Ilford, Essex, of all places.
His name was James Cooper and he was the son of a Barking
brush salesman. He claimed to have worked with Coward during
the war, as a stage manager in Nairobi, and had been employed,
before then, as a dancer on the south coast and a dogsbody in the
West End. The influence of Coward the all-rounder was too
much to sustain him in a walk-on capacity, so he decided to
become a big fish in a small pond and to run his own small theatre
in Ilford.

He did so with tremendous aplomb, directing and designing all
the plays – he also built all the sets, ran the box office, fixed the
lights and the sound and invariably took the leading role. In fact,

he made Garry Essendine – whom he often played – look like a bit of a wilting violet. Cooper, whom Alan Dent of the *News Chronicle* once described as 'certainly not the worst of the eight Hamlets I have seen this year', used to swagger round the Ilford Broadway and up the Cranbrook Road impeccably turned out in a blazer, perfectly creased slacks, highly polished shoes and a slick, satiny hairstyle. He chain-smoked a brand of cigarettes called Perfectos and is the only person I have ever known so to do. His favourite actor was Laurence Olivier, his favourite entertainer Frank Sinatra. But he modelled his public persona on a mixture of Danny Kaye – whom he resembled facially – and Noël Coward. Coward was for him the supreme man of the theatre and he echoed many of his sentiments as expressed in the finger-wagging lecture to Roland Maule, the wannabe playwright from Uckfield in *Present Laughter*.

Cooper, like Coward, pooh-poohed the whole idea of subsidy in the arts as a guarantee of slackness, self-indulgence and putting on rubbish nobody wanted to go and see. One of the plays he presented with some regularity was that classic wartime British farce *See How They Run* by Philip King and Falkland Carey. This contains the imperishable line, 'Sergeant, arrest most of these people' and such exchanges as 'How mad are you?'; 'I don't know, but I was perfectly sane when I arrived' and 'I have not come here to be insulted'; 'Oh, where do you usually go?' Well, it ain't Coward, but it ain't bad! It also contains a fascinating revelation of the extent to which Coward had percolated down into the cultural life of the country, as the farcical shenanigans in the sleepy village of Merton-cum-Middlewick are enlivened with a reanimated touring theatrical romance, enacted in Coward's *Private Lives*, between a vicar's wife and her long-lost soldier buddy.

Not only was Coward a permanent fixture in ordinary people's lives, he became a background to other people's plays. In some cases, as in James Cooper's, he became incorporated in a demonic, even vampiric sort of way. This phenomenon could be illustrated by a comparatively recent play on just this subject by the actor Sean Mathias, who would later become a director of

Coward and other classics. And again, *Private Lives* was invoked.

Mathias's *Cowardice* opened at the Ambassadors in London in 1983 to a fairly torrid reception. It was less than perfect, but it was interesting in the way it rewrote the legend of Noël Coward and Gertrude Lawrence as the tale of two South London showbiz urchins who never, unlike Noël and Gertie, managed to cross the tracks. So they played at being them instead, rather as Jimmie Cooper did in Ilford. Mathias's characters, Boy and Babe, were brother and sister. Boy was played by Ian McKellen and Babe by Janet Suzman. Playing out a grim parody of *Private Lives*, they are also rehearsing a new Coward play, *Public Death*, which Boy is receiving through the ether, rather like that odd woman Rosemary Brown recording the posthumous doodles of Beethoven and Brahms.

An all too convincing aroma of failure hovered over the proceedings, although I remember much enjoying a bizarre scene where Janet Suzman administered oral sex to a Shakespearean bore played by Nigel Davenport before securing his promise to speak well of her brother's play at the Arts Council. A whole new world of Ortonesque possibilities opened up surrounding the provision of project grants to new playwrights.

Still, the point remained that Noël and Gertie might have been like this without the flair and the talent, but also without the opportunity. And no critic at the time, least of all myself, pointed out that the ironical homage to Coward had a double-edged potency: it acknowledged Coward's cult status in the lives of ordinary people and underlined how the period trappings and trimmings, in their absence, were part of the essence.

Or were they? Twelve years later Mathias was a director and was responsible for a production of *Design for Living*, the play which Coward wrote for himself, Alfred Lunt and Lynn Fontanne (who, as it happens, came from Barking, just like Jimmie Cooper and, for that matter, Maggie Smith). This 1930s sexually ambiguous comedy enshrined the whole colour magazine ethos of 'making it' as an artist and a personality. Coward lived with the idea for this play for some years and even considered placing the entire action in one gigantic bed: 'This, however, was hilariously discarded,' he said, 'after Alfred had suggested a few stage directions which if followed faithfully, would undoubtedly have landed all three of us in gaol.'[1]

The play was produced on Broadway in 1939 but not in London until six years later when the Lord Chamberlain relaxed a ban imposed because of the dubious morals of Otto the writer, Leo the painter and Gilda, the girlfriend who shuttles between them like an enchanting androgyne, a sort of divine intellectual slut. A fine revival, starring Vanessa Redgrave and directed by Michael Blakemore in the year Coward died, went some way to establishing the play as a really well-sprung comedy about friendship and ambition, as well as about art and fashion, and Coward's perennial theme of putting the dullards to rout. One reviewer at the time complimented the director on a delicate, yet uproarious treatment of the drunk scene at the end of the second act when a present-day audience – in 1973 – might have expected Otto and Leo to fall into bed together.

Almost twenty years later Sean Mathias directed a quite different sort of evening, one that had some reviewers reaching for their machine-guns. Mathias ended each act with an explicit sexual embrace on the floor. The art connoisseur whom Gilda marries was presented not as a glum bore but as a good-looking, confused outsider. Somehow, the shock of the new had become the contemporary cool. Rachel Weisz as Gilda was a stunning new voluptuous actress, disporting herself on top of the fridge in the Paris studio and basking in the fridge's electric glare; and the two lads were lanky Welsh Paul Rhys and chunky Northern Clive Owen, each a far cry from the traditional H. M. Tennant ideal of a juvenile lead. There is a libertarian credo at this play's heart that was totally honoured in the execution.

The text was well delivered and it was refreshing to hear Coward's effetely clipped phraseology lightly unmoored from its predictable rhythms, rather as the radical pianist Glenn Gould makes you hear Bach or even Telemann in an entirely new way while not departing from the score, or the fundamental spirit of the music. Some critics wailed on behalf of a traduced author and one – my distinguished colleague and literary adviser to the

Coward Estate, Sheridan Morley – advocated the formation of a critics' mafia, along the lines of John Osborne's playwrights' mafia, aimed at disposing of unwanted nay-sayers. These censorious gangs, Morley suggested, might roam the streets and physically dispose of young directors in a hurry who had decided to make their reputations at the expense and in often blatant disregard of those they have been hired to stage.

It seems to me that if the practical theatre proceeds on the basis that a Coward play should be produced in a manner that would have pleased the Master, the practical theatre is doomed. Even apparently conventional productions find themselves taking liberties and creating distortions he would have loathed.

One such was a 1993 revival of *Present Laughter*, directed by Tom Conti and indeed starring Tom Conti as Garry Essendine. Conti perforce bent the play to his personal style of undercutting diffidence while suggesting that the real subject under discussion was not a matinée idol's vanity but his promiscuity. This Garry was not a Cowardesque brittle popinjay so much as a dark and insolent Don Juan, close relation of Marcello Mastroianni in Fellini's 8½. The action was moved forward from 1939 to 1951, with the mixed results of a new cultural seediness and servants much more impatient for the classless society John Major would one day advocate.

There were a lot of changes and insertions that in fact were far more barbaric than anything proposed by Mr Mathias. Jenny Seagrove as Joanna Lyppiatt, for instance, played the adulterous vamp as a thickly accented Russian émigrée, so that the recurrent mating call of 'I've forgotten my latchkey' became 'I have lostet my latchkey', which sounded as though a Jewish potato dish had gone missing from the dinner table. More interestingly, and not at all at odds with the play's meaning, Roland Maule, the ridiculous playwright, became a sort of celebrity stalker and potential assassin.

Thus we can see how easily, and inevitably, a Coward production can move away from the initial and perhaps more innocent comic premise. The Mathias approach, the extreme antithesis of his own writing experiment in charting the appeal of

Coward to suburban idolaters was a more wholesale effort to engage with the notions of sexual ambiguity, social poise, arrogance and cool of Coward's characters. But he was not the pioneer in this field.

As a young actor Mathias had worked at the Citizens Theatre in Glasgow, the most consistently interesting, adventurous and influential repertory theatre in Britain over the past thirty years. It is here, if anywhere, we should look for an underpinning contemporary aesthetic in the reassessment of not just Coward, but also of Oscar Wilde, Tennessee Williams, Jean Genet and even Proust, whose masterpiece *A la recherche du temps perdu* was presented as a four-hour salon epic with the gloriously insouciant title *A Waste of Time*.

The Citizens in the Gorbals slum area of the city has thrived, in my view, as a theatre of opposition within a variety of contexts. They believe in audiences before artists. The seat prices are the lowest in Britain. They recycle costumes and sets, all of which are made and built on the premises, in order to operate within the most astringent of budgetary restrictions. Paradoxically, this theatre on a shoestring made a reputation as the most flamboyantly visual in Britain during a period when theatrical extravagance was regarded in the subsidised sector as anathema to good intentions. The Citizens defies, in particular, the assumption, that a living theatre must be some kind of lickspittle, torch-bearing collaborator in the reputations of dead playwrights.

The defining moment in terms of Coward arrived with the world première in 1977 of *Semi-Monde*. *Semi-Monde* was written in 1926. Originally titled *Ritz Bar*, it was eclipsed eventually by Vicky Baum's *Grand Hotel*, a far more innocent and palatable collection of foyer follies. Although Max Reinhardt had been keen to direct the play in Germany, it had slipped quietly into oblivion, unperformed. In 1957 Coward informed Beverley Nichols: 'Ritz Bar was as jagged with sophistication as all get out; the characters were ether demi-mondaine or just plain mondaine, shared their apartments and their lives with the opposite, or the same sex, and no wife dreamed for one instant of doing anything so banal as living with her husband.'[2]

The idea of social subversion, as well as sexual inversion, is lightly paraded but evidence nonetheless of a deep aesthetic antipathy to the status quo, the everyday norm, the acceptable social practice. The American scholar Terry Castle has demonstrated convincingly how the bisexual and lesbian high life in *Semi-Monde* reflects Coward's close intimacy with Radclyffe Hall, Una Troubridge and their glamorous international lesbian milieu.[3] Philip Prowse took this further, stretching Coward's skim across three years between the wars into a parable of doomy foreboding across twenty, from 1919 to 1939. The piano music went from the Charleston to wistful romance. A pageboy previously in search of Mrs Simpson finally called for Madame la Duchesse de Windsor. Sirens mingled with Debussy and the hotel vacuum cleaner. Beige flower bowls of pink and blue lilacs were restocked with tiger lilies. And in one vintage scene – one of the best examples of Coward's small talk and prattle fluttering in the emotional void – an ageing novelist took his farewell of a socialite while fighting back tears with banal comments about the latest revue.

It was absolutely typical that the glittering first night of *Semi-Monde* was greeted by a group of local urchins setting fire to a vehicle in the theatre's car park. Inside, on the stage, butch lesbians screamed their heads off, highly strung young men hit each other with handbags and jumped on tables, two married couples exchanged partners, a Russian was shot dead by an irate rival and so on. I remember thinking that while the RSC was admirably busy with Gorky and Shakespeare, and new plays by the likes of David Edgar, Stephen Poliakoff et al., here was a theatre making Coward a central strand of an even bigger world of drama which had already ranged from Lermontov and De Sade to Brecht (always a sell-out in the Gorbals), Gogol, Seneca and the more recherché Jacobean repertoire.

For Glasgow, Coward was not a diversion after dinner, but a writer with something serious to say about the way we live and the way we should interpret the past. At the time, I was editing a theatrical magazine and I invited one of Coward's biggest admirers, and indeed one of his friends, the musical comedy composer and author Sandy Wilson, to review the show. Like Coward, and later Lionel Bart, Wilson, best known for *The Boy Friend*, was – is – a one-man band of musical theatre, usually writing his own libretto, music and lyrics.

Wilson half regretted what he saw as the portentous overloading of Coward's little charade, but he was amazed by the costumes of gold lamé and chinchilla, hard black hats and eye-veils, stunning lace gowns, one in that intrinsically Thirties shade known, he believed, as saxe blue. One actor, he said, conveyed just the right air of bewildered outrage as the wronged husband and Pierce Brosnan – yes, the future James Bond – came on as a dead ringer for Clark Gable, 'dimple on the chin, ears and all'.

Oscar Wilde once said that one should either be a work of art, or wear a work of art, and the moral and habitual narcissism at the Citizens got up many critics' noses, often it has to be said, the noses of critics who never even went near the place. In the Camp of Coward, there is a problem for interpreters that the Citizens' have always met head on: that is, how best to rescue Coward from Coward himself and prove that his artistry works in contemporary terms.

In the theatre this is especially difficult because of the tone and temper of the plays, very much of their time, and the sound of Coward's affected voice behind them. And yet they rarely seem all that dated. Cyril Connolly has been proved wrong in his 1937 judgement that 'One can't read any of Noël Coward's plays now ... they are written in the most topical and perishable way imaginable, the cream in them turns sour overnight'.[4] But the earliest comedies and the middle-period classics all share a snappy, elliptical daring that was unprecedented on the stage and remains caustically alive today. As Tynan said, 'Coward took the fat off English comic dialogue; he was the Turkish bath in which it slimmed.'[5] It was left to Harold Pinter to apply the birch.

Having anticipated the recent rush to claim Coward as a camp contemporary icon in their *Semi-Monde*, the Citizens tackled *Private Lives* for the second time in 1994. Rupert Everett played Victor, the boring one, as a bespectacled loon looking like both John Hegley and Elvis Costello. He entered singing, under his breath, Kylie Minogue's 'I Should Be So Lucky'. And the yacht that was spied from the balcony was not the Duke of Westminster's but Robert Maxwell's. Philip Prowse's salon design style had moved on by now to a more postmodernist brutalism, brashly revelling in a riot of grey art deco, with silver strips, flower pots, naked light bulbs and pop art sleaze.

These productions were punctuated, in 1988, by the Citizens' definitive revival of *The Vortex*, a play which, said Philip Prowse in an interview in the *Financial Times*, 'was a yuppie piece then, and it's a yuppie piece now'. He hit on the important fact that Nicky Lancaster, who returns home from studying music in Paris in a mood of feckless irritation, was some kind of new European. Rupert Everett as Nicky, who appeared to be stoned, and damned, from the moment he entered his mother's boudoir, gave new meaning to the line, 'I'm a little beyond aspirin.' This performance injected a study of the pathology of addiction into a play that toyed with the subject of drugs without confronting it directly. Miraculously, the production also sustained the *echt* Coward style, its brittleness and fizz, its perennial decadence, while imparting a sense of absolute modernity.

Coward had described the colours and decorations of Florence Lancaster's London flat as 'on the verge of being original'. Philip Prowse covered the Citizens' stark black walls with new paintings suggestive of Juan Gris and Kandinsky, adjusting the locations with white sofas and gauze screens, vases of white flowers and, for the final traumatic Oedipal bedroom encounter, a low-hanging, tilting mirror above the pink silk sheets and pillowcases. Maria Aitken gave the performance of her career as Florence, a woman fighting off loneliness with a hectic determination to stay in the swim. Prowse supplied her with a stunning array of dresses in pink and black silks, satins and taffetas, as well as a plunging, backless white gown for the country house dance. Aitken projected an exact and critical sense of being both a symptom and victim of the enervating social charades. The production was remounted in London after a short delay ironically caused by Miss Aitken's appearance in court to defend, successfully, a charge of cocaine smuggling.

Sometimes, when the show transferred to the Garrick Theatre in London, audiences complained of not hearing Rupert Everett all that clearly when he overdid the realism of his far-gone, far-out state of befuddlement. An irate correspondent was surprised to receive a reply from the actor in which Everett enclosed a snippet of his pubic hair as a mark of his esteem and gratitude. Coward might well have turned in his grave, but he might also have applauded this little act of tasteless defiance.

And so to this centenary year at the Citizens, where Philip Prowse fulfilled a long-held ambition to direct *Cavalcade*. We knew Noël Coward was a patriot, but the centenary celebrations unearthed no bigger surprise than his anger at lost life in brutal war, the bitter-sweet taste of his puffed-up London pride. *Cavalcade* was conceived in 1930 as a test of his production powers on a large scale. It covers our century as a nation, upstairs and downstairs (indeed the popular television series of that name was said to be inspired by the piece), in the Boer War, then the trenches, ending with a sardonic wail of the jazz age, 'Twentieth Century Blues'.

At Glasgow, Michelle Gomez squawked out this number as a transsexual cabaret singer, Fanny Bridges, both summarising and prophesying our nerve-racked era as large computer lights counted out the century from 1931 to 1999. As with his *Semi-Monde*, Prowse took creative liberties with Coward's time-span, utterly transforming an apparently skimpy, underwritten piece that pits the upper-class Marryots and their servants, Alfred and Ellen Bridges, against the tidal wave of history.

The stage, and the partition of gathered curtains that advanced inexorably and quietly towards the audience, were blood red. Derwent Watson, the excellent musical director, moved between two grand pianos, one on the stage, one in the stalls, that enclosed the domestic and outside action.

Coward's tempi and consummate stagecraft met their match not only in Prowse's inspired fluency of staging but also in a precise and sentimental vocal pitch among the actors that sounded neither too dated nor too twee. The cast played the truth of Coward's pride and patriotism without, amazingly, suggesting

for one minute that this is, as I always thought it was, an absurdly
jingoistic affair. No one did this better than Jennifer Hilary as
Jane Marryot, seeing in each new year with redoubled sorrow and
diminishing fervour.

The Great War was presented with a mixture of music hall
relish and subdued dignity, as a procession of corpses on stretchers
crosses the stage. At the Relief of Mafeking and on Armistice
Day, a crowd of extras flooded the theatre, from back-stage to
front of house, then vanished, gone, as in a sudden nightmare.
Prowse nearly presented the piece without any crowd at all and
was prepared to do so, before striking lucky with a bunch of eager
local amateurs at the last minute. He used them sparingly,
without exposing any amateurism, and the rest of the cast list was
covered by sixteen actors. Hardly a line was cut or altered. The
running time was ninety minutes.

The famous scene where a honeymoon couple talk of their
hopes and fears on board a ship was stunningly evoked with two
long strips of light bulbs on rigging. Coward's mawkish stage
direction, where the lady moves a coat to reveal a lifebelt on the
Titanic, was ignored. We knew this was the *Titanic* at once, and
the scene was loaded afresh with pathos and poignancy.

With minimal resources, Prowse conjured a wealth of visual
detail, using showers of tiny petals (red, white and blue, as in the
Union Jack), exquisite satin costumes and fox furs, superb
lighting (by Gerry Jenkinson) and his own impeccable, spatial
instincts. There was no better staged production all year in the
British theatre, nor one more magically in tune with our
millennial misgivings and exhausted end-of-termism as the clock
clicked round to a new century.

There were two really intriguing revivals of comparatively
unknown Coward at either end of his career. The Chester
Gateway dug up *The Young Idea* (1924) while Sheridan Morley
moved his revival of *Song at Twilight* (1966) into the West End
after a bumpy try-out at the King's Head fringe theatre in north
London. In the latter, Vanessa Redgrave, magnificent and
magnetic, stormed the London stage as the former lover of a
hypocritical novelist played by her own brother Corin. Moral

cowardice is the charge, a phrase that echoes throughout Coward's plays. Vanessa Redgrave brought an electrifying air of moral righteousness to a flaccid script. For Coward was not writing all that well at the end, for all the pertinence and poignancy of his theme.

Sir Hugo Latymer (played by Corin) is a successful novelist who has published a self-serving autobiography. Carlotta Gray (played by Vanessa, succeeding a far wispier reading by Nyree Dawn Porter at the King's Head) is a half-successful actress seeking some form of emotional justice for a barely acknowledged homosexual lover of Hugo who has died of drink-related hepatitis.

The scene is a Geneva hotel in 1965. Morley presumably approved a rather shallow bit of tinkering with the text as Carlotta sang a snatch of the Beatles and also a song from *Camelot*, 'How to Handle a Woman', in which Vanessa appeared on film. The personal echoes in this production seemed infinite. Corin's real-life wife, Kika Markham, played his stage wife and secretary, the butch German Hilde. And much was made in the pre-publicity of the fact that the Redgraves' father, the bisexual Sir Michael, was a casual lover of Coward. On top of which, Coward's biographer and literary executor, Sheridan Morley, was the director!

At the Chester Gateway, *The Young Idea* was a really interesting rescue job by director Deborah Shaw. The play was openly inspired by Shaw's *You Never Can Tell*, but even Shaw recognised the talent in the writing, which bounces along with a lively freshness. Two young siblings (Simon Quarterman and Chloe Newsome) try to reunite their divorced parents (Benjamin Whitrow and Jane How). They do so in a symbolic shift from English country house stuffiness to Italian sensuality or, as the designer Paul Edwards superbly suggested, from George Stubbs to Renaissance frescos.

All the Coward themes are here, as well as the tension between discretion and blatancy, bursting to be harnessed in the stylistic genius of his great comedies. There was another great act of rediscovery at the Royal Exchange in Manchester, where *Nude with Violin*, conventionally viewed as one of those Coward plays where his reactionary conservatism gets the better of him – another of the same 1950s period, *Relative Values*, ends with a toast to 'the final inglorious disintegration of the most unlikely dream that ever troubled the foolish heart of man – Social Equality' – was gloriously reconsidered. This revival by Marianne Elliott came across as much less a reactionary polemic than a keenly observed and very funny comedy of manners.

The holier-than-thou kneejerk response to *Nude with Violin*, perfectly expressed by Michael Billington in his *Guardian* review, is that the play is an antedeluvian philistine whinge in which modern art is seen as a conspiracy against the public. Coward seeks to prove this, it is alleged, by assembling the family of a legendary painter, Paul Sorodin, after his death and exposing him as a fraud. It is of course useless to pretend that most people don't find the whole concept of modern art funny, or at least in part a con trick. Just think piles of bricks, Gilbert and George, stone circles and sheep in formaldehyde. But the Manchester production allowed the central character, Sorodin's multi-lingual Martinique manservant, Sebastien Lacreole, the upper hand with a twist of irony.

This role was first played by John Gielgud and then in the States by Coward himself. But in the casting of Derek Griffiths, a waspishly funny black actor, as Sebastien, Coward's play was reinvented as a triumph of the servant over his fraudulent master while preserving the central thesis as a moving paean to creative talent. 'No one knows anything about painting any more,' sighed Griffiths in a quiet heart-to-heart with the dead painter's daughter. 'Art, like human nature, has got out of hand.' The snooty Coward tone was replaced by a non-controversial expression of true sorrow. And in a magisterial irony of presentation, a play about art was itself a beautiful work of art, with a sumptuous in-the-round art deco design in cream and black, and costumes every bit as good as any of Philip Prowse's at Glasgow.

Again, this proved that you don't have to do Coward in a period vacuum, in fact you'd better not, in order to make him live on the stage. There were differences of opinion as to how this had applied in the National's *Private Lives*. But the biggest uproar this year has been that surrounding the revival of *Hay Fever*, directed by Declan Donnellan in the West End. 'Coward trashed and travestied,' screamed the *Evening Standard*. Other words cropping up in reviews included 'dire, dismal, fiasco, shambles' and 'bare-faced cheek'.

What had Donnellan actually done? He prefaced the comedy in which the weekend guests of the Bliss family are humiliated in a game of charades and leave the next morning with an extract from the grotesque melodrama in which Judith made her farewell as an actress. He tacked on a grinning finale of 'Tea for Two', a song that bubbles away under the action, or rather, non-action. He added thunderclaps and lightning, and instead of the familiar cosy cottage on the Thames at Cookham, we were plunged into a grim Gothic hallway. Taking as a cue the remark that the Bliss family are all artificial to the point of lunacy, Donnellan presented a freak show not unlike the Addams Family. Interestingly, one reviewer hailed this similarity as a delightful plus, another used it as a stick to beat the production over the head. Judith Bliss and her husband, the philandering novelist, were clearly big drinkers, not joined at the hip, but the hip flask. There were dark tensions between father and son, while daughter Sorel appeared to have taken up man-eating as a dietary precaution against anorexia.

Some thought the play could not stand this level of psychological intensity; others, that the approach highlighted the innate essential flippancy. Either way, the play would survive on the page. And surely this was as good a way as any to test the critical axiom that Coward's plays might mean little beyond his native shores. You could imagine Donnellan's production winning prizes at foreign theatre festivals. Had he trangressed the spirit of the play to access its meaning? Even the first production in 1925 was criticised for presenting the outsiders as more grotesquely eccentric than their hosts. I think the same was broadly true of the National's 1964 version. Declan Donnellan's production categorically and outrageously reasserted the Bliss family as the real weirdos, which is surely the basis on which the comedy of humiliation and expulsion crucially depends.

Finally, two anecdotes. The first touches on the musical rhythm of Coward's phrasing and the importance of getting the lines, if not necessarily the inflections, absolutely right. In the first production I saw of *Hay Fever*, that famous one at the National in 1964, very much part of Dad's Renaissance, as Coward called this period of rehabilitation, Dame Edith Evans played Judith Bliss. She was far too old for the part, almost eighty, and very insecure with her lines. She insisted on saying in rehearsals, apropos of the cottage's Thames-side situation, 'On a very clear day you can see Marlow.' This drove Coward to distraction until, past breaking point, he yelled from the back of the stalls, 'Edith, dear, the line is "On a clear day you can see Marlow". On a *very* clear day you can see Marlowe and Beaumont and Fletcher.'[6]

And the other, one I hold dear to my heart, is a classic encounter between critic and artist that I often feel should be taken as a model of etiquette between the factions of those who do and those who comment. In 1959, Kenneth Tynan was in New York, writing reviews for the *New Yorker*. After the curtains went up on Broadway, and before they came down later, he popped into Sardi's, the theatrical restaurant, for a bite to eat. That very day, his column had carried a scathing review of Coward's disastrous adaptation of Feydeau, *Look After Lulu*. As he perused the menu, he noted with horror that Coward, also alone, had entered the virtually empty restaurant and sat down at another table. Tynan himself takes up the story: 'I knew him too well to ignore his presence, and not well enough to pass the whole thing off with a genial quip. No sooner had he taken his seat than he spotted me. He rose at once and came padding across the room to the table behind which I was cringing. With eyebrows quizzically arched and upper lip raised to unveil his teeth, he leaned towards me. "Mr T," he said crisply, "you are a cunt. Come and have dinner with me."'[7] The couple proceeded to have a merry time discussing everything under the sun except Tynan's lousy review.

That's what I call real style.

NOTES:

1. Coward's Preface to *Design for Living*, quoted in Noël Coward, *Plays:Three* (London: Methuen, 1979), p.xii.
2. Coward's Preface to *Sweet and Twenties* by Beverley Nichols (London: Methuen, 1957), quoted in Noël Coward, *Plays: Six* (London, 1999), p.ix.
3. Terry Castle, *Noël Coward & Radclyffe Hall* (New York: Columbia University Press, 1996), passim.
4. Cyril Connolly's review of *Present Indicative* quoted in Cole Lesley, Graham Payn and Sheridan Morley, *Noël Coward and his Friends* (London: Weidenfeld & Nicolson, 1979), p.127.
5. Kenneth Tynan, *The Sound of Two Hands Clapping* (London: Jonathan Cape, 1975), p.60.
6. Tynan, ibid., p.61–2.
7. Tynan, ibid., p.58.

PART TWO
Practitioners on Coward

1   Round Table

The following comments are excerpted from two round-table sessions, 'Directors on Coward' and 'Performers on Coward', hosted as part of the University of Birmingham's Noël Coward Centenary Conference (1 and 2 November 1999). The editors are grateful to all participants and to session co-ordinators Steve Nallon and Dr Russell Jackson.

PHILIP FRANKS
Director
Private Lives, Royal National Theatre, 1999

It's very difficult to know who Coward actually was and you don't get any sense, I think, by listening to recordings of him. Nothing dates so quickly as theatrical styles. To hear that very clipped tone and the strangulated voice or to look at the slicked-back hair, the cigarette holder and the elegant dressing gown, is not to look at Coward at all. It's to look at a construct of Coward.

. . .

I found a useful way into *Private Lives* in something Philip Hoare said on a television documentary. He showed us a bronze of Coward's head and said, 'Look at the strain around the eyes – and he was only thirty.' *That*, I thought, was very interesting. Underneath the polished surface it was possible to get a sensation of deep strain. So I thought maybe it's not a question of looking at 'cocktails and laughter', maybe it's a matter of looking at what came 'before' and 'after', and addressing *Private Lives* as a text like any other. If you go to it with some half-baked notion of 'Coward style', or what Coward would have wanted, you're on the same dubious ground as the current cult of Jane Austen, reducing all those witty, insightful, passionate and troubled books to the pattern of English Heritage. So you have to put the caricature to one side and ask what Coward was actually writing about. In the case of *Private Lives* I think he was, appropriately for his time, writing about creatures dancing on the edge of a volcano, as someone once said of the characters in Waugh's *Vile Bodies*. I looked at a lot of stuff from the middle to late Twenties and fed it through to my cast. One particular doorway in was Fitzgerald's *Tender Is the Night*. From out at sea, on the beach, Fitzgerald's characters are the most beautiful, witty, sexy, gorgeous creatures you ever saw in your life. When you get up close, one's an alcoholic, the other's a victim of child abuse and both will be insane in five years' time. That seemed to me to be pretty much what was going to happen to Elyot and Amanda.

. . .

Refinement is a funny word to use in connection with *Private Lives*. One review of the first production described the play as a bucket of stable manure thrown in the audience's face. Clearly they didn't think it was refined then.

. . .

You ignore Victor's and Sybil's attractiveness and sexuality at your peril. I've seen productions in which Victor has been what Amanda accuses him of being, a fat old gentleman in a club armchair. This ignores the fact that what she's doing is looking ahead and saying that he will *become* a fat old gentleman in a club armchair. What she's married, considering what we know of her sexual appetite, is a hunky dish. Coward's Victor, remember, was Laurence Olivier, the most attractive actor of his generation.

. . .

The idea of 'rescuing Coward from Coward' is fraught with the pitfalls of vanity and arrogance. Coward was an extremely good writer, and wonderful theatrical technician and tactician. Listen to him. He knew what he was doing. We tried lots of different ways of staging the tea party at the end of *Private Lives*. Eventually you have to pass the sugar when he says 'pass the sugar'. You have to pour the milk when he says 'pour the milk'. But just because you observe his scaffolding doesn't mean that you have to be imprisoned by it. On the contrary, it can make you freer. What any director, or actor, has to get away from is impersonating an impersonation. But in terms of stagecraft, where the furniture is, where the doors are, he knows. And if you try to shunt it around you'll find it feels wrong.

. . .

Coward's best plays are terrifically good and insightful, and their psychology is complex. What they have to say about the vagaries and pains of the human heart are universal, and not fixed in brilliantine and a dressing gown . . . His songs are more artefacts of the period. They seem, to me, to be stuck more firmly in the past.

CORIN REDGRAVE
Actor
Sir Hugo Latymer in *Song at Twilight*, directed by Sheridan Morley. The King's Head, with Nyree Dawn Porter, 1998; the Gielgud, with Vanessa Redgrave, 1999

What I think is interesting about *Song at Twilight* is that it's Coward's last play, certainly his last full-length play. And, as far as I'm aware, he knew that it would be. That is unusual. Here, Coward takes the opportunity to put a full stop or line after his work, saying, in effect, 'Take it, or leave it. That's all I have to say.' To a large extent, it's his dramatic last will and testament. Coward, it seems to me, is also fighting a kind of tiredness, which sometimes surfaces in the lines. But I think that he transcends it. It is the tiredness of a man writing his last play and having something he very much wants to say.

. . .

The play gains from being seen at a distance. When it was first performed in 1966, the year before the Sexual Offences Act was passed, it was treated rather solemnly as what used to be called a 'problem play'. Yet *Song at Twilight* isn't about the actual repression of gay men under laws which criminalised their behaviour. Hugo Latymer, like Coward himself, is at one remove from the men who were regularly harassed on that account. But there's an internal oppression, a form of self-censorship operating here – the kind of thing that caused Coward to burst into tears when listening to Gore Vidal speak openly as a gay man on a television talk show. It makes Hugo wonder how honest a writer he has been, and how honest a man, and what he *might* have been in *other* circumstances. These are enormously powerful issues and they transcend the question of what was legal then or now. The play goes much deeper than that.

. . .

Song at Twilight is the first Coward play in which I've performed. So I can only share my experiences of that piece. I did find it helpful to research the context of the play and Coward's state of mind when he wrote it. Sheridan, Kika [Markham, who played Hilda] and I went to the hotel in Switzerland where the play is set. We had very expensive drinks on the shores of Lake Lausanne and watched a woman of a certain age – clearly over fifty – chain-smoking menthol cigarettes and feeding crumbs from a biscuit to a tiny dog. It was an almost Chekhovian image. We also lunched with Graham Payn, Coward's long-term companion. All this helped enormously. So did my research on Somerset Maugham who served in part as Coward's model for Sir Hugo. I don't know that this approach would work for the comedies . . . The other thing I found out about performing Coward, and this I think would be applicable to his other plays, is that it's very important to speak the text with as much accuracy as one can manage. You need to get it right word for word. If you misplace a single syllable it won't work. I'll give you one example. When Carlotta tells Hugo that she has written her memoirs, she says: 'I too have written an autobiography.' For three or four performances

Vanessa slipped into saying 'I too have written *my* autobiography'. You wouldn't think it would make a difference. It's
the kind of thing actors do all the time. But it did and we stopped
getting laughs on the line. As soon as we restored Coward's word
the laughs returned. You have to be very, very accurate.

. . .

You ask if it made a difference playing Sir Hugo opposite two very
different Carlottas. The answer is yes. Nyree's reading was very
gentle, very soft. Vanessa's was more forceful, more what Hilda
has in mind when she says 'you have a very forceful personality'.
And that does change the balance. As far as Hugo was concerned
it meant a considerable alteration. I'm not sure how much of this
was visible to the audience, or needed to be. But Nyree's Carlotta
brought out an urge, a vindictive pleasure on Hugo's part to
stomp on her vulnerability. With Vanessa I had to adopt very
different tactics, playing from the baseline rather than coming up
to the net and smashing each return as hard as I could . . . But
don't forget that it's not just a question of different actresses. At
the King's Head we used a shorter version cut by Coward himself.
It's very skilfully cut, an object lesson, in fact, in how to cut a
play. But it reduces the piece to melodrama. In the full-length
version there is more room to develop the characters.

CHRISTOPHER NEWTON
Artistic Director, Shaw Festival, Canada
Director
Easy Virtue 1999

What attracted me to *Easy Virtue* was the play's ambiguity. The
plot's very simple. It takes place in a country house in the home
counties between the wars. The son goes off to the South of
France and marries an older divorcee. He brings her back home
and she doesn't fit. She simply doesn't fit. The difficulty is that she
is deeply in love with him. It presents audiences with an obvious

(and a not so obvious) clash of values; those of an older Edwardian world with those of a sophisticated, worldly kept woman – an anticipation in some ways of Mrs Simpson or Jackie Onassis. When I started rehearsals at the Shaw Festival my cast didn't know what to make of it. The only way to begin was by asking them to forget about Coward and treat it like Ibsen – extremely seriously, because the characters feel deeply. The difficulty of approaching much Coward is that he moves very quickly from being serious to being funny and you have to speed up your thinking accordingly. His characters think in quarter-seconds. And if the characters think in quarter-seconds the actors must think even faster. Actors must also like the characters and this comes not from attempting imitations of Coward himself, but from trying to understand why characters behave as they do.

. . .

You don't quote Coward the way you quote Wilde, or Shaw. He's not a particularly witty writer. The funniest lines in Coward are things like 'this haddock's disgusting' and 'very flat, Norfolk'. And they're not funny unless you know the context. However different they may be from us, Coward gives us real people, in real situations. Their problems are different from ours – as are Richard III's – but a director's and an actor's job is to bring them to life within their world. Once you do this you realise that there's a kind of continuum and the past is now.

. . .

I directed *Cavalcade* at the Shaw Festival in 1985. I think it was the play's first professional revival, although we did it with a cast of forty-four rather than four hundred. David Edgar, I know, has commented upon some crucial weaknesses in Coward's history plays. Yet we need to recognise the very different lines upon which they're built. It's important, for example, to remember that the most moving and effective scenes in *Cavalcade* have no words at all. There is an extended episode in the middle of the piece in which people in mourning dress walk about in a park after the death of Queen Victoria. The Marryot family meets another

family, they greet one another and pass on. It's an extraordinary
five minutes of people just moving on stage, and can reduce an
audience to tears. Coward is a complex and complicated writer,
and we need to begin by acknowledging that he knew the theatre
backwards and forwards, and understood how it worked from
moment to moment much better than someone like Shaw.

. . .

We listen to the old Coward recordings in Canada, but we hear
them differently. And are less influenced by them. We're
fortunate in that respect. We Canadians are a bit of the old
Empire, but we left early on. Besides we're not English, we're
Scots – as the Australians are Irish – Scots and French. Coward is
very popular in Canada, but we approach him by a different route.

. . .

We don't know how Coward will be done in twenty years' time.
But we do know that in twenty years we'll all be twenty years
further away from the details. Coward's a naturalistic writer and
the details are important. So how will we do Coward as they begin
to slip away? Well, how do we do Strindberg? Or Ibsen? Or Shaw?
At the outset we will need to do more homework. In directing a
recent production of *Lady Windermere's Fan* I realised that I didn't
know where women kept their dance cards – hanging from their
wrists? Tucked into their gloves? When the play was first done this
was the sort of thing everyone knew. And a correctly or
incorrectly worn dance card could tell worlds about its wearer.
The same thing will happen with Coward. But as the period
becomes less readable, as it retreats into the mist, Coward's
characters and situations have the potential to stand out all the
more clearly. In the end it doesn't matter how well documented a
period is if audiences don't know it. You can have the beauty spots
in all the right places and the correct kind of boots. It's good for
the actors, but it doesn't help audiences. They go for the people.

MALCOLM SINCLAIR
Actor
Richard Greatham in *Hay Fever*, directed by Declan Donnellan.
Savoy, 1999

Some twenty years ago I played Simon in *Hay Fever* here in
Birmingham. I thought I was rather good. But after one
performance when I went round to have my head patted, Harold
Innocent, an actor some of you will remember, took me to one
side and said, 'You know, you don't play Coward by imitating
him.' Which was, unfortunately, exactly what I had been doing.

. . .

Coward is not an epigrammatic playwright. In *Hay Fever*, which
I think is his funniest play, there are no epigrams at all. It's all in
the rhythm, the music. You need, above all, to get the rhythm of
the lines right. As Richard, in Declan's production of *Hay Fever*,
one of my funniest lines was 'Russia used to be a wonderful
country before the War'. If I stumbled ever so slightly there was
no way I could recover. On the other hand, all I had to do was say
the line – winking, smirking, anything like that would have taken
away from it. The rhythm, the music is absolutely crucial . . . A
lot of younger actors, trained for television, slide into a part by
muddying the edges, by injecting 'ers' or 'wells' or 'yeahs' before
they say a line, or beginning with a shrug or a raised eyebrow.
They're tools, I know, for getting into a role. But in Coward they
don't work. Clarity and precision are everything.

. . .

Declan's *Hay Fever* was tremendously controversial. It divided
audiences, critics and some of the cast. It didn't, however, make
much of a difference for my character. Richard Greatham is
quietly appalled by everything that happens to him at the Bliss
household. So no matter what 'outrages' we put on stage I could
be honestly thunderstruck. If we had bananas for tea, I could, in
character, play it as 'Oh, yes, we're having bananas for tea'. . . .
Richard also has no sense of humour. This can be terribly funny.

But you must play it straight. You can't wink at the audience, saying 'I'm a bit stupid, aren't I?' The whole thing has to be played absolutely straight . . . For the final scene Declan gave me the wonderful idea of playing Richard with a sort of smile plastered across his face, just as everything was crashing down around him . . . If you're in a farce and don't get laughs, you're left with egg on your face. If you play *Hay Fever* without laughs – well, it wouldn't be good, but you shouldn't feel exposed or vulnerable. You should be able to play it absolutely, completely truthfully.

. . .

What I found interesting about *Song at Twilight* – and, I suppose, this is true of Declan's *Hay Fever* as well – was the way it wrong-footed audiences, threw them off balance. Presenting them not with the expected two hours of delightful, inconsequential conversation, but something often darker about topics that matter enormously. We don't usually think of Coward that way. Though I suspect that when the whole cannon is performed, as it will be over time, it won't be such a surprise. It certainly isn't with Wilde. In a play like *Lady Windermere*, Wilde lets us know, often portentously, when the solemn bits are about to arrive. You don't have that with Coward. An audience stumbles unprepared into the Goodwyn Sands of serious drama. It's quite wonderful.

SUE WILSON
Producer
Tonight at 8.30, BBC Radio 4, 1999

Mine was a different task. I was looking for a way we could celebrate Coward on radio. Because we couldn't possibly do all his plays – even in the Centenary – I decided to look at *Tonight at 8.30*. It's a wonderful cross-section of Coward's work, reaching from the theatricality of *Red Peppers*, to the sophistication of *Hands Across the Sea*, to the reflection of Coward's working-class origins in pieces like *Fumed Oak*. I wasn't trying to 'rescue

Coward from Coward', or in any way debunk his style. While I absolutely agree with what's been said about not wanting an imitation I did want to look at when the plays were written and the society Coward was writing about. I wanted to do justice to that. The other thing that influenced me and my partner Malcolm McKee – who actually 'radiofied' the plays – was the fact that *Tonight at 8.30* had been conceived by Coward as a vehicle for himself and Gertrude Lawrence. Coward wanted to create fresh challenges for them both within the context of a repertory company. We didn't use two actors for all the main parts, but we did create a functioning company for the project. We never tried to reproduce the Coward–Lawrence recordings, but we were influenced by the period and its affectations. For me there would be no point in doing Coward if I was trying to 'de-Cowardise' him. What I set out to do was to locate the truth and joy in these plays, and to recreate Coward's wonderful artificiality. I also find a curious foreboding in Coward's work, a realisation of how abruptly the periods he embodied would come to an end. I tried to impart this as well.

. . .

It was our intention at the outset to have the plays broadcast together. Unfortunately such decisions are not always in the hands of those who make radio drama. I would defend, however, our decision to use different principals in each work and to experiment with Coward's ordering of pieces. Indeed, Coward himself played around with the sequence. And he was overtaken by events. *Family Album*, which has a funeral setting, was pulled after the death of George V made it seem inappropriate as entertainment. Coward also had second thoughts about the stage-worthiness of *Star Chamber*, which looked better on paper than on the stage. As for casting – well, I didn't have Noël and Gertie. And the best actors available for a play like *Still Life* weren't necessarily the best for *Fumed Oak* or *Shadow Play*. *Tonight at 8.30* embraces an impressive range of styles. Noël and Gertie, of course, had the advantage of having had each of the plays written to show them – and the peculiar chemistry of their partnership – to best advantage. I'm not sure that using two actors for the sake of doing so is the best way to serve the plays today.

. . .

The plays work very differently on radio where, of course, you have only the voice. *Hands Across the Sea*, which is in many ways the most straightforward of the lot, was extremely difficult to do. Much of the time is occupied with Piggy Gilpin on the telephone, and we weren't able to take on board the reactions of other characters in the room to create Coward's complex cross-cutting of conversation. On the other hand *Shadow Play*, the most experimental of the pieces, might almost have been written for radio. Using different acoustics to travel in space and time enabled us to do a lot that Coward couldn't do in the theatre of his day. Its absolute artificiality contrasted nicely with the gritty realism we used for plays like *Fumed Oak*.

. . .

What we wanted to do was to revisit the plays in the same way that we revisit Restoration comedy. We wanted to look at them and their period from the perspective of our own time. The excitement lay in uncovering it all and peeling the layers away. Although we were in a recording studio we still had to learn the lines and build the sets. Take *Red Peppers*, for example. There's no way you can tap-dance and hold a script at the same time. In the end we had to know as much about Coward's sets as Philip or Christopher.

2   Interviews

JUDY CAMPBELL
Actress
created roles of Joanna Lyppiatt in *Present Laughter*
and Ethel Gibbons in *This Happy Breed*
played opposite Coward in *Blithe Spirit*
talking to Maggie Gale, 16 March 2000

Q.   When did you first work with Noël Coward?
A.   I joined Noël in 1942, playing opposite him in his two new plays, *Present Laughter*, in which I played a glamorous bitch in a Molyneux dress, and *This Happy Breed*, a homely tale of the Gibbons family settling back into Clapham between the wars. Noël was Frank Gibbons; I played Ethel his wife and Joyce Carey played his whining sister. In *Present Laughter* Joyce played Noël's wife – wise, witty, a perfect companion, and this was the role she played in real life. *Present Laughter* was very autobiographical; it's a day in the life of Noël Coward ... Both plays were to go into the Haymarket for three months, but this would be preceded by a seven-month tour the length and breadth of the British Isles. Noël thought that if the provinces could no longer come to the West End, then the West End must go to the provinces. For the tour we added *Blithe Spirit* – in case we got bored with only two plays to do. Noël played Charles Condomine, Joyce his wife Ruth, and I Elvira, the one who died young and comes back to haunt Charles. We had a read-through of all three works and were asked to learn them before rehearsals started. This is not very popular with a lot of actors. It's much better to have a script in your hands and make notes about the moves. But on this occasion we only had one week to rehearse each play and then a

week of dress rehearsals. After this, Noël always asked his cast to learn their lines before rehearsals began.

Q.   *Blithe Spirit* was already playing in the West End, wasn't it?

A.   Yes. It had been playing for some time, which is why we decided to do it first. We'd all seen it, and the moves and make-up had already been set. In fact, I went round to Kay Hammond, the first Elvira, to learn about the ghost make-up. She had created it herself, melting sticks of greasepaint over a candle and mixing them together. It was green but went grey over pink skin.

Q.   What was Coward like as a director?

A.   Well, to begin with he was director, actor and author – so you didn't get into the predicament you often get into with a new play when someone says, 'Do you think we could alter this? Or cut that?' And the director says, 'I'll have to call the author.' With Noël on the spot we could change things at will.

Q.   How amenable was he to suggestions from the actors?

A.   Very. He paid us the compliment of thinking we were bright enough to contribute and to pick things up fast – we had all been in weekly rep. For group scenes – four or more people on stage together – he would begin by mapping out moves to save time. But in two-handers we could do as we pleased and see what happened. This was the way Noël and I rehearsed our long seduction scene in *Present Laughter*.

Q.   Was this true of the text as well?

A.   No. He wanted the text to be absolutely as written. He wrote wonderful dialogue, and you wreck it if you start mucking it about ... Later on, rehearsing *Relative Values*, he got into tremendous rows with Gladys Cooper about not being line perfect.

Q.   *This Happy Breed* is set in working-class south London, *Present Laughter* amid society debutantes, *Blithe Spirit* in the country. Did you find it difficult moving between three such different worlds?

A.   We all had nightmares that we would come on in the wrong costume – that I would come on in my pinny and little brown skirt and my hair done up at the back for Ethel and find Noël elegantly playing the piano and singing ... On the long train journey up to Scotland we used to play a game, going through our lines from one play and seeing if we could find cues to jump to the next. It was a dangerous idea.

Q.   Did you find the roles equally challenging?

A.   They're very different. I remember shaking like a leaf before the London opening of *Present Laughter*. It's much more nerve-racking playing high comedy than something like *This Happy Breed*. Not that you can afford to be slow with that play, but you can relax into it. It's an altogether cosier piece. Noël and I talked about this at the time. *This Happy Breed* was far easier to play.

Q.   I know that Coward was very precise about the look of his productions. What kind of a veto did he exercise over design or costume?

A.   Edward Molyneux, the couturier, designed the high-fashion clothes for our plays. He had made a lovely grey chiffon dress for Kay Hammond in *Blithe Spirit*, and he made gowns for both Joyce and myself in that play and in *Present Laughter*. For *Present Laughter* he made me a glorious dress with a cloak of scarlet satin. The cloak was pre-war material and he told me that he'd been saving it for something really special. When I wore it at the costume parade before the dress rehearsal Noël said, 'I refuse to play opposite a scarlet bathing tent.' Cecil Beaton was there and said he liked it. But Noël wouldn't let me wear it. Apparently it went orange under the stage lights. So in the end I had to wear a chinchilla cloak Gladys Calthrop found for me ... Noël didn't like my hair either. For *Present Laughter* I had long hair with an extra bit added on to make it longer. Noël called it bedroom hair. Again, Cecil stuck up for me. This time Noël reluctantly agreed. But whenever I lay back on the sofa with my hair over the back he'd lean on it with his arm so I couldn't move. And I had to play it like that.

Q.   Was he being difficult?

A.   He was keeping us on our toes. We were doing a different play each night, but even so actors can go on auto-pilot – you know, saying your lines but thinking about a telephone call you have to make. It's something that happens in a long run. So to keep us up to the mark Noël would, for example, refuse to interrupt us on broken sentences. In *This Happy Breed* I had a line about a taxi coming – something like 'Why isn't he here? Why is he late?' Noël was supposed to come in with 'Don't fuss, Ethel', but he didn't. And I was left stranded – 'Can't think where that taxi's got to. It didn't have far to come. I should have thought Fred could have gone and got it' – until he decided to let me off the hook. But he never did anything to interrupt the rhythms of a scene, or obscure a cue line, or detract from another actor's performance. He was far too professional for that.

Q.   Was there a secret to working with him?

A.   I think the secret to working with him was that he con-tinually set you challenges. Not enormous challenges – things like making cuts as he went along and expecting you to pick them up, or altering a move, flinging himself on the floor instead of into the corner of the sofa. He expected you to adapt. If you did, full marks. And, yes, he would adapt to you as well . . . All this was done in actual performance. When you got off stage he'd just say, 'I think that was rather good, you sitting down before you lit the cigarette. Keep it in' or, 'That was a mistake, we won't do it again.'

Q.   Did you ever disagree?

A.   He only once took me to task. When Cecil Beaton was taking his photographs of *Blithe Spirit* he posed one with a number of stagehands holding me up. They were all covered with a black velvet cloth and choking to death, poor things. I was flying like a bird. Cecil liked all the flowing chiffon and ghostly presences. This clearly went to my head and I began 'floating' a bit in performance. One night, as we sat in the wings, Noël said to me, 'I know that you're a very tall girl and so you studied to be graceful.' I took it the wrong way. I said, 'Studied to be graceful? I don't know what you're talking about. If I move gracefully it's because it comes to me instinctively. That's the way I move.' 'Well,' he replied, 'I think you should stop it and move like an ordinary person. It's much funnier. And when you're in a rage, stamp about as if you were wearing gumboots, but looking like a ghost. It's funnier if you're in a temper.' 'Oh, very well,' I said rather miffed. The cue came, we went on to the stage and I tripped over the doormat and fell over. Noël, I remember, leaned

on the piano and went 'Tee-hee-hee'! Well, I struggled to my feet
and stamped about, very cross. And, of course, he was right, it was
much funnier.

Q.   Did he have strong feelings about how actors prepare for
performance?

A.   He believed that actors should be free to find their own way
to a role. Anything was acceptable as long as it worked. Noël
didn't have much patience with method acting, which he
thought was pretentious. But if it helped an actor to a better
performance, fine. I do remember, though, Noël using up his
precious Chanel No. 5 – it was very scarce during the war – when
playing the working-class Frank Gibbons in *This Happy Breed*.
His point was that he wasn't a slave to 'the method'. That his
acting was just that – acting.

Q.   You knew many of the principal women in Coward's life,
including Joyce Carey, Gladys Calthrop, Clemence Dane and
Lorne Lorraine. How central was their contribution to his work?

A.   Very. Gladys, for example, was more than a designer. She
was his mentor, friend, companion, fought his battles with him,
everything. When I knew him she was very much present. If
something was wrong with the set, she'd be there, rebuilding the
fireplace or something half an hour before the curtain went up.
She did the costumes as well, except for the designer gowns, and
was particularly good on period clothes. But she made me rather
nervous. She was cool. Cool in the present sense and cool in the
accepted sense. You didn't flurry her. I remember her driving, her
hands on the steering wheel in the correct position, but relaxed
and beautiful with a very big ring. Gladys was there at *The Vortex*,
at the beginning. It was the play that put Noël on the map and
she was very much part of it. She wasn't afraid to disagree with
him. Joyce was there from the beginning as well. She was sixteen
when her mother, Lilian Braithwaite, played Florence in *The
Vortex*. Both Gladys and Joyce were involved in practically
everything Noël did. Joyce didn't always perform – she was a
writer as well – but she was always around.

Clemence Dane was an astonishing woman: large of stature in
every way, she wore long, flowing garments Victor Stiebel

designed for her and she would float down to the Ivy like a galleon in full sail. Multi-talented – playwright (most famously for A *Bill of Divorcement*, the film that brought early success to Katharine Hepburn) – poet, artist – her painting of Noël is in the National Portrait Gallery. It was at a party in her Covent Garden flat that I first heard Noël playing songs later to become famous. She was a tremendous enthusiast. I remember being swept off to a picnic in the park with Noël and Joycie, sitting on the grass eating sausage rolls and Winifred (her real name) saying, 'What a pity we're not in the country, I could have made baked hedgehogs.' (Noël said thank God we're not!) And I can see her now, sitting on the floor with the tortoiseshell combs tumbling out of her hair telling us about a ballet she had seen. Noël called her Winnie, teased her and loved her. She was the role model for Madame Arcati.

Q.   Why do you think Coward surrounded himself with such individual, strong-willed women?

A.   It's a very good kind of relationship for a gay man. Sex doesn't get in the way. You don't get involved in predictable emotional entanglements. For the woman you have a male to go around with. And if he looks at other men, it's all right because you look at them too. It's lovely. A gay man can admire your clothes without wanting to take them off.

Q.   Have you had a chance to see any of the centenary revivals of Coward's plays?

A.   I very much liked *Song at Twilight*. I thought that was wonderful. But I'm never quite sure how I feel about revivals. It's certainly a mistake to try to do the plays as they were done when they were first performed. Perhaps you shouldn't do them unless you have something new to say, something that can be said now but couldn't be said sixty or seventy years ago. The one that immediately springs to mind is *Design for Living*. Noël wrote it about two men in love with one another and with a woman who loves them both. But it couldn't be played like that at the time. Everything had to be implied, not spoken. It's much more fun if they can be openly bisexual. And it changes the ending when all three end up on the sofa together roaring with laughter at the starchy, prudish Ernest.

Q.   You've worked with Coward's texts as both an actress and director. Do you feel that there is a preferred or 'authentic' way of performing Coward? And if so, how far can one stray from it without destroying Coward's work?

A.   I think that there's an identifiable Coward music, an inescapable rhythm. Most of the plays are rooted in period, but not in a society that was ever real. Therefore you do have considerable leeway. I never feel that there are all that many givens, except for that essential music. You can't bugger that up.

Q.   One of the panellists at the Coward Conference spoke about the need 'to rescue Coward from Coward,' to prevent the plays from becoming museum pieces, or crude imitations of Coward himself. Do you think that this is a danger?

A.   Yes. But there's a tremendous 'gutsiness' in Coward's work that can be easy to miss. Coward wrote for actors he knew and he relied upon them to take care of this side of things. Sometimes we think that he's taken care of it all, but he hasn't. It's up to us to warm up his characters from underneath, to root them and make them real. And this has to do with our own period, our own time. This is our chance at modernity. I don't think that there's any point in doing the plays if there isn't some connection made between who we are now and who they were then. It's the jokes and rhythms that look after themselves in Coward, nothing else . . . When I was playing Elvira at the National – the production [of *Blithe Spirit*] directed by Harold Pinter – I got a card from Judy Campbell, the only person to play the role opposite Coward. It said, 'Elvira's a ghost in gumboots.' It's a wonderful note, because, of course, if you flitter about being all ethereal you miss the whole point. Elvira is the most earthy and rooted of creatures. Every time anybody plays the role I pass on the advice. I feel I'm sort of in the line of succession.

Q. The point about 'gutsiness' is well taken. It's easy to forget that when Coward's plays were first reviewed it wasn't their elegance that was remarked upon but their coarseness and vulgarity.

A. Absolutely. It's nothing to do with whisking about a lot of props and cocktail glasses. It's to do with human behaviour seen through a prism of manners which Coward reinvents in each work. It's a terrific game to play, but it's different each time. I don't think I've ever acquired knowledge from one play that has been terribly useful in the next. I've always had to begin anew ... If there's a secret about acting in Coward that applies to more than one play it's that as an actor you have a sort of gun at your back, something the other characters don't know about. You possess a secret that gives you authority, something that informs you with both a sense of reserve and of specialness. To possess an unspoken secret is part of the skill of performing Coward. Beyond that it's a matter of questioning Coward's individual play worlds. Some of the questions one asks would be the same – what kind of behaviour gets rewarded in this play? What kind of behaviour gets punished? What do you have to do to get by in this society? – but the answers will be different for each play.

Q. Looking at some of this year's Coward revivals critics seemed to cite Ibsen, Strindberg and John Osborne as fellow dramatic travellers rather than the expected trinity of Congreve, Sheridan and Wilde. Do you feel that this has been helpful in placing Coward at the century's close?

A. Well it's certainly different. I'm not sure I agree with it. But I can see the Strindberg, I can see *Dance of Death* in *Private Lives* ... And I loved the way that Simon and Sorel were played in Declan Donnellan's *Hay Fever* – absolutely modern. The initial impulse is to do something phoney, a kind of imitation poshness. That never works ... I wish younger directors would take more liberties. Just because there are certain rules doesn't mean that they can't be broken. I found Declan's *Hay Fever* maddening in some ways but thrilling in others. And he got some very special performances.

Q.   What was it that drew you to *Easy Virtue* for your centenary production?

A.   To begin with, I thought that it would be interesting to direct a Coward that's hardly ever done. I reread it just about the time that Princess Diana was killed and the notion of someone just not fitting in seemed particularly poignant. I did it first for radio, then for a gala in New York. People seemed hypnotised by it. I thought, good heavens, this old warhorse has still got something going for it.

Q.   When you directed it at the Chichester Festival with Greta Scacchi as Larita critics accused you of baiting the Chichester audience – casting a black actor in the role of Charles Burleigh and introducing a wild jazz dance in the party scene at the play's close. Audiences, apparently, gasped at both.

A.   My production deliberately fastened on to the African aspect of the Twenties. It was a conscious attempt to replace a shopworn 'flapper' image. Casting Evroy Deer as Charles was not at all out of period. It went hand-in-glove with a specific jazz age view of Larita's world – and a Larita modelled upon someone like Nancy Cunard . . . We also did an enormous amount of research, which some people might think ridiculous for a Coward play. I had the entire cast read through *The Lady* for 1923 and 1924. Etiquette books were studied. Even the extras for the dance scene watched videos about the period so that the background conversation at the Whittakers' party was about the right kind of things. We also needed to sort out the rules that divided public from private morality and establish attitudes towards things that are only hinted at in Coward's text, such as the truth behind Marion's failed engagement . . . All this contributes to the texture of a production and prevents things from becoming tiresomely second-hand.

Q.   So it wasn't your intention to provoke middle-class spectators?

A.   I think that the play itself does that. I find *Easy Virtue* quite an angry work. This is not a case of Coward [in John Lahr's phrase] 'gumming the hand that feeds him'. He's biting with a young man's viciousness. The Whittaker household, Coward's principal target, is the upper-middle class at its most bourgeois. Larita and Charles may be shut out of that society – and in Charles, Coward may be offering us a coded version of his own predicament of being gay and lower-middle class. But there's nothing glittering or glamorous about the Whittakers and their circle, nothing here that Coward lusts after.

Q.   Are Coward's targets too easy?

A.   Yes, I think perhaps they are, although at Chichester I did hear people commiserating with Wendy Craig [as Mrs Whittaker]. On stage it can be a fairer fight than it looks on paper ... Also things are complicated by the figure of Colonel Whittaker. After serving as Larita's ally through the piece he mysteriously disappears at the close. Instead there's a curious exchange just before Larita leaves in which Furber, the butler, agrees to do what she asks. Larita and Furber have not spoken a word to one another up to this point. He says 'Yes, ma'm' and it's the end of the play. What has she asked? There is absolutely no explanation. Furber has a good relationship with the Colonel. Is he a go-between? Is the Colonel the chauffeur driving Larita's car? Will he get in and make his escape with her? At Chichester I tried at least to raise the issue, to make clear that Larita's line was about the Colonel. . . . It's a very interesting and unexpected ending.

Q.   *Easy Virtue* dates from the same period in Coward's career as *The Vortex*, a play you and Philip Prowse rediscovered in a very impressive production in Glasgow and London a few years back. Did your playing of Florence Lancaster in any way inform your direction of *Easy Virtue*?

A.   Not really. They're very different works. *The Vortex* still has the power to shock. And what's daring there is Coward's willingness to pit three kinds of unpleasantness against one another. There's really not a lot to be said for the weak husband or even for Helen, the fairly sensible family friend. And then there's Pawnie, a sort of piranha fish, and Nicky who in his own way is equally unattractive. It's a gamble to do and curiously

modern. But again, catching the Coward music is essential . . .
Philip made a brilliant distinction between the way the older and
younger characters talked. As Nicky, Rupert [Everett]'s accent
was much less posh than mine. Mine was squawked up to
kingdom come and we both worked at top speed.

Q.   I saw it in London and recall a particularly breathless last act
between mother and son played out on silk sheets beneath an
enormous overhead mirror.

A.   Rupert and I dreaded doing that scene at the outset. It's very
melodramatic. Philip took one look at Coward's text and said this
is too embarrassing – we can't let audiences hear it. So we simply
rolled over each other's lines, picked up cues in the middle of
speeches and went like trains on a ski jump of emotion. He
thrashed me about the room and we got through it in less than
fifteen minutes. Audiences were shocked, deeply shocked. The
curtain would come down each night on a really horrified silence
before people began to applaud. It was wonderful and turned out
to be the easiest part of the play.

Q.   Michael Coveney called your Florence Lancaster the
performance of a lifetime. Is it your preferred Coward role?

A.   That and Amanda. I'm lucky to have done the young ones
and the old ones. I don't think anybody else has had that chance.

Q.   Are you considering other Coward projects at the moment?

A.   I always think, gratefully, you know, thank you very much,
Noël – but this is the last one. And then something else comes
along. I am interested in doing *Semi-Monde* but Philip did a
wonderful, definitive production some years back. . . . I would like
to do a production of *Private Lives* with one extra man, presenting
the Elyot–Amanda couple as gay.

Q.   The Coward Estate has rejected similar proposals in the past –

A.   I think it would be a very interesting experiment. So much
of Coward's sexuality is coded in his psyche. I don't know how
consciously it appears in his writing, but it's there. And it crops
up in various ways, in Nicky's drug-taking, for example, or
Charles Burleigh's sudden proposal in *Easy Virtue*. A bisexual
Elyot seems a perfectly reasonable proposition. Eventually it will
be allowed.

PHILIP PROWSE
Director, Glasgow Citizens Theatre
Director and Designer, *Cavalcade*, 1999
talking to J. Kaplan and S. Stowell, 21 February 2000

Q. Your work on Coward over the past two decades has included some surprising choices, not only *Private Lives* and *Design for Living*, but *Semi-Monde*, *Sirocco*, *The Vortex* and now *Cavalcade*. What is it that has attracted you to these pieces?

A. Well, *Semi-Monde* was a world première. I knew that Max Reinhardt had wanted to do it, but never got round to it. And that intrigued me.

Q. More generally, what interests you about Coward?

A. Coward was writing to make a living and to be a huge success. It would have been unthinkable for him to be in the theatre without being a success. But he was also working his way up, finding out how to make his way in the world as a lower-middle-class homosexual from south London. I think that he was bound to have a double view of the world he inhabited. And it shows, particularly in his attitude towards the upper classes, which is partly critical and partly boot-licking.

Q. Does this appear in his writing?

A. Absolutely. It's what distinguishes Coward from his contemporaries. He always, or almost always, works on two levels – or at least two. If you're not directing one level, you can direct the other. Or if the actors are playing one, you can direct the other . . . *Cavalcade*, which we've just done, is a case in point. It's written as a celebration of the Empire and its aspirations. But, as I hoped we showed in our production, it can also be a critique of Englishness, and a condemnation of those same values and aspirations.

Q. Do you suppose Coward was aware of these alternative texts?

A. I don't know, perhaps he was. Perhaps he thought 'Oh well. They won't notice. I'll just leave it.' But they're very much there

and create a resonant subtext for his work . . . Maugham and
Lonsdale, by comparison, don't have this dimension.

Q.   Does updating Coward's work help to recover these 'other'
texts?

A.   Sometimes. *Design for Living* was updated and worked very
well. Today's audiences can empathise with the predicament of
Gilda, a woman used by two men who are really more interested
in one another. It was a play that Coward couldn't write openly
in his own day, but if you update it audiences can fill in the gaps.
Too much period fussiness, fiddling around with cocktails,
cigarette holders and the like, simply gets in the way. It can
prevent us from seeing the 'other' play . . . *The Vortex* is possibly
an exception. It has to be done in period. Actually, I did push it
forward slightly from the Twenties to the Thirties, because
Thirties fashions look better to modern eyes. But the shock value
of mothers with lovers and drug-taking sons is more effective in a
period setting. No one is really horrified by either nowadays.

Q.   Does a director have the same latitude with the delivery of
Coward's text?

A.   No. There's only one way to say each line and that's the way
Coward heard it when he wrote it – in his inner ear. Or the way
he'd have said it if he played the role. I don't think that there's
any room for manoeuvre here at all. There's an upper-middle-
class pre-war way of talking that has to be reproduced.

Q.   Is this as true of a history play like *Cavalcade* as it is of
Coward's comedies?

A.   Language and class are tremendously important in
Cavalcade. And they're particularly acute because the scenes are
so short. They're written very, very economically, almost too
economically. There's no time for explanation or discovery – you
come on, say your piece and you're off. Every speech, every
moment has to work.

Q.   Did you find it difficult making what is so obviously an
English play work in Glasgow?

A .   We made it work, I think, in quite a different way. For the
audiences who first saw the play at Drury Lane, *Cavalcade* was a
vast spectacle that supported their beliefs and way of life. I

remember that sort of patriotism very well. It was unquestioned. Jane Marryot's sacrifices, including the loss of her sons, would have been seen as an ennobling vindication of the Empire. I wasn't going to have any of that. It wouldn't have worked in Scotland in any event. The play's entirely English. Not a mention of anyone else. It's one reason why we delayed doing *Cavalcade* at the Citizens. It was only when I decided to strip it down, do away with the pageantry and focus on Coward's 'other' play that I saw how it might work.

Q. And what is Coward's 'other' *Cavalcade* about?

A. Waste and loss. That's what the play seems to be really about. The wretched Mrs Marryot at the end – there she is, celebrating the new year, her children are dead, her husband's decaying. And what's it all been for?

Q. What changes did you make?

A. I cut two wordless scenes. One consisted of walking about in mourning after the death of Queen Victoria, the other was a ball scene in which Robert Marryot gets his title. But they were pure spectacle. There were virtually no changes made to the text. Two or three lines were cut here and there, and we dropped some Edwardian brand names. No one today knows what a Worth gown or a Redfern gown is. If you leave in topical references like these you end up distracting your audience. People stop to puzzle things out and they miss something else. The play's too tightly written to chance this. But aside from a minor tweaking of the text from time to time nothing was altered. That's the point I was trying to make before. You can do Coward's 'other' plays without changing a thing. It all depends upon how you ask the actors to think about what they're doing and saying. Critics thought we must have dropped entire scenes. But we didn't. We simply stripped the play down, did away with the intervals, and got through it in one hour and twenty minutes.

Q. Some critics were particularly impressed by the sheer power of your final tableau – a juxtaposition of Fanny's cabaret-style delivery of Coward's 'Twentieth Century Blues' with a posed Victorian portrait of the Marryot family while a vast light board counted out the old century.

A.   For that final family portrait I brought back Joe Marryot as a ghost in his army uniform. That's not in Coward. When Joe touches his mother's shoulder at the close it's a gift for her. All she really has left. Fanny's singing of 'Twentieth Century Blues' was for the rest of us – moving us into a bleak future Coward didn't know at the time but we do. That's why we took the countdown to 1999. Perhaps Coward did suspect. He certainly knew that everything finishes, everything changes. There's a great sense of mortality, of doom, in his work, a feeling that we're all on the same ship going down together.

Q.   Was that why you decided to forgo the element of surprise in the *Titanic* episode. Coward's scene of two lovers on shipboard doesn't let us know it's the *Titanic* until the very close when a cloak is removed revealing the name on a lifebelt.

A.   We did talk about it and decided not to play the surprise. Anyhow, whom is it going to surprise nowadays? It worked, no doubt, in Coward's day. But he didn't have that movie to contend with.

Q.   There were tears in the audience the night we saw it.

A.   Good. There were meant to be. But not tears of pride.

Q.   Philip Hoare, reviewing for the *Times Literary Supplement*, concluded his notice by saying 'Philip Prowse has done a brilliant job of making us all feel very depressed indeed' – or words to that effect. Was that your intention?

A.   Absolutely.

Q.   Has a quarter-century of directing and designing Coward's work changed your attitude towards Coward as a playwright?

A.   I take him more seriously now than when I started. I think that I've really learned to respect his work. His writing is remarkably clear. He has specific objectives to achieve in each scene, each encounter and each piece of dialogue. If you achieve them it works, if you don't it doesn't. It's as simple as that. And there's only one way to do it. That's what I meant before when I said that there isn't much room for manoeuvre. Every successful production – well, it isn't one's own, it's Coward's.

Q.   So regardless of your take on a particular play, all good productions will arrive at the same point?

A.   Yes. I think Coward wrote to safeguard himself against exploitation or directorial innovation.

Q.   But doesn't this fly in the face of what you've said about new readings, or directing the 'other' Coward?

A.   Not really. You can't direct the 'other' play if it's not somehow already there. It's an odd position to take, I know. But it goes back to Coward working to earn a living in the commercial theatre. He had to have audiences and they had to be entertained. But he was better than that and he knew it. Which is why he wrote, perhaps even in spite of himself, these subtextual 'other' plays. They're there to be found.

Q.   Is Coward a great playwright?

A.   Yes. *Private Lives*, certainly, can stand alongside anything by Congreve, Wilde or Shaw. That's the one in which he struck absolute gold. It's shorter than Shakespeare and much funnier.

Q.   Are there Coward plays you would like to do in the near future?

A.   We've done it before, but I'd quite like to do *Blithe Spirit*. And I would love to do *This Happy Breed*. It's about Coward's early life, the world he left behind. There's a central bit in which a father talks to his son about values, British – English – values. Coward thought that the sentiments were right but the way that he'd written them was all wrong. That would be challenging.

JULIET STEVENSON
Actress
Amanda Prynne in Royal National Theatre's
production of *Private Lives*, 1999
talking to Russell Jackson, 3 March 2000

Q: What ideas did you have about Noël Coward before you started work on *Private Lives* at the National?

A: I'd never played Coward before and I had little interest in him. I was sure he was inventive and witty, but I'd been put off by associations with a certain class and with conventional forms of theatre that I wasn't very interested in.

Q: So what persuaded you to accept the part?

A: Well, as soon as I picked up the play and began to read it, I fell instantly in love with it really. My preconceptions fell away. I found it to be wonderfully witty, fresh, moving and complex. The dialogue seemed so vibrantly alive, just as resonant now as it ever was and when I began to speak it aloud, I discovered the rhythmic brilliance of it. In that first reading, I moved in about twelve minutes from being someone with no interest in Coward to being in a frenzy of excitement about doing it. I had been longing to do something really funny for some time, having felt periodically frustrated by labels like 'serious' and 'classical', so Amanda felt like a gift. The fact of her being such a bad girl appealed very much too.

Q: What do you make of Amanda's marriage, and the situation she's in at the start?

A: The first scene that she has in the play is the most difficult one by a long shot. She's only been married to Victor for a few hours but she already knows it's a disaster – she's trying to make it work but it just doesn't. Everything Victor does or says seems to compound this fear. So the challenge of that first scene between them is that the audience has to get to know you while you're sort of in disguise. She's trying hard to be Mrs Victor Prynne, but she's a size nine foot attempting to squeeze into a size three shoe, and you have to persuade the audience both of the possibility and impossibility of this marriage, simultaneously.

Q: What about the moment when you first see Elyot?

A: Well, I guess it is one of those moments of which there are quite a few in *Private Lives*, where you are under some pressure to meet high comedic expectations from the audience . . . They can be a little nerve-racking if you stop to think about them in that way. I think the clue is not to, but just to play the character's truth at that moment, shaped by a bit of careful timing. Amanda's truths are often pretty extreme, since she is highly reactive, impulsive and hungry for incident, so exploring them for all they are worth usually paid dividends. I did a shamelessly big double take on Elyot on first spotting him, which depended critically on timing for its comic success or failure – sometimes it worked a treat, others I mistimed it by a sliver of a second and it fell short.

Q: What are the most difficult sequences from the point of view of emotion?

A: The whole of Act Two is something of a mountain to climb from that point of view. Emotionally both characters are functioning at such extremes and reeling from one to the next – from ecstasies of happiness to jealous rages to unstoppable laughter to intense mutual irritation, etc. – the whole act is a kind of roller coaster of the heart. It is structured in so many cycles, each cycle culminating in a row, before they kiss and make up and begin the next. It is a challenge to keep each of these true and particular to itself – if the audience starts to sense the repetition of these patterns then they might tire of them a little. You mustn't as an actor anticipate what's coming, but commit emotionally to the moment and go wherever the play takes you. What is rather exhausting about the structure of the act is that by the end of it the two of you have been slugging away out there for an unrelieved forty-five minutes and then you have a massive fight to perform! The fight in this production was longer and more elaborate than usual – it sort of evolved that way in rehearsal. The fight director didn't come with a finished piece of choreography in his head – we worked on it together, with the geography of that particular room and whatever in it that could be hurled, smashed or used as a weapon. Almost everything, as it turned out. It was very good fun. We could have been a bit more selective perhaps, and conserved our energies a bit, but neither Anton [Lesser] nor I could bring ourselves to discard any of it . . . which we sometimes regretted when we got past the hundredth performance mark and were on our knees.

Q: And Amanda's dance to Stravinsky's *Rite of Spring*?

A: Well, we'd worked on the dance at the beginning of Act Two a great deal, but this one – this moment towards the end when Amanda dances purely to enrage Elyot – we didn't resolve till late on in the rehearsal process. We weren't quite sure what it should be and were perhaps waiting for something to arise organically out of the moment once the play was in running shape. Then one day I saw Marguerite Porter, the choreographer, sort of physically doodling in a corner. She was making fantastic, spiky, angular shapes to the syncopated rhythms of that bit of Stravinsky. I loved it and instantly thought it was right for that moment in the scene. She looked like a sort of mad, ecstatic, frenetic little leprechaun. Marguerite told me it came from Kenneth MacMillan's choreography for *The Rite* and was a bit worried about copyright, etc., but what the hell, we used it anyway. What I especially liked about the design for this production was that it placed Amanda's and Elyot's world – or her world – not in a sort of grand apartment with elegant balconies overlooking the Seine, but in much more bohemian terrain. This was the Paris of political radicalism, intellectual debate, the culturally avant-garde – of café life and cigarettes and lots of sex . . . every form of experimentation. Of course Amanda and Elyot are not ideas people, intellectuals at all, but you feel they would have been at the cutting edge, wherever that was. So the Stravinsky and Amanda's dance as a crazy hopping goblin were somehow part of that picture.

Q: What qualities in Anton Lesser's Elyot did you find you responded to?

A: Anton and I have worked together a lot, including two previous incarnations as a couple, so we're quite familiar with each other, which was a bonus for these roles because we could quite easily behave like people who've been married before. We were not perhaps an obvious pairing for these roles on the face of it, but I think there is a kind of chemistry between us as actors that worked well. Anton's Elyot was quirky, wry, quite eccentric – it seemed clear to me that for Amanda other men might seem dull and predictable by comparison. We tried to keep the relationship very alive on stage, changing things to some extent from night to night, allowing some volatility in. We got very preoccupied with the rhythms of the dialogue – Coward's rhythms are so precise, almost like a musical score. We found again and again that when we served those rhythms without interfering with them, the scenes surged into life, the rhythm doing quite a lot of the work for you. But when we broke lines up, took pauses on an impulse, imposed our own dynamic on the dialogue, the scenes didn't work anything like as well.

Q: How long did you have for rehearsal?

A: About seven weeks. The first few were largely spent doing different kinds of research – looking at the period and reading from other contemporary writers like Scott Fitzgerald, Evelyn Waugh, etc. We also read *Easy Virtue* and *The Vortex*, and spent some time reading and talking about Coward's life. Looking at the ways in which the First World War impacted on the 1920s and generated that extraordinary reckless, hedonistic spirit was what I found most helpful and illuminating. The way in which that war had witnessed the establishment's slaughter of an entire generation of young men gave rise to a subsequent explosion of radical political thought, upheaval and sexual liberation. The craziness of that slaughter in the name of some spurious morality made nonsense of all morality thereafter, in a way. So the sensual, amoral and anarchic behaviour of Amanda and Elyot has its roots in this reaction. They live as though they have won their lives on the lottery and are spending them with wild gay abandon, heedless of all consequences, moral, physical, or of any other kind. And this is I think where the play achieves its stature and why it is more than a light comedy – because although Amanda and Elyot are addicted to the greatest forms of fun, this addiction has its dark origins and somehow they recognise this in each other.

Q: Was there any discussion of Coward's homosexuality?

A: Yes, a bit, but it didn't seem particularly useful for Amanda or Elyot. I think perhaps that the issue of his class origins is more revealing for *Private Lives* than the issue of his sexuality. He was a refugee from his lower-middle-class origins from quite an early age, and the tenacity with which he identified himself with certain attributes of the upper classes is reflected a bit in Amanda and Elyot and their snobbish relationship to Victor and Sybil. Victor, I think, is of old-school upper-middle-class stock, and Sybil seems to smack of the petty bourgeoisie. Amanda and Elyot would consider themselves thoroughbreds and much fun is unashamedly had in the play at the expense of these differences. Coward's biting contempt for the class he came from has the hallmark of intimate knowledge of that class and its preoccupation with shoulds and oughts and appearances.

Q: What about the idea that Sybil and Victor are, as it were, 'normal' while Amanda and Elyot are 'abnormal' people who belong together?

A: I think that's true, and it's not just that Amanda and Elyot are both outrageous. They are driven by something darker than the other two and in Amanda's case – perhaps Elyot's too – joking is crucially important to their survival. Her wit is like a rubber ring around her waist in an ocean full of sharks. There is a very vulnerable side to her, because in a way she's out of control. I think she's perhaps more damaged than Elyot. For both of them, humour is their weapon against everything – the world, each other, themselves. He is a great trivialiser, which is also part of his defence, and this sometimes drives her batty. But then you get that great tirade of his towards the end of Act Two against the pontificators and the morality men and the law-makers, in which you glimpse something much more interesting. That's where you get a sense of what fuels both Elyot and Amanda – again, it is to do with the period, I think. They're on the edge. I doubt whether Amanda goes on to live to a ripe old age, or would even want to – she'll probably die in a car accident, or overdosing on something, or perhaps choking on a croissant while laughing too much. If she can't live for ever then I think she'd probably rather live to about forty-five and then throw in her chips. In a way they're both dangerous people. But like a lot of dangerous people I think they are frail, or have been exposed to their frailties and therefore use their powers to conceal them and to make sure they stay on top of what frightens them. That's all there in the play, but it needs so light a touch that if you over-weight it when you play it you will kill the spirit of the thing. Nevertheless, it's sustained by this stuff. It's the magma in the very core of the particular planet on which these characters live. Once you've rooted yourselves in that I think you can sort of forget it and play the play.

Q: And it has to be played lightly?

A: Oh yes. The beauty and the difficulty, plaited together, of playing it, is to observe the delicacy and precision of those rhythms. Coward's ear is unbelievable – he has a kind of Mozartian clarity. You mess with that at your peril. The rhythms in the writing will take you to places you will not reach if you impose your own. It is more like a musical score than any play I've ever done, except perhaps Samuel Beckett's.

Q: Were any passages particularly difficult

A: I think Act Three, interestingly, is not brilliantly written. It's really not exquisite farce writing (with the exception of a few moments) and it's full of difficulty. I think Coward had a problem. He had a great idea that he launched in Act One and played out to the hilt in Act Two, but now what's he going to do? How is he going to sustain it all the way through to a conclusion? You have to work hard at Act Three. It's a sponge, it absorbs an enormous amount of energy. And then finally you've got the dreaded breakfast scene, which is fun but unbelievably complicated to play. It's to do with the elaborate timing of coffee and croissants, jam and butter and marmalade and milk – all being passed to the right person at the right second and fitting in seamlessly with the dialogue. On good nights the audience, high on Acts One and Two roared through Act Three and so it sort of sustained itself. But if they didn't, because they were shyer or cooler, then the weakness in the fabric really did begin to reveal itself.

Q: The play was written for Noël Coward himself and Gertrude Lawrence. Does this show?

A: Well, you're very aware of that in Act Three, because time and time again Coward gives himself as Elyot the best gags and suddenly he doesn't give Amanda any! It's a most peculiar thing. And I don't know what Gertrude Lawrence felt about this. Maybe that was Coward making sure the audience went out singing his tunes.

3 The Coward Centenary on Stage:
a selective catalogue

1 **Present Laughter** West Yorkshire Playhouse, 10 December 1998. Daphne Stillington: Claudie Blakley; Mr Erickson: Willie Ross; Fred: Will Keen; Monica Reed: Susie Baxter; Garry Essendine: Ian McKellen; Liz: Clare Higgins; Roland Maule: Rhashan Stone; Henry: Timothy Walker; Morris: Paul Bhattacharjee; Joanna: Clare Swinburne; Lady Saltburn: Ellen Wik [acronym for Will Keen]. Director: Malcolm Sutherland; Designer: Robert Innes Hopkins; Lighting: Peter Mumford; Sound: Mic Pool.

2 **Song at Twilight** King's Head Theatre, 29 December 1998. Hilde Latymer: Kika Markham; Felix: Mathew Bose; Hugo Latymer: Corin Redgrave; Carlotta Gray: Nyree Dawn Porter. Director: Sheridan Morley; Designer: Saul Radomsky; Costumes: Serena Brown. Revived Gielgud Theatre, 20 October 1999 with Carlotta Gray: Vanessa Redgrave; Designer: Simon Higlett; Costumes: Shirley Russell; Lighting: Leonard Tucker.

3 **Ace of Clubs** Wimbledon Studio, 12 January 1999. Pinkie Leroy: Claire Carrie; Harry Hornby: Russell Wilcox; Felix Felton: Peter Gale; Rita Marbury: Ellen O'Grady; Benny Lucas: Anthony Jordan; Sammy Blake: Paul Todd; Det. Insp. Warrilove: Nick Burnell; Jo Snyder: Ronnie Letham; Gus: Stephen Lockwood; June: Zoe Shepherd; Doreen: Caroline Aslett; Baby: Saskia Butler; Dawn: Sarah Lloyd; Police Officer: Nick Burnell. Director: Jenny Lee; Designers: Rodney Cottam and Trelawnie Mead; Costumes: Dean Morgan and Jaqueline Waite; Lighting: Roger Frith; Choreography: Angela Hardcastle; Musical Director: Paul Todd.

4 **Blithe Spirit** Salisbury Playhouse, 21 January 1999. Edith:

Sarah Flind; Ruth: Celia Nelson; Charles: Robin Kermode; Dr Bradman: David Crosse; Mrs Bradman: Ursula Smith; Madame Arcati: Fenella Fielding; Elvira: Mairéad Carty. Director: Gareth Armstrong; Decor: Russell Craig and Kate Hawley; Lighting: Jeanine Davies; Sound: Gina Hills; Music: Simon Slater.

5 **After the Ball** [Concert performance, Covent Garden Festival]. Peacock Theatre, 27 May 1999. Chorus/Duchess of Berwick: Penelope Keith; Lady Plymdale: Rosie Ashe; Lady Stutfield: Fiona Kimm; Lady Jedburgh: Frances McCafferty; Mr Dumby: Christopher Saunders; Mr Cecil Graham/Parker: Tom McVeigh; Lord Augustus: Gordon Sandison; Lord Windermere: Eric Roberts; Lady Windermere: Linda Kitchen; Mr Hopper: George Dvorsky; Lord Darlington: Karl Daymond; Lady Agatha: Nina Young; Mrs Erlynne: Marie McLaughlin. BBC Concert Orchestra, Conductor: John McGlinn; Director: Paul Curran.

6 **Private Lives** Lyttelton Theatre, The Royal National Theatre Company, 13 May 1999. Sibyl Chase: Rebecca Saire; Elyot Chase: Anton Lesser; Victor Prynne: Dominic Rowan; Amanda Prynne: Juliet Stevenson; Louise: Darlene Johnson. Director: Philip Franks; Decor: Stephen Brimson Lewis; Lighting: Howard Harrison; Sound: Adam Rudd; Choreography: Marguerite Porter; Music: Matthew Scott; Fights: Malcolm Ranson.

7 **Hay Fever** Savoy Theatre, 14 June 1999. Judith Bliss: Geraldine McEwan; David Bliss: Peter Blythe; Myra Arundel: Sylvestra Le Touzel; Richard Greatham: Malcolm Sinclair; Jackie Coryton: Cathryn Bradshaw; Sorel Bliss: Monica Dolan; Sandy Tyrell: Scott Handy; Simon Bliss: Stephen Mangan; Clara: Anne White. In *Love's Whirlwind*: Mavis: Caroline Lennon; George: Andrew McDonald; Victor: Giles Smith; Nurse: Barbara Wedel. Director: Declan Donnellan; Decor: Nick Ormerod; Lighting: Tanya Burns; Sound: Paul Arditti; Choreography: Jane Gibson; Musical Arranger: Paddy Cunneen.

8 **Easy Virtue** Festival Theatre, Shaw Festival, Niagara-on-the-Lake, Ontario, Canada, 2 July 1999. Mrs Whittaker: Patricia Hamilton; Marion: Kelli Fox; Colonel Whittaker: David Schurmann; Hilda: Fiona Byrne; Furber: Richard Farrell; John

Whittaker: Kevin Bundy; Larita: Goldie Semple; Sarah Hurst: Glynis Ranney; Charles Burleigh: Todd Waite; Philip Borden: Brian Elliott; Mr Harris: Patrick R. Brown; Hugh Petworth: Larry Herbert; Nina Vansittart: Patty Jamieson; Bobby Coleman: Randy Ganne; Letty Austin: Risa Waldman; Algy Prynne: Alistair James Harlond; Lucy Coleman: Karen Wood; Henry Furley: Allan Craik; Mrs Hurst: Nora McLellan; Mrs Phillips: Gabrielle Jones; Mary Banfield: Robin Hutton. Director: Christopher Newton; Designer: William Schmuck; Lighting Designer: Alan Brodie.

9 **Nude with Violin** Royal Exchange, Manchester, 5 July 1999. Sebastien: Derek Griffiths; Marie-Celeste: Janie Booth; Clinton Preminger Junior: Nick Caldecott; Isobel Sorodin: Marcia Warren; Jane: Tamzin Malleson; Colin: Ian Shaw; Pamela: Dariel Pertwee; Jacob Friedland: John Bennett; Anya Pavlikov: Rosalind Knight; Cherry-May Waterton: Gay Soper; Fabrice/George: Martin Pirongs; Obadiah Lewellyn: Joe Speare; Stotesbury: Dale Meeks. Director: Marianne Elliott; Decor: Lez Brotherston; Lighting: Chris Davey; Sound: Rob Tice; Fights: Malcolm Ranson.

10 **Easy Virtue** Chichester Festival, 27 July 1999. Furber: Michael Stroud; Mrs Whittaker: Wendy Craig; Ellen: Pauline O'Driscoll; Colonel Whittaker: Michael Jayston; Marion Whittaker: Jenny Quayle; Jackson: Paul Doust; Hilda Whittaker: Elisabeth Dermot Walsh; John Whittaker: Andrew Clover; Larita Whittaker: Greta Scacchi; Louise: Joanna Stride; Sarah Hurst: Lou Gish; Charles Burleigh: Evroy Deer; Philip Bordon: Paul Moody; Hon. Hugh Petworth: William Buckhurst; Nina Vansittart: Alex Rittner; Mrs Phillips: Zulema Dene; Bobby Coleman: Simon Cole; Mrs Hunt: Pauline O'Driscoll; Rev. Henry Farley: Paul Doust. Director: Maria Aitken; Decor: Frank Hallinan Flood; Costumes: John Bright; Lighting: Peter Mumford; Sound: Matt McKenzie; Choreography: Struan Leslie; Music: Howard Davidson.

11 **The Young Idea** Gateway Theatre, Chester, 15 October 1999. Huddle/Eustace: Andy Greenhalgh; Roddy: Mark Payton; Cicely: Celia Montague; George Brent: Benjamin Whitrow;

Gerda: Chloe Newsome; Sholto: Simon Quarterman; Priscilla: Sasha Waddell; Claud/Hiram: Graham Seed; Julia/Maria: Jane Karen; Jennifer: Jane How. Director: Deborah Shaw; Designer: Paul Edwards; Lighting and Sound Designer: Alan Jackson.

12 **Sail Away** Carnegie Hall, New York, 3 November 1999. Joe: Jonathan Freeman; Mimi Paragon: Elaine Stritch; Elmer Candijack: Bill Nolte; Maimie Candijack: Anne Allgood; Alvin Lush: Paul Iacono; Mrs Lush: Alison Fraser; Sir Gerard Nutfield: Herb Foster; Lady Nutfield: Gina Ferrall; Johny Van Mier: Jerry Lanning; Mrs Van Mier: Jane White; Barnaby Slade: James Patterson; Mrs Sweeny: Jane Connell; Mr Sweeny: Gordon Connell; Elinor Spencer Bollard: Marian Seldes; Nancy Foyle: Andrea Burns; Passengers, Stewards, etc.: Danny Burstein, Tony Capone, Dale Hensley, Jennifer Kathryn Marshall, Bill Nolte; The Little Ones: Tanya Desko, Paul Iacono, Alexandra Jumper; Adlai: Phyllis Gutierrez. Music Director: Ben Whiteley; Director: Gerald Gutierrez; Dance Arrangements: Peter Matz; Vocal Arrangements: Fred Werner.

13 **Waiting in the Wings** Colonial Theater, Boston, 17 November 1999; Walter Kerr Theater, New York, 16 December 1999. May Davenport: Rosemary Harris; Cora Clarke: Rosemary Murphy; Bonita Belgrave: Elizabeth Wilson; Maudie Melrose: Patricia Conolly; Deirdre O'Malley: Helena Carroll; Almina Clare: Bette Henritze; Sarita Myrtle: Helen Stenborg; Lotta Bainbridge: Lauren Bacall; Topsy Baskerville: Victoria Boothby; Osgood Meeker: Barnard Hughes; Dora: Victoria Boothby; Zelda Fenwick: Crista Moore; Alan Banfield: Anthony Cummings; Sylvia Archibald: Dana Ivey; Perry Lascoe: Simon Jones; Doreen: Amelia Campbell; Ted: Geddeth Smith; St John's ambulance man: Collin Johnson. Director: Michael Langham; Scenery: Ray Klausen; Costumes: Alvin Colt; Lighting: Ken Billington; Sound: Peter Fitzgerald.

14 **Cavalcade** Citizens Theatre, Glasgow, 26 November 1999. Jane Marryot: Jennifer Hilary; Robert Marryot: Stephen MacDonald; Edward Marryot: Tim Chipping; Joe Marryot: Jay Manley; Margaret Harris: Ellen Sheean; Edith Harris: Lorna McDevitt; Bridges: Andrew Joseph; Ellen Bridges: Patti Clare;

Fanny Bridges: Michelle Gomez; Mrs Snapper: Brendan Hooper. Director/Decor: Philip Prowse; Lighting: Gerry Jenkinson; Choreography: Geoffrey Cauley; Musical Director: Derek Watson.

15 **Volcano** The Palace Theatre, Westcliff on Sea, Essex, 26 April 2000. Robin Craigie: Richard Bacon; Ellen Danbury: Louise Butcher; Guy Littleton: Antony Edridge; Adela Shelly: Elizabeth Elvin; Melissa Littleton: Faith Flint; Keith Danbury: Ryan Philpott; Grizelda Craigie: Emma Powell. Director: Roy Marsden; Designer: Simon Scullion; Lighting Designer: Robin Carter; Costume Designer: Adrian Lilley; Costume Co-ordinator: Helen Ryan; Sound Designers: Neil Douglas and Lisa Westerhout.

CONTRIBUTORS

Maria Aitken has played leading roles at the Royal National Theatre, the Royal Shakespeare Company and in the West End. Her Coward productions include *The Vortex, Blithe Spirit, Private Lives, Design for Living* and *Hay Fever*. Among her directing credits is the Chichester Festival centenary production of *Easy Virtue*. She is Visiting Professor at the Yale School of Drama and the author of *Style: Acting in High Comedy*.

Judy Campbell worked with Noël Coward in the 1940s and 1950s. She created the roles of Joanna Lyppiatt in *Present Laughter*, Ethel Gibbons in *This Happy Breed*, and Miranda Frayle in *Relative Values*, and played Elvira opposite Coward's Charles Condomine in *Blithe Spirit*. Her recitation of 'If Love Were All' concluded the London Centenary Gala at the Savoy.

Jean Chothia is University Lecturer and Fellow of Selwyn College, Cambridge. She is author of *Forging a Language: A Study of the Plays of Eugene O'Neill, Directors in Perspective: André Antoine* and *English Drama of the Early Modern Period: 1890–1940*, and editor of *The New Woman and Other Female Emancipation Plays*.

Michael Coveney is theatre critic on the *Daily Mail* and former theatre critic on the *Financial Times* and the *Observer*. His books include *The Citz: A History of the Glasgow Citizens Theatre, Maggie Smith: A Bright Particular Star, The Aisle is Full of Noises, Knight Errant* (with Robert Stephens), *The World According to Mike Leigh* and, most recently, *Cats on a Chandelier: The Andrew Lloyd Webber Story*.

David Edgar is a playwright and a general commentator on the cultural scene. His plays include adaptations of *Nicholas Nickleby* and *Dr Jekyll and Mr Hyde*; a version of Gitta Sereny's biography of Albert Speer for the National Theatre; and the original plays *Destiny*, *Maydays* and *Pentecost*. He founded and chaired the University of Birmingham's postgraduate course in Playwriting Studies and recently edited and introduced *State of Play*, a collection of papers from the course's annual theatre conference.

Philip Franks is both an actor and director. He recently directed Coward's *Private Lives*, with Juliet Stevenson and Anton Lesser, at the Royal National Theatre. He has himself appeared at the RNT, with the Royal Shakespeare Company and in the West End. He has edited two anthologies, *Shall I See You Again* (with Juliet Stevenson) and *An Actor's Life*.

Maggie Gale is Senior Lecturer in Drama and Theatre Arts at the University of Birmingham. She is author of *West End Women: Women on the London Stage 1918–1962*, and co-editor of *British Theatre Between the Wars* and *Womens' Theatre and Performance: New Historiographies*.

Frances Gray is Senior Lecturer in Drama at the University of Sheffield. She has written books on Noël Coward, John Arden and feminist laughter, and is currently working on a book about crime writing. She is also a playwright and winner of a *Radio Times* Comedy Award.

Philip Hoare is author of *Noël Coward: A Biography* (1995), praised on publication by Sheridan Morley as 'the definitive biography'. In 1998 he was consultant to Adam Low's BBC2 *Arena* trilogy on Coward. He works as a writer, obituarist, curator and broadcaster in London and Hampshire, and is currently writing a book on the Royal Victoria Military Hospital, Netley.

Peter Holland is Director of the Shakespeare Institute, Stratford-upon-Avon and Professor of Shakespeare Studies at the University of Birmingham. His most recent book is *English Shakespeares*, a study of Shakespeare on the contemporary English stage. His article on Noël Coward and comic geometry appeared in *English Comedy* (1994), edited by Michael Cordner.

Russell Jackson is Reader in English at the University of Birmingham and Deputy Director of the Shakespeare Institute. He has a particular interest in Shakespeare on film and has worked as text adviser to Kenneth Branagh and Oliver Parker as well as on *Shakespeare in Love*. His publications include editions of plays by Oscar Wilde and Henry Arthur Jones, the source book *Victorian Theatre* and (with Jonathan Bate) *Shakespeare: An Illustrated Stage History*.

Joel Kaplan is Professor of Drama and Theatre Arts at the University of Birmingham and Director of the University's Postgraduate Centre for the Study of Drama. Recent publications include *Theatre and Fashion: Oscar Wilde to the Suffragettes* (with Sheila Stowell) and *The Edwardian Theatre* (with Michael Booth).

Sheridan Morley is a Trustee of the Noël Coward Estate and author of Coward's first critical biography, *A Talent to Amuse*; he is drama critic of the *Spectator* and the *International Herald Tribune*, and author of *Noël and Gertie*. In 1999 he directed Vanessa and Corin Redgrave in Coward's last full-lenth play, *Song at Twilight*, at the Gielgud Theatre where it ran for six months.

Christopher Newton has been Artistic Director of the Shaw Festival in Niagara-on-the-Lake, Ontario, Canada for the past twenty-one years. At the Festival his Coward credits include *Cavalcade*, *Private Lives*, *Present Laughter*, *Easy Virtue* and *Point Valaine*.

Philip Prowse is a Director of the Glasgow Citizens Theatre. Over the past two decades he has directed and designed Coward's *Semi-Monde* (a world première), *Sirocco*, *The Vortex*, *Private Lives*, *Design for Living* and *Cavalcade*.

Peter Raby is Reader in Drama and English at Homerton College, Cambridge. He has written extensively for and on the theatre, and is editor of the Cambridge Companions to Oscar Wilde and Harold Pinter.

Dan Rebellato is Senior Lecturer in Drama and Theatre at Royal Holloway College, University of London. He is author of *1965 And All That*, a re-examination of British theatre before *Look Back in Anger*, and editor of the selected plays of Terence Rattigan for Nick Hern Books. He is also a playwright and translator.

Corin Redgrave recently played Sir Hugo Latymer in Coward's *Song at Twilight* at the Gielgud Theatre, with his sister Vanessa Redgrave and wife Kika Markham. He has written three plays for BBC radio and a memoir, *Michael Redgrave, My Father*, which became a documentary film for the *Omnibus* television series.

Malcolm Sinclair read Drama at Hull University and trained at the Bristol Old Vic Theatre School. He has most recently appeared in Coward's *Hay Fever* (Savoy), Nicholas Wright's *Cressida* (Albery), Alan Ayckbourn's *House and Garden* (RNT) and, on television, *Anna Karenina*. His latest radio project, M. Kahan's *Design for Murder*, had him playing that well-known sleuth, Noël Coward.

Alan Sinfield teaches English and Lesbian and Gay Studies at the University of Sussex. He is author of *Out on Stage: Lesbian and Gay Theatre in the Twentieth Century*, *Gay and After*, *The Wilde Century: Effeminacy, Oscar Wilde and the Queer Movement* and *Cultural Politics – Queer Reading*.

Juliet Stevenson trained at RADA. Her theatre work has included leading parts with the Royal Court, the Hampstead Theatre, the Royal National Theatre and the Royal Shakespeare Company as well as in the West End. She has also worked extensively in film and on television. Her appearance as Amanda

Prynne in Philip Franks' 1999 Royal National Theatre production of *Private Lives* marks her first role in a Coward play.

John Stokes is Professor in the Department of English, King's College London. His books include *Oscar Wilde: Myths, Miracles and Imitations* and *Eleanor Marx: Life, Work, Contacts.* He reviews regularly for the *Times Literary Supplement* and, in collaboration with Russell Jackson, is editing Wilde's journalism.

Sheila Stowell is Senior Research Fellow at the University of Birmingham. Her publications include *Theatre and Fashion: Oscar Wilde to the Suffragettes* (with Joel Kaplan) and *A Stage of Their Own: Feminist Playwrights of the Suffrage Era.*

Dominic Vlasto graduated in music from Cambridge University, and worked extensively with the late Norman Hackforth on the performance of Coward's music. He now combines musical interests and freelance teaching with the conservation management of a small wetland nature reserve on the Norfolk Broads. He is co-author, with Alan Farley, of a forthcoming catalogue and compendium to the music of Noël Coward.

Sue Wilson is the Senior Radio Drama Producer at BBC Birmingham. She is also a writer and theatre director, and has been Artistic Director of the Pitlochry International Festival Theatre, the Chester Gateway and the Nuffield Theatre, Southampton. Her stage productions have included *Private Lives* and *The Vortex.* During the Centenary, she directed six plays from *Tonight at 8.30* for Radio 4.

Index